BRISTOL
SCOUT
1264

BRISTOL SCOUT 1264

REBUILDING GRANDDAD'S AIRCRAFT

DAVID BREMNER

FONTHILL

Fonthill Media Language Policy

Fonthill Media publishes in the international English language market. One language edition
is published worldwide. As there are minor differences in spelling and presentation, especially
with regard to American English and British English, a policy is necessary to define which form
of English to use. The Fonthill Policy is to use the form of English native to the author. David
Bremner was born and educated in the UK; therefore, British English has been adopted in this
publication.

Fonthill Media Limited
Fonthill Media LLC
www.fonthillmedia.com
office@fonthillmedia.com

First published in the United Kingdom and the United States of America 2018

British Library Cataloguing in Publication Data:
A catalogue record for this book is available from the British Library

Typeset in 10.5pt on 13pt Sabon
Printed and bound in England

Acknowledgements

Many of those who helped to bring this project to fruition are mentioned in the book, and to all of them, of course, I extend my grateful thanks.

Yet some contributions are not, and in this respect, I would like to give grateful thanks to Geoff Hill, Norman Burr, Sir George White, and Paschalis Palavouzis who have given up a great amount of time and expertise in editing and correcting the book, as well as offering encouragement and moral support.

Yet two who are in the book deserve particular mention here as well. Theo Willford features prominently since it was he who sparked the project into life, and has been the unacknowledged backbone of it ever since. As it is my Granddad's aircraft, I tend to end up in the limelight, but this has always been Theo's project as much as mine, and he has been happy to accept that he gets less of the attention.

My wife Sue is another major unsung contributor. Aeroplanes are pretty much boy's toys, but she has been an active and enthusiastic supporter and contributor to the project, and an essential member of the team, creating the associated social media and keeping them lively and up to date, manning the stand and drawing the public—particularly the children—in, sorting out merchandising, urging us ever onwards when we started to flag, and enthusiastically backing the expenditure required.

The bonds of friendship between us might well have been strained over the years, but instead they have matured and strengthened and become one of the most precious and permanent parts of my life.

CONTENTS

Introduction

5.30 a.m., 23 June 2016. Thassos, Greece

In the pre-dawn light, Theo Willford and I stood on a hastily prepared airstrip and looked failure squarely in the face.

Theo is a solidly built man in his mid-sixties with a thatch of black hair streaked with grey. His personality matches his physique; solid, imperturbable and utterly reliable. We met more than thirty years ago in the early days of microlighting, and have flown and built aeroplanes together much of the time since. There is no one I would trust more than Theo.

Yet fourteen years previously, the normally level-headed Theo had suggested an astonishingly ambitious project—to rebuild a Great War Bristol Scout aeroplane using the three parts my grandfather had brought back with him as souvenirs of his favourite machine from the Greek island of Thassos in 1916, where he had been a pilot with the Royal Naval Air Service. Equally improbably, we had been invited by the Greek government to fly it from the identical spot 100 years later.

At this time of year, the weather on Thassos is normally calm, but the Meltemi winds, most frequent during August, were forecast to blow for the remainder of our time here, ruling out any flying in our fragile machine. This morning was likely to be the last time flying might be possible, and even now, the windsock was streaming out, indicating quite lively winds.

In addition to this, the airstrip had been roughly levelled using a grader, so the majority of the surface was uneven dirt—not ideal for a machine designed 100 years ago.

We stood and pondered. Normally, we would not even dream of flying such a delicate and historic machine in these conditions. Yet these were far from normal circumstances. We had been invited by the Greek government who had made huge efforts to prepare everything for us. Exactly 100 years ago to the day, Granddad had flown in this aeroplane and we would be following in his footsteps. A film crew had come with us to film the event.

Theo and I drove the car up and down the strip to assess its smoothness, and at 30 mph, the bumps nearly made our heads bounce off the roof. The sun crept ever higher until it just peeped above the crest of the hills ahead. In an hour or so, it would start to create strong thermals which would add a further level of risk to any flying.

It was now or never. Standing on the very spot where my Granddad had been exactly a century ago, my memories of him came flooding back. Exactly 100 years ago to the day, he had written this:

> Escorting H.F.s dropping petrol bombs on crops. Good fires started. Dropped four bombs on seaplane sheds, shooting bad, but one bomb fell very near small pier. Machine well t'ed up. Very bumpy, landing good.

Granddad

My grandparents lived only half an hour away, and as boys we used to visit them very regularly. Along with my brother Rick, I used to listen to Granddad's stories about flying in the Great War, and although we did not understand them fully at the time, they must have caught our imaginations, because both Rick and I became, and have remained, fascinated with aviation ever since (Fig. 1).

There was the story, for example, of Granddad's friend who went to visit a colleague in another squadron where they flew Sopwith Camels:

> In those days it was all very informal. People used to borrow an aeroplane in order to fly home for the weekend, and in this case my friend was invited to go and take a Camel for a spin. He'd never flown one before, and of course the Camel was renowned as being one of the trickiest types to fly. But he managed okay, and got halfway through a loop when he realised he'd not fastened his seat belt correctly. He started to fall out of the aeroplane, and let go of the controls in order to save himself. The Camel was very unstable flown normally, but it was pretty stable upside down, so he wasn't in immediate danger; it was just that he couldn't let go with either hand to grab the controls to sort himself out.
>
> In the end, he managed to grab the stick at its base and pull it back, but did so very roughly. The Camel was very, very manoeuvrable, and turned the right way up in the blink of an eye. My friend was thrown back into the seat with such force that he broke the frame and it began to fall through the bottom of the aeroplane! He had to fly all the way home

with his feet braced against the rudder bar, and his head leaning back over the headrest in order to keep his bottom off the seat ...

There was the other one about the mad Serbian pilot:

> I flew with No. 2 Wing Royal Naval Air Service (RNAS), and in the spring of 1916 we were stationed at Thassos, a Greek island off the Macedonian coast at that time occupied by Bulgaria, which had recently joined the Axis powers.
>
> The most common target was the crops in the fields—it was early summer after all—and we lashed up home-made incendiary bombs and attached them to home-made bomb racks on our aeroplanes.
>
> A Serbian pilot called Stephanovitch HATED the Bulgarians, and he wanted to drop more bombs on the Bulgarians than anybody else. So in addition to bomb racks under the wings, he filled the front seat of his two-seat aeroplane with more bombs, and took an umbrella along with him. Then when he'd dropped all the bombs from his bomb racks under the wings, he would hook the extra bombs in the front cockpit out with his umbrella and hoick them over the side too.

Of course, we asked Granddad what type he flew, and he told us 'the Bristol Bullet'. At that time, without the internet, our primitive research (probably in I-SPY books) did not turn up the Bullet, and I am afraid we may have wondered how much of the rest of his stories were true. It was only later—much later—that we came across the Bristol Bullet as a nickname for the Bristol Scout, on account of its high speed when it was introduced.

His favourite stories about the Bullet were about the unsynchronised Lewis machine gun that fired some of its bullets into his own propeller, so they had doped fabric strips to the propeller 'to stop the splinters coming off in your face', and how he had acquired a German Bosch magneto from an Italian who had achieved international fame as a motor racing driver before the war:

> This Italian's name was Meo Costantini, and while he was serving with the French squadron on Thassos he'd managed to acquire this Bosch magneto via his German racing friends, and I did a deal to swap it for some bombs and some food. The Bosch was much more reliable than the ones fitted on British machines, and since there was only one magneto on these early aeroplanes, a failed magneto inevitably meant you wouldn't be getting home by air. I switched it from machine to machine thereafter.

In retrospect, it seems odd that Granddad did not regale us with much of his other memorabilia at the time; we were clearly very interested, and we now know that his recollection of the events of 1915–1916 was crystal clear. He had kept in touch with the RNAS Association, went to regular reunions with his contemporaries, and in 1974 was interviewed by David Lance from the Imperial War Museum, sharing much of his memorabilia between them and the Fleet Air Arm Museum at Yeovilton.

However, we did not find out the full details of his service until after he died in 1983. It was then, as we were clearing out his workshop after his death, that we came across three items that set us on the long, long trail that led back here to Thassos. They were the control column or stick (the term 'joystick' was derided by the RNAS), rudder bar, and the Bosch magneto taken from his favourite machine: Bristol Scout Type 'C', RNAS serial 1264.

Now, exactly 100 years later, they were back in the identical machine on the identical spot, waiting to take to the air above Thassos once more (Fig. 2).

The Bristol Scout

The fighter aircraft is the preening glamour boy of the aviation world. Even the least aviation-minded person has heard of the Sopwith Camel, the Fokker Triplane, and the Supermarine Spitfire. Sleek, fast, powerful, and well-armed, the supreme flying qualities and one-to-one combat of the fighter aircraft engages the romantic in all of us.

The Bristol Scout was not a fighter, but it, more than any other single design, pointed the way to what was needed. It was, if you like, the John the Baptist for the ultimate flying machine.

Up to the outbreak of the First World War, the Army specified three main types of aeroplane.

The two-seat reconnaissance machine would be the backbone of the fleet, providing detailed strategic reconnaissance information with some armament for self-defence by the observer. In the absence of radio, the aeroplane would have to land back at base to deliver the information.

The fighting aeroplane was a two-seat pusher with the gunner in front, able to operate a machine gun with a maximum field of fire to attack the enemy's reconnaissance machines and defend their own. Speeds for both machines, based on the power of the engines available at that time, were around 60 mph.

The third type was a fast single-seat scout to provide up-to-the-minute tactical information; as a single-seater was capable of up to 80 mph, it would not need to be armed.

Up to that point, aircraft were generally flown in as straight a line as possible; any violent manoeuvres would likely send the machine out of control. So the idea of aiming the whole aeroplane at a fast-moving target would have seemed quite preposterous—apart from the famous technical problem of getting a gun to fire through the propeller. However, the Bristol Scout changed all that.

Just two machines were given to the RFC before the outbreak of war in August 1914. Immediately, its pilots were delighted with its speed and nippy handling, nicknaming it the Bristol Bullet. They quickly found ways to mount rifles on them to give some sort of offensive capability, and this would continue to be story of the Scout throughout its service career.

The Bristol was not the only Scout in service; Sopwith's Tabloid, the Nieuport 10, the Martinsyde Scout and others were all produced in small numbers. Yet the Bristol outlived them all, despite its lack of factory-fitted armament and the relatively small numbers produced, and achieved a number of important firsts.

The first Victoria Cross for aerial combat was awarded in 1915 to Lanoe Hawker flying a Bristol Scout (Fig. 36). Albert Ball, the first British Great War ace, won his first victory in a Bristol Scout. Charles Gordon Bell was the only Bristol Scout ace, with five kills.

The Bristol Scout was the first wheeled military aeroplane to take off from an aircraft carrier (HMS *Vindex*) in 1915 (Fig. 37). It was also the first aeroplane to be launched from another aeroplane in 1916 (Fig. 38).

Unlike most of the other first-generation Scout machines, it remained a popular mount long after its operational usefulness had come to an end, and was much prized by good pilots (and the senior officers who considered themselves good pilots) as a personal runabout. Cyril Uwins, Bristol's chief test pilot, who flew every Bristol type until he moved up to a senior management position, was asked at the end of his career which the nicest aeroplane he ever flew was, and he unhesitatingly picked out the Scout, as did my Granddad.

Its designer was Frank Barnwell, who achieved iconic status in the aeronautical industry; his story, too, is compelling.

The Barnwells:
Early Days (1880–1907)

If Frank Barnwell had been born 100 years later, his childhood might well have been labelled 'dysfunctional'. At the time, however, it would have seemed perfectly normal, and indeed very privileged.

Frank's father, Richard, was what today would have been called a management whizz-kid. Born in Canterbury, he married Anne Sowter from Lewisham in south London, but in 1878, aged only twenty-eight, he was employed at the John Elder shipyard on the Clyde, possibly based on his banking training.[1,2] Presumably he was living up there, but his first two children, Harold and Frank, were born at their maternal grandmother's house in Lewisham: Harold on 3 April 1879 and Frank on 23 November 1880; the whole family had moved to Gravesend at the time of the 1881 census.[3,4,5]

The next child, Archibald Stonham, was born in Scotland in 1882, and twin girls (Elizabeth Ann and Amy in 1886), a son (Frederick Crofts in 1889), and another daughter (Dora in 1890) were also born there.[6] They appear to have lived in Kippen, near Stirling, at first, and then moved to Inchinnan by the 1891 census. At some point the family moved to Elcho House, Balfron, which is the address often given in accounts of Frank's life, though the only documentary evidence is the 1901 census at which point it was only occupied by Harold and his aunt Elizabeth.[7,8] By the 1891 census, all three boys were boarders at the Edinburgh Academy; Frank went from there to Fettes College in 1895, the world-famous school in Edinburgh.[9,10]

In 1885, John Elders had been restructured as Fairfield Shipbuilding and Richard had been appointed managing director, aged only thirty-five. It was one of twenty-eight yards on the Clyde at the time, capable of turning out the largest ships, from transatlantic liners to battleships, and employed around 4,000 men (Fig. 3). He was also a director of many other companies—British Explosives, Isle of Man Steampacket, Northern Pacific Steamship, Scottish Oriental, etc. He and Fairfield Shipbuilding's chairman were active Freemasons, holding several senior positions in the Glasgow Lodge.[11]

Yet on 18 December 1893, Frank's mother Anne died.[12] She was only forty-two, and hers was the first of many premature deaths in the Barnwell family. On 17 April 1897, Frederick also died, aged only eight.[13] On 7 March 1898, so did his father. Richard was only forty-eight and died 'of a long illness', having spent the last year in the south of England.[14]

By this time, Harold had left school, and was working as a shipbuilding apprentice in his father's firm. Frank joined him; it seems likely this was something his father had arranged before his death.[15]

It is hard to know how much influence his parents had on his personality, but it seems clear that his father was a fairly remote figure who would not have provided much emotional involvement. He had been at boarding school since the age of eight and his mother had died when he was thirteen. The one constant family member was his older brother Harold, and the two of them had become very close, and would remain close for the rest of their lives.

Richard's estate was worth £82,538 (equivalent to about £9 m in 2016), so despite the large number of siblings and the newly introduced Estate Duty (which amounted to only 5.5 per cent), both of them were in line for a substantial inheritance from their father, and at that age it would not have been surprising if they had blown the lot on high living.[16] Yet as we have seen, Frank joined Harold as an apprentice at the shipyard, and lived with his brother in digs in Govan, round the corner from the yard.[17] This must have been a bit of a shock after Elcho House and Fettes College, but it is clear both boys were intelligent, modest, and capable of getting on well with people from all walks of life. I am sure any rough edges would have been quickly knocked off at the shipyard, where their privileged position as sons of the managing director would have marked them out for serious ribbing among their workmates.

Of the two, it was Harold who was the natural leader. His two years' start at the shipyard had given him a natural authority, and he suggested what they should do in their spare time. Frank was the more introverted, but also the more academic, and he enrolled in Glasgow University to study natural philosophy and chemistry, matriculating in 1900. When he had finished that, having become interested in the engineering aspects of shipbuilding, he decided to re-enrol in 1902 to study naval architecture and engineering, graduating with a BSc in 1905.[18]

It is not clear exactly when the brothers' interest in aviation was sparked, but this was the time when it became a hot topic, and for young men of an adventurous spirit, the prospect of trying to be the first to achieve controlled flight was the ultimate dream. The desire to move quickly from place to place is hard-wired, particularly into the male psyche as a hangover from the hunter-gatherer days.

Horses, boats, ships, carriages, trains, and cars have always been highly prized, and flying pressed all the buttons. It was unlikely that anyone would consider making a ship or a car by themselves, but it was starting to look as if all you needed for an aeroplane was an engine from a car or motorcycle (and these were starting to become quite easily available), a few pieces of bamboo and some fabric, and you would have the complete freedom of the skies. It was a heady mix, and everyone with a spark of adventure about them wanted a piece of the action.

Of course, it was not until 17 December 1903 that another pair of brothers—Wilbur and Orville Wright—claimed to have actually achieved the goal of controlled flight in a powered, heavier-than-air machine, and even then they kept the details so quiet that no one knew how it was done, and many doubted it had been done at all.

It is a fair guess that Harold and Frank were no exception, and the university would have provided fertile ground to discuss the ideas being put forward. It is my guess that it was Harold who was the driver in this, buying magazines and talking up the possibilities of trying to be the first to fly in Scotland.

At any rate, around 1905, they designed and built a couple of gliders (which gave them plenty of experience in how not to build), which Harold tried (and failed) to fly near their old home in Balfron.[19]

After Frank's graduation, both brothers then headed across the Atlantic to work at the Fairfield Shipbuilding company's other yard in Quincy, Massachusetts.[20, 21] It is difficult to know whether they were still interested in shipbuilding as a career, or if this was a way of finding out more about flying at someone else's expense. It is said that while there they got the opportunity to meet the Wright brothers, but this has never been verified.[22]

Leo Opdyke (1960–1986)

The last surviving Bristol Scout was taken off the register in 1930 when it was regarded as being incapable of being brought up to current airworthiness standards and was scrapped. The story might have come to an end there, except for a bloody-minded lecturer by the name of Leo Opdyke from Poughkeepsie, New York (Fig. 4).

The story of Leo's Bristol Scout would fill another book, but boiled down to its essentials, he had always been fascinated by early aviation, inspired, no doubt, by Cole Palen's Old Rhinebeck museum up the road. He had always fancied building a Bristol F2B fighter, but was talked out of it by another early aviation buff, Ellic Somer, who suggested the Bristol Scout as a more practical alternative, the F2B being larger and more complex.

Leo's qualifications to take on this project were somewhat limited—no workshop, no previous building experience, and not many flying hours—but that was not going to stop him. Leo started work in the garage of his house in Rochester, NY, later moving to a fairly spacious nineteenth-century house in Poughkeepsie, where he continued making and assembling parts in the basement.

The drawings Leo used had come from the Smithsonian Institute. Ellic transcribed some of the information from these on to modern drawings for ease of interpretation, and they obviously arrived piecemeal at the Opdyke home, complete with encouraging and witty comments about his interpretation of the drawings and Leo's progress.

In those days, there was no computer-aided drawing or manufacturing—not available for private individuals, at least. Today, you can get a good deal of the laborious jobs done this way, but for Leo, it involved sitting in his basement with a saw, a file, and a vice. Leo has a reputation for single-minded tenacity, no doubt gained in his basement at this time.

In a good building group, you can get mutual support; when one of you gets down or depressed about a particular part, the others will muck in with suggestions, and very often they will be achieving success with another bit, which will buck you up and get you going again. This was not the case for Leo. Every time he came across a problem, he had to solve it on his own. Every time he let the size of the project get him down, he only had his own resources to rely on, though I am sure his wife Sandy provided a good deal of moral support and encouragement.

The build process took around fifteen years, and it was not until 1986 that the machine was ready to fly. Painted in the olive drab PC10 colour used later in the First World War, it was identified as N4519, the very last one to come off the production line in December 1916. There were some compromises: Leo will tell you that it is a bit of an amalgamation of Type 'C' and Type 'D' features, and the tanks were welded, not riveted. Yet it was a very good reproduction indeed, complete with 80-hp le Rhône engine.

Leo packed it on to a trailer and shipped it to Old Rhinebeck aerodrome about half an hour away, where he rigged it ready for flight.

Unlike today, an airfield in 1915 was a field large enough for an aircraft to take off in any direction. Before considering flying, you consulted the windsock. Granddad said that if the windsock showed any signs of activity, you put the aircraft away, but this is something of an exaggeration as you can gather from his own logbook, which indicates he was flying at one point in a 40-mph wind.

Assuming the wind strength was considered acceptable, you would push (well, normally your ground crew would push) your aircraft to the furthest point of the field in the direction of the windsock. There you would clamber in and the engine would be started. You got the engine running sweetly at full power as quickly as you could, and then waved away the chocks and took off directly into wind.

You had little directional control during take-off, and if the wind was coming from anywhere other than straight ahead, one wing was likely to lift and it would end in an undignified ground loop, possibly terminated by turning upside down. Landing was even more critical; trying to land when you were not pointing directly into wind was courting disaster.

Today, airfields have generally been replaced by airstrips, with one or two runways in defined directions, and aircraft are generally capable of dealing with crosswinds to a greater or lesser extent. Yet if you want to operate an aircraft of this vintage, it is generally advisable to find somewhere with as much freedom as possible to take off into wind, and as much clear area as possible in the immediate vicinity in case it all goes quiet in the engine department.

Old Rhinebeck fulfils none of these requirements; it is a tiny strip cut out of a large forest. It is short, narrow, and sloping, surrounded for miles around by trees. Nevertheless, Cole Palen satisfied his passion for antique aircraft by clearing the strip and filling it full of a simply astonishing collection of rare and ancient flying machines. In order to fund their maintenance, he started an old-fashioned flying circus, which involved putting these machines through their paces in ways which they had not seen since they were new. There were regular casualties, but Cole and his devoted band of volunteers kept them going somehow, and visitors filled the place twice a week to watch the extraordinary antics based on extraordinarily corny storylines, and the occasional accident.

When Leo turned up with his Scout, Cole, who by now knew more than most about operating rotary engines in fragile airframes, looked it over carefully and suggested that Leo might want to get the seventy-year-old magneto re-wired, since he only had one and if it failed the engine would stop. Yet Leo was convinced the magneto was in good shape and after some ground trials, which resulted in a small accident requiring repairs, he got in.

The propeller was swung, the engine fired up, and Leo—who had never flown a rotary-engined aircraft in his life—headed down the strip and lifted off. It was the culmination of fifteen years of hard labour, and Leo was ecstatic. There are a couple of air-to-air photographs from that first flight and even if you cannot see the details on Leo's face, the delight and astonishment shine through like a beacon (Fig. 5). Leo flew around the area getting used to the handling. He found it to be so perfectly aligned that he could take his hands off the controls for extended periods.

Then, after twenty minutes in the air, the engine went unexpectedly quiet. With a rotary engine, there are a number of possible causes, and (unlike a modern engine) the propeller will keep it rotating at all times. Yet nothing brought it back to life, and Leo and his beautiful Scout ended up in the trees.

Thankfully, Leo was not hurt, but there was, of course, significant damage to the machine, and when it was recovered and surveyed, it became clear that it was beyond Leo's resources to repair it. Therefore, after fifteen years building and only twenty minutes flight time, poor Leo had to put it up for sale, having never had the opportunity to use the wheels for their second function: to land. The cause of the malfunction—as I am sure you have guessed—was the magneto.

Thankfully, his work was not entirely in vain. It was brought to the UK and examined by the Royal Air Force (RAF) Museum's Tim Cox, who produced a report based on the premise of trying to restore it to flying condition and concluded that it would be prohibitively expensive to do so.

Given the fact that it was the only reasonably accurate reproduction of a Bristol Scout, it seems a little sniffy, but the regulations for airworthiness in the UK and the USA differ considerably, and it might not have been practical to get it flying.

Yet the report does not appear to consider the option of returning it to a non-flying exhibit. In the end, it was bought by Sir George White, great grandson of the founder of the British and Colonial Aeroplane Company (B&CAC) that had designed and built the Scout. It was restored to non-flying condition by the Fleet Air Arm Museum in Yeovilton, where it resides today, prominently displayed hung from the roof above the prototype Concorde, one of the first aircraft produced at Filton and one of the last—a vivid reminder of the pace of progress in just fifty years of aviation.

So in spite of all Leo's hard work, there was still no airworthy Bristol Scout in the world.

3

The Barnwells: Stretching Their Wings (1907–1911)

It is not clear exactly what precipitated the Barnwell brothers' next fateful step in their careers, or exactly when. Yet around 1907, on their return from the United States, the brothers (possibly together with their younger brother Archibald) set up a company—Grampian Motor and Engineering in Causewayhead, Stirling—to concentrate on making aeroplanes, and to service cars in order to keep the books more or less straight.[1]

Both of them were more than qualified for a successful career in shipbuilding, which would have provided them with a secure income and a satisfying life. Aviation was dangerous and the future of it must have seemed very uncertain. Perhaps they had come into their inheritances from their father. Maybe they were two young men with no family responsibilities fired up with enthusiasm and decided to give it a go. At this stage, it is impossible to know, but the two of them were very close, understood each other perfectly, and their skills—Harold's drive and enthusiasm and Frank's more intellectual approach—complemented each other perfectly.

Their first aircraft was a canard biplane design powered by a 7-hp Peugeot motorcycle engine and seems to be similar in concept to the successful June Bug design by the American Glenn Curtiss, though both were being designed about the same time (Fig. 6). Details are sketchy, and the only known photograph appears to show it rigged in the grounds of a house with enormous hedges behind, but the records suggest it was tested at Cornton Farm in Causewayhead in 1908.[2]

With only 7 hp, it is scarcely surprising it did not fly; it would have been surprising if it moved at all. At any rate, they decided on substantial modifications and by December, they had a canard monoplane that looked as if they simply modified the top wing of the earlier machine and one of the original two foreplanes (Fig. 7). It was a radical design powered by a 40-hp twin-cylinder air-cooled engine designed by Harold, and seemed to prefigure early microlight designs from the 1980s, with its single-surface wing and crude canard mounted on long outriggers. The engine is mounted under the wing leading edge driving a pusher propeller via a long shaft, with the pilot seated in what looks suspiciously like a leather armchair right at the back.[3,4]

There is no vertical stabilisation, and the centre of gravity looks to be about a couple of feet too far aft. It is not clear how it was controlled, but a long stick seems to end just in front of the pilot's chest, ready to impale him on a hard landing. Pitch is controlled with the canard and roll control by wing warping. Since there are no vertical surfaces, there would have been no means of yaw control.

It is certainly very different from contemporary aircraft designs. These were normally of the type that came to be known as the boxkite, and although Blériot was developing monoplane designs, the boxkite was a much more rigid structure. The brothers were certainly adventurous, and it's tempting to suggest that the design owed more to Harold's enthusiasm than Frank's more intellectual approach. At any rate, it is Harold who is credited with it.

The following is what the *Aberdeen Daily Journal* had to say on 2 December 1908:

Experiments at Stirling

Experiments with an aeroplane were conducted yesterday in a field adjoining the Grampian Engineering and Motor Company's works at Stirling. The machine is the joint production of Messrs Harold and Frank Barnwell, two of the partners of the company. It is of the monoplane type, and is driven by a forty horsepower, air-cooled engine. From tip to tip the machine measures forty feet. The engine was designed by the inventors, and manufactured by the company. The machine is compact and strong, and when fully equipped weighs about 10 cwts.

The experiments yesterday were of a preliminary nature and they were not intended to be anything more than that. The aeroplane made some smart runs along the extensive field, and a speed of about 25 miles an hour was attained, the machine showing a strong tendency to lift. The engine emitted a sound like that of a Maxim gun in operation. There was some trouble with the engine, but, on the whole, the trial was regarded as satisfactory.[5]

The location, as for their previous effort, was Cornton Farm, Stirling. They had calculated they needed to reach 35 mph to achieve take-off; apparently, it only reached 25 mph with Harold in the armchair. Perhaps this is just as well.

They clearly decided that the design was not worth pursuing. One lesson they may have learned from the exercise, particularly judging from the long grass in the rough field the aircraft was standing in, was the amount of power needed to drive bicycle wheels across rough terrain and long grass at 35 mph. Therefore, the next year's machine could not have been more different, in that they had clearly decided to return to the Wright brothers' designs with another canard biplane pusher (Fig. 8).

The span increased to a massive 48-foot wing divided into three bays. Instead of wing warping, roll control was by ailerons mounted between the two wings. The foreplane had two horizontal surfaces and three vertical, and was mounted on the end of a pair of enormous planks. It is difficult to see that there was any significant torsional rigidity, and one suspects it would have twisted from side to side alarmingly in use.

The pilot sat on the leading edge of the lower wing with the engine (a 40-hp Humber four-cylinder car engine) behind him driving two 10-foot diameter propellers by chains. The wing section is more or less the arc of a circle and very sharp edged. The whole thing is mounted on an unusual bicycle undercarriage, with small stabilisers under each wing about halfway along.[6]

The purpose of the undercarriage becomes clear when you read in the contemporary description that it was designed to take off from a rail, which is what the Wright brothers had done in all their early experiments. Clearly this was one of the lessons they had taken from their earlier trials in the long grass.

They had more success with this machine, though it was not without its problems. The first flight was at Causewayhead, and was described in the *Evening Telegraph and Post* of 29 July 1909 as follows:

Flight at Stirling

In December last Messrs Harold and Frank Barnwell, of the Grampian Motor and Engineering Company, Causewayhead, Stirling, completed an aeroplane of the monoplane type, but a series of trials led the inventors to abandon the particular form of machine with which they were making experiments, and since that time nothing has been seen of the aeroplane.

It was, however, known that Messrs Barnwell were working upon another machine, in the conception of which they were hoping by their previous experience to eliminate the defects which characterised their first venture. In a large shed on the Gorton Road they have been quietly working for months past, and yesterday morning at an early hour the public got the first glimpse of their new machine, which was run out of its shed for the purpose of testing the engine and other fittings. Later in the forenoon preparations were made for attempting a flight. The final touches were given, a screw was tightened here and there and a nut adjusted there, and at last the aviator—Mr Harold Barnwell—took his seat in the machine, which was now trembling and vibrating with the throb of the engine. A wooden track had been erected to give the better chance of the aeroplane's rising, and upon this it was placed.

The machinery was set in motion, and the aeroplane, like some huge, white-winged bird, rushed forward and with a rapid upward sweep rose into the air. The nose was pointed very highly, and after travelling about 80 yards the machine suddenly dipped and came rushing to the ground. The aeroplane was badly damaged but Mr Barnwell escaped with a few cuts and bruises.

Mr Barnwell was highly delighted with the results shown on the first test, and his explanation of the accident is that when he left the track and rose into the air he thought the upward sweep was too much pronounced, and fearing that the machine would topple backward he adjusted the controlling plane to correct the too rapid ascent. The controlling plane, however, appeared to be too sensitive, with the result that the aeroplane came rapidly to the ground. The improved construction by the Bros. Barnwell is of the biplane type, somewhat similar to the Wilbur Wright machine and is fitted with a 40-horsepower water-cooled petrol engine. The initial tests are considered highly satisfactory, and immediately the necessary repairs have been executed other trials will follow.[7]

One suspects that had he managed to take control of it in pitch, the lack of any vertical surfaces except on the foreplane would have rendered it totally unstable in yaw. This is now recognised as being the first flight in Scotland. The next we hear is as follows:

After repairs and with the wingspan reduced to 45 feet further trials were carried out on 8 September 1909 using a starting rail. A height of 25 feet was reached before the machine was damaged beyond repair on 10 September 1909.[8]

By now, experience in flying was making rapid advances, so the boys started with a blank sheet of paper once again. This time, they produced a very much more conventional machine. It was a midwing tractor monoplane like Louis Blériot's XI which had crossed the English Channel that summer, with a 40-hp twin-cylinder engine that Harold had designed and built himself. The rear fuselage was fabric-covered and the tail surfaces were entirely conventional (Fig. 9).

Roll control was by warping, and the undercarriage had two wheels with a skid in front and one under the tail. In fact, it looked pretty much like a modern single-seat sport aircraft. One unconventional feature was the radiator, which was situated over the pilot's knees, presumably to help to keep the draught off him and keep him warm into the bargain.

For the first time, this machine looked well-designed and utterly practical. The wing area looked pretty much on the mark, the aerofoil section was reasonably practical, and the tail surfaces looked as if they might be about right too. Although this design, like the others, was often credited to Harold, it is tempting to spot the more rational influence of his younger brother having some effect.

At any rate, the first flight was not until 14 January 1911, which, after their longest-ever flight of 600 yards, ended in disaster when it turned over. Damage was minimal, however, and on 30 January, Harold made another flight of a mile; for this, he was awarded the J. R. K. Law prize by the Scottish Aeronautical Society. Even this flight was not without incident, however, as he crashed again trying to avoid telegraph wires and the railway line at Bridge of Allen.[9] Harold had not had an opportunity to learn how to make turns.

Up to now, the boys had given all their time and attention to the business of building aircraft while servicing cars to make a living. Yet in 1910, Frank had met Marjorie, the daughter of Major Sandes who lived locally, and their relationship had flourished to the extent that Frank had proposed to her.[10] It was clear that the income from the Grampian Motor and Engineering Company was not going to be enough to support the daughter of a major in the style to which she had become accustomed, and so Frank started looking for employment with a better income.

With his engineering degree and his flair for engineering drawing, he decided to apply for jobs in the design departments of the larger aeroplane manufacturers. The growth of the industry was phenomenal. The first manufacturer, Short Brothers, had been set up in 1908, and by the end of 1911, there were around twenty. They came and went with bewildering rapidity.

He was offered a position as chief draughtsman at the British and Colonial Aeroplane Company (B&CAC) in Bristol, and by March, he was engaged at the Filton design office carrying out modifications to an existing machine. By the time of the 1911 census, he and Marjorie, newly married, were living in digs at 28 Lion Hill, Clifton.[11]

Meanwhile, Harold soldiered on at Grampian Motor and Engineering. He knew the latest machine was good, and made a couple more flights at Cambusdrennie Farm, Blair Drummond on 16 August and 13 October, but without Frank's support and help, he was never going to make a success of aeroplane building or motor car repairs.[12] By now, he was hooked on the experience of flying, and—like so many people since—decided it was the only way to make a living.

This was the first time the brothers had lived and worked separately, and it must have been stressful for both of them. One wonders whether Frank's relationship with Marjorie had unbalanced their relationship. There is no indication that Harold had a serious relationship with a woman at this or any other time, and perhaps he had come to rely too much on the support of his younger, quieter brother. They would always share a passion for aeronautics and ultimately their bond of blood would survive, but undoubtedly this was a defining moment in their lives. Therefore, in the winter of 1911–12, Harold closed down Grampian Motor and Engineering and moved south to take flying lessons at the Bristol school at Brooklands.

Another phase of the brothers' life was finished but it was not forgotten. A wing strut (presumably from the biplane) and various other parts are on display at the Stirling Smith Art Gallery and Museum in Stirling, and a statue was erected in 2005 at Causewayhead next to the site of their factory to commemorate their achievements. The original marble sculpture was replaced by a steel one following vandalism, and is a more accurate representation of the prize-winning machine.[12]

4

Research (1983–2007)

Granddad died in March 1983, a day short of his ninetieth birthday. He had left the RAF in 1919 to get married, and had had a varied and interesting career in engineering, working in the UK, India, and South America. On the outbreak of war in 1939, he pushed hard to get back into the RAF, but served in the Air Ministry ordering aircraft instrumentation. After the war, he became an expert in dealing with patents for the electrical equipment manufacturer Creeds. He remained interested in mechanical things all his life and had a succession of motorbikes and cars, including a 1927 3-litre Bentley in which he used to commute to work up until the 1950s.

Although he never flew again, he retained his connection with the RNAS and No. 2 Wing; I can remember his reminiscences about flying throughout my childhood. He also gave interviews and left much of his memorabilia to the Imperial War Museum in London and the Fleet Air Arm Museum in Yeovilton, which have proved invaluable in getting an accurate picture of his service there and of the details of the aeroplanes he flew.

After he died, Dad and I were clearing out his workshop and found a stick, rudder bar, and magneto. Although he had enjoyed sharing his reminiscences with us, he had never mentioned these parts to us and it was only thanks to our interest in aviation that we recognised their potential importance (Fig. 10).

The magneto was mounted on a piece of propeller blade with a couple of large copper wires leading from the high voltage output, underneath the wood and up to pointed ends over a recess intended to allow one to light a candle using the spark. I cradled it in one hand and spun the gearwheel with the other, and the spark earthed through my hand, causing me to drop it.

For twenty years, they remained treasured possessions on the mantelpiece, the magneto being spun for visitors to demonstrate its ability to produce a fat healthy spark—though I was careful never to hold it in my hand while doing so.

By now, Rick and I had built a number of microlight aircraft, and we had formed a close friendship with Theo Willford. Since reading Biggles as a child, Theo had always dreamed of flying a Great War aircraft and realised that the only practical way of achieving that was to build his own. So in 2002, he suggested we investigate whether we could rebuild a Bristol Scout incorporating these parts. In truth, we did not know anything about them, not even the type of aircraft they came from, though the fact that the magneto was a Bosch one made it likely that it was the one he had acquired from Costantini.

We pored over everything we could find, including a copy of his logbook, and from this, together with his photographs and an article in *Cross and Cockade* magazine based on his interview with the Imperial War Museum, it was clear that of the ten types he flew for the RNAS, his favourite was the Bristol Scout Type 'C', and that his favourite example of the type was known by its RNAS serial number: 1264. It seemed likely, therefore, that the souvenirs had come from 1264, and that this would be the machine we would set ourselves to rebuild. Yet we were still not certain of anything. There would be no point in starting to build if the parts had come from something completely different. We needed much more information about the Bristol Scout before we could make any decisions.

So where to start? I had been to the Yeovilton museum and seen Leo's machine, and it was not that difficult to get his contact details since he still edited *WWI Aero* magazine, one of the world's premier resources for authoritative work on aviation in 1914–1918. I wrote to him, and managed to acquire a first set of drawings. Although they were not enough to allow us to go ahead with the build, they did at least confirm that the parts we had were from a Bristol Scout. Theo and I continued to look.

There were two leads to follow up: we knew that the Bristol Aero Collection at Kemble might have a parts list, and Leo had told us that the Royal Aeronautical Society (RAeS) held Barnwell's notebooks from which the prototype had been built. Neither seemed particularly hopeful, but they were, at least, leads of a sort. Still, it seemed a shame not to follow them up, and so we persevered.

The Bristol Aero Collection at that time was a slightly ramshackle collection of memorabilia relating to anything aeronautical produced at Filton. They did indeed have a parts list, but it proved to be a rather poor photocopy and by the time we had copied it again, it was virtually indecipherable.

On a business trip to London, I had taken the opportunity to visit the archive of the RAeS, which had some original manufacturer's documents relating to the Scout, one of which was the sketchbooks in which Barnwell had designed the prototype. We did not have much confidence that would be able to read across to the Scout Type 'C', since we did not know which parts would have been modified subsequently, but it seemed worth a try. The box of documents, when it came up from the archive, had that indefinable smell of old paper that sends a thrill down the spine of anyone who takes an interest in old things, and handling the notebooks themselves was a real privilege. Barnwell writes in a clear round hand that is a pleasure to read, and each page is carefully laid out with an artist's eye, so that the information is presented clearly.

Neither lead had produced sufficient information for us to be able to go ahead with the project. Yet you never know what is awaiting you around the corner, and things were about to change for the better, in ways we simply could not have expected.

While I was at the RAeS, the archivist, Brian Riddle, said that he had received an email from a man in Houston, Texas who was interested in the Bristol M.1C Monoplane asking for details of entries in the notebooks relating to this machine. Could I keep an eye out for references while I was going through the sketchbooks and get in touch with him?

This I did, and sent the list by email to Derek Staha in Houston, who replied promptly to thank me. He also said that he understood that I was interested in the Scout, and asked if I would like copies of the drawings. I could not quite believe what he said, but answered in the affirmative, and the result was a cornucopia of over 200 scanned copies of drawings; some were original Bristol drawings, and some were redrawn by an American draughtsman in 1917 for the benefit of Americans who did not understand metric dimensions. Derek sent the drawings in a series of emails without any charge, and it completely transformed the practicability of the project.

It seemed a highly improbable connection, but presumably these were the drawings used by Leo Opdyke in the 1970s, which had somehow found their way into Derek's hands. At any rate, this was a phenomenal piece of serendipity and a gift horse whose teeth we did not care to examine.

There was one last link in the chain of information. Leo had told us that a set of plans had been drawn up by Stan Teachman, using the original Bristol drawings obtained by Leo. Stan was a modeller, and the plans were intended to give detailed assistance to those who wanted to build fully accurate models of the Scout. Leo did not have Stan's drawings, but gave me his contact details, and I wrote only to discover that Stan had died some time before.

Once again, serendipity came to the rescue. I had discovered that the only other Bristol Scout replica in the UK—one built by RAF apprentices using modern materials and never intended for flight—was being restored by one Keith Williams. When I contacted him, I discovered that he had the original ink Teachman drawings. We came to a deal, and while we had to be careful to cross-check them against the originals, they were easy to read and provided an excellent way of understanding the general layout of the machine.

Incidentally, we were able to see Keith's restoration at the Shuttleworth collection. Even though it is not intended to be accurate, it gives an excellent idea of the size and sit of the finished article. I was slightly perturbed to note, however, that the apprentices had made a very significant engineering blunder. On a biplane, the wings are braced by diagonal wires. Those going from the bottom of the fuselage to the top wing are called 'flying wires', since they do all the work in the air, while those going from the top wing in the centre to the outside of the bottom wings are called landing wires, since they hold the wings up on the ground. The Bristol Scout was one of the first to have double flying wires, to give added security in the air. However, the replica has double landing wires and single flying wires.

I spent a great deal of time studying the drawings, since strictly speaking only the drawings for the Type 'C' were relevant, and we would only be able to use the Type 'D' drawings if we could be confident that they were simply transpositions with no amendments in between. There were fifty-four Bristol drawings for the Type 'C' and twenty-seven for the Type 'D'. Ninety-five were Type 'D' drawings transcribed into American, and there were forty American detail sketches that were not related to Bristol drawings. We also had the drawings done by Ellic Somer in the 1960s for Leo Opdyke and the 1984 transcription by Stan Teachman.

The Bristol drawings for the Type 'C' were exactly contemporaneous with 1264, and were used wherever possible. Yet there were a number of significant omissions from these, and I consulted the Bristol drawings for the Type 'D' next. If they did not provide the answer, I went to the American transcriptions; the most significant case where this was required was the main fuselage drawing. There was no evidence that the overall dimensions had been altered when the Type 'D' was produced, so I cross-checked between all the available sources. As expected, there was a change between the Types 'B' and 'C', but there was a discrepancy between Ellic Somer's drawing and the American one around the tail. By comparing with the original tailplane drawing, one could see where the American draughtsman had introduced a 1-inch error in converting from the metric dimensions.

The undercarriage (known at that time as the chassis) was another area where original drawings were a bit sketchy, but thankfully Ellic Somer had done a beautiful and very detailed set of drawings that checked out with all the available information from the originals, so we went with those.

The only other element where we had to rely on non-original drawings were the petrol and oil tanks, and in this case, I was happy to go with the Bristol drawings for the Type 'D', since there were also drawings of the combined petrol and oil tanks that were introduced at that time, so that the single tanks were unlikely to have been modified from the Type 'C'.

Eventually, I was reasonably confident that we had sufficient information to build a reproduction of 1264 to museum standard, but before we went ahead, we needed another breakthrough; that was the parts list. The photocopy we had obtained from the Bristol Aero Collection was a start and had been of use in establishing the veracity of the drawing information, but a significant amount of it was indecipherable, and in particular there were photographs—of sub-assemblies and individual parts—that were likely to prove invaluable.

About this time, it seemed a good idea to take a closer look at Leo's machine, which was hanging in the Fleet Air Arm Museum in Yeovilton. We contacted the curator, Dave Morris, who kindly arranged for us to visit when it was closed to the public, and to provide a cherry picker so that we could get up close and personal with it.

When it arrived in the UK, fresh from its close encounter with the trees near Old Rhinebeck, it was certainly in need of significant repairs, but was far from irretrievable, though Leo had sold the engine (by far the most valuable part of the remains) separately. The RAF Museum had made a preliminary assessment of the structure, coming up with a list of remedial work, which was very, very thorough and conservative in its assessment of what was needed to bring it up to their standard. The museum baulked at the likely cost, and there it sat.

At this point, in stepped Sir George White, great grandson of the founder of the B&CAC, who was keen to preserve his family's illustrious heritage and recognised that this was the only reasonably accurate representation of one of their most important designs. He therefore purchased it in order to ensure its survival, and it is now on loan to the Fleet Air Arm Museum in Yeovilton.

It was repaired to static condition, and left with the structure largely uncovered (except for the centre section and rudder), with a dummy engine. Today, it hangs over the prototype Concorde, giving an almost perfect illustration of the advances made in aviation within a fifty-year period by illustrating one of the first and one of the last products of the Bristol company's Filton works. The uncovered airframe is the most graphic way of showing the fragile structures in which our grandparents went to war. For us, who needed to see every detail of the construction, it was the greatest piece of luck.

In early January 2007, Theo and I went down, camera and notebook in hand, and had a great day measuring and photographing every part, admiring Leo's workmanship and attention to detail, and making that essential bridge in understanding between the two-dimensional drawings and the third dimension of the real thing.

Dave Morris also let us get up close and personal with another of his Great War treasures: a Sopwith Pup that had been built to museum standard and flown, before being grounded to live out its days in the Yeovilton museum. We particularly remembered Dave's infectious enthusiasm for the authenticity of the work. Even the screws attaching the plywood cockpit surround were at the correct spacing; this was something of a driving force behind the decisions we made during our own build process. Finally, Dave gave us the contact details for the Scout's owner, Sir George White.

Later that year, we contacted Sir George, who invited us to his house. Nothing could prepare us for the simply astonishing document he showed us. The original parts list was a working document, copies of which would have been circulated around the factory. What he owned was a coffee table book, printed on top-quality photographic paper, bound in maroon linen paper and complete with 'photoshopped' images of parts, sub-assemblies, and the internal construction of the Scout.

Dated November 1915, it said on the front 'Price 20/-'. Clearly, it was not a working document, and clearly it was not actually for sale, since the information would have been top secret at that time. Sir George had found it in the bottom drawer of his great grandfather's desk, and it was, so far as we knew, the only copy in existence. It is, and remains, a mystery, though my suspicion is that it was a Christmas present to the first Sir George in 1915 from his brother-in-law Edward Everard who ran a print works in Bristol and did all of B&CAC's publicity.

At any rate, to us it was worth far more than 20/-, since it gave every detail, not just for any Bristol Scout, but for 1264's precise batch. Sir George carefully photographed every page for us, and it has formed the backbone of our entire project. The photographs have proved invaluable in providing any number of precise manufacturing details, from the seat and safety belt to the petrol tank and many, many other things.

With this information, we were finally confident of being able to remanufacture 1264 exactly as she had been, and it was time to see if we could get the piece of paper which would allow her to fly.

5

Frank Barnwell:
Bristol Beginnings (1911)

When Frank Barnwell started work at the B&CAC in 1911, aeroplane manufacture was not a run-of-the-mill business, and manufacturers could be broadly divided into two types: the large firms with strong links to the military (such as Vickers) and those started by aeronautical enthusiasts (such as Shorts and A. V. Roe). There were many others dipping their toes in the water, but any businessman worth his salt would have looked at the prospective market for the aircraft of the time and decided it was far too speculative.

One exception was Sir George White, who, having started life as a solicitor's clerk, had built up a very successful business empire in public transport (trains, trams and buses) in many English towns as well as Dublin. He was also a well-known benefactor to the district having made handsome contributions to the Bristol Royal Infirmary, the Red Cross, and others, and it was for this public service he received his baronetcy.

His investment in aviation was not primarily for financial gain or indeed because he wanted to fly. Sir George was fifty-four when he sent a Bristol Tramways delegation to meet Wilbur Wright in France in October 1908 and spent 1909 laying the foundations for his new business. In February 1910, he launched the B&CAC, primarily because he understood that aviation was going to be of critical importance to Great Britain's defence, and he wanted to ensure that there was a strong manufacturing base for the fledgling industry. The family is said to have invested half a million pounds (around £50 m in today's money) into the company before they saw a penny back.

The Board consisted of Sir George, his younger brother Samuel and his son G. Stanley White (later Sir Stanley White, 2nd Baronet). Sir George was unquestionably the visionary and driving force behind the enterprise, but he and Samuel had to balance their involvement in aviation with tramway and many other business interests. It was Stanley, becoming managing director in 1911 at the age of twenty-nine, who took all the day-to-day decisions. Stanley was well-qualified for the job, having been brought up in business by his father. He was also a fearless horseman and carriage driver, who had taken up the new hobby of motoring with enthusiasm. He liked nothing better than to exercise both his managerial and his practical mechanical skills in this thrilling new technology (Fig. 11).

They decided from the outset to use Bristol as the brand name, so all their aircraft were called Bristols in the same way that aircraft produced by A. V. Roe Ltd were called Avros; however, I shall continue to use B&CAC as the company name and Bristol as the brand name throughout this book.

B&CAC had been set up in the Bristol Tramways omnibus depot and repair shop at Filton near Bristol. The general office was in the adjacent Filton House, a private residence which had been bought for the purpose. Sir George also established top-class flying schools at Larkhill on Salisbury Plain and at Brooklands near Weybridge in Surrey, which was a hub for aeronautical activity at the time. By the outbreak of war in 1914, the Bristol schools had trained more than half of all British pilots.

By March 1911, when Frank started, B&CAC was the largest aeroplane manufacturer in Great Britain employing about 100 people, and had enough space to build five machines at a time. It had been in existence for only a year, and yet it had already turned out sixteen Boxkites at a price of £1,000 each (of which £520 was for the Gnome engine), and at the training schools, seven pupils had obtained their Royal Aero Club brevets. Stanley had been appointed managing director in January and the company's capital had been increased to £50,000. It had won an order from the Russian government for Boxkites in November and they had been demonstrated as far afield as India and Australia. They had been used for trips round Malaya and South Africa, and were being regularly used in competitions in Great Britain, as well as in both schools. Several of the instructors had been hired in France.

Nevertheless, it was clear that the Boxkite was rapidly being outdated, and the design office was a hive of activity. George Challenger, the chief engineer, had been drafted in originally from the Bristol Tramway company and had learned to fly. Pierre Prier, an outstanding pilot and engineer, joined in June 1911 to design a fast monoplane to compete in the Gordon Bennett race.

Gordon England, a top competition pilot on Bristol machines, was also drafted in to the design office in August when he showed talent as a designer.[1] Others also contributed: Archibald Low had mathematical talents and Frenchmen Robert Grandseigne and Léon Versepuy were also designing the Bristol Racing Biplane at this time.

When Frank joined, Grandseigne and Versepuy were completing work on the Bristol Racing Biplane, Challenger and Low were starting work on the Bristol Monoplane, and Gordon Challenger was also working on the Bristol Biplane Type 'T', a development of the Boxkite. It is therefore easy to see why Frank would have been delighted to be offered a position there.

So what did the Whites see in him? Frank was not above average height, of slight build, and with a spectacularly receding hairline that left him with a tonsure of fair hair and a moustache. He was slow to speak because he liked time to think carefully about his response. He had a habit of tugging his earlobe when he was thinking. He was polite and considerate, and there was a natural authority about him which, with his premature baldness, soon earned him the nicknames 'Daddy' and 'The Old Man'. Stanley White may have seen in him a kindred spirit, since both men were quiet and introspective and felt (unlike Stanley's father) uncomfortable in the public eye.

Yet what else would he bring to the business? Clearly a degree in engineering had the potential to be useful, and he had a natural talent as a draughtsman. If he had shown them the photographs of the Barnwell machines, they were unlikely to have been particularly impressed, except possibly for the last one. Not only was he not a pilot, he had never flown, which would have been a significant drawback. Nevertheless, they must have seen something in him, and took him on in March as chief draughtsman.

The last time he had been in a design office was at Fairfield Shipyard, which would have been calm and orderly, with a rigid hierarchy and well-established procedures. The contrast between that and the design office in Bristol must have been remarkable; the aviation industry was changing rapidly, and even in B&CAC which was well-funded and run by men who knew how to organise a business, people were coming and going all the time, as we have seen.

Frank must have felt a little overawed by this array of early talent, all of whom were capable and even exceptional pilots who could bring a wealth of practical experience to their designs. He had never flown, and the Barnwell machines were primarily Harold's; they were very primitive in comparison to the machines being turned out here. So although he was not employed to design aircraft on his own, about six different designs by all of the other men in the office were going through the office, and he was involved, at least as a draughtsman, in some or all of them.

By the end of 1911, Challenger, Low, and Leslie MacDonald had been poached by Vickers, which had set up their own aeroplane factory, and Prier had returned to France. In January 1912, Henri Coandă, son of the Romanian War Minister, would join the company and six months later, Gordon England would leave.

Although Frank was quiet, affable, and polite, and had spent much of his life in a supporting role to his older brother, a steely core of ambition was beginning to flower in him, perhaps as a result of being married. He wanted to design aeroplanes, not just be a draughtsman, and it must have appeared that his talents were being overlooked in Filton, so on 28 November 1911, only seven months after joining B&CAC, he approached H. V. Roe, managing director of the A. V. Roe Company in Manchester founded the year before, with an offer to invest £2,500 in the company.[2] He also paid half the cost of a 45-hp Viale engine for installation into a Roe biplane, designed a mount for it, and was offered a job by Roe in Manchester.

A. V. Roe and Company had been founded by early pioneer aviator Alliot Verdon Roe and his brother Humphrey.

However, although H. V. Roe also managed the successful family firm manufacturing webbing, compared to B&CAC, it was a shoestring operation and one suspects that Frank, who was familiar with the idea of senior management from his father and large organisations through his shipbuilding, would have instinctively known that B&CAC, with eighty employees, sufficient space to build five machines at a time, and a seemingly bottomless pocket of capital available would have been preferable if only he could do more rewarding work.

Nevertheless, he was on the point of accepting the position at A. V. Roe when, in December 1911, he received an offer he could not refuse from B&CAC, and the die was cast.

Many accounts claim that Frank Barnwell joined B&CAC in the autumn of 1911 as Chief Draughtsman for the top-secret X Department (of which more later), but this does not fit the facts. There is no question he was he was in Stirling in January 1911 when Harold flew their final machine, and the census shows him in Bristol by May, which supports C. H. Barnes who states that he joined the company in March. The X Department was not set up until December, and there is no evidence he was given responsibility for design work until then.

Incidentally, the Viale engine was used in 1912 on the Avro Type 'F', a radical, fully enclosed two-seater that crashed in 1912 with Harold Barnwell at the controls. The damaged engine was apparently acquired by Frank in 1919, repaired, and used in his single-seat Babe design which was intended for sale to private pilots. A replica of the Type 'F' is now at the Museum of Science and Industry (MOSI) in Manchester, and the Viale engine—the one acquired by Barnwell—is on display at the Science Museum in London.

6

Registration (2007)

One of the first questions you need to decide when approaching a project of this type is the degree of care with which you want to replicate the original aircraft. Generally, there are three classes into which they might fall.

Original

To fall into this category, you need to have at least one part that can be shown unequivocally to have been part of the original aircraft, together with documentation that shows the complete history of the machine. The most extreme example of this is the maker's nameplate, around which you then rebuild the entire machine from scratch.

You might think that is a bit absurd, but you should bear in mind that an aircraft which is unquestionably original may have very few—if any—original parts. Aircraft are lightweight and highly stressed, and over the years parts will naturally have been replaced due to wear and tear, corrosion, or accidental damage.

No one questions their authenticity, so you see the scenario suggested above is not significantly different; it is just that the replacement process (provided you can show that the aircraft has been rebuilt according to the original design and materials) happens all at once, instead of over a period of years. The constructor may even decide to incorporate modern features (digital instruments, updated engine, etc.) but it would still be an original machine.

Replica

A replica is a newly built machine that looks like an older one but, even though it may contain some original parts, lacks the continuous history to connect it with an original aircraft.

These two categories are the only ones recognised by the UK's Civil Aviation Authority (CAA), though many would like them to introduce a third category. The problem is that the definition of a replica is too broad. Some are built with incredible attention to detail, replicating every part of the original, actually being more accurate than some original machines, while others may bear only a superficial resemblance to the original. For many machines, it is the original engine that is the sticking point; they are very difficult to get hold of, and difficult and expensive to operate if you do.

Yet original airframes can be pretty impractical too. The undercarriage will be very fragile by modern standards; linen fabric can sag in damp weather; and a wooden tailskid is quite impractical if you need to operate the aircraft anywhere other than on grass. So a replica can involve substantial redesign, even to the extent of using modern welded steel tube construction instead of wood, and a relatively modern radial or in-line engine to replace the original rotary.

Reproduction

Those for which every effort has been made to replicate the original in every detail are commonly called reproductions, and many think it is time the CAA adopted this definition when registering aircraft.

We had to decide very early on which route we were going down. We spoke to Ernie Hoblyn, who flew a replica Sopwith Triplane at air displays, and he said that, even with a modern engine, the 'Tripe' (as the Triplane is commonly known) was difficult to operate owing to its limited (well, basically non-existent) crosswind capability.

If you have not come across the problem before, here is a quick rundown. An aircraft flies because of its speed through the air, not over the ground so it is always best to take off or land an aircraft facing into the wind. That way, the wind gives you a head start in achieving airspeed, even before you start moving. Conversely, if you take off downwind, the wind is actually hindering you, so that you have to go much faster over the ground in order to get flying speed through the air.

It is even worse when the wind is blowing across your take-off path—the crosswind situation. An aircraft is designed to fly straight ahead otherwise it would be almost impossible to steer it. Yet if you try to take off or land with a crosswind, there will come a point where the wheels are taking you in one direction and the wings are trying to fly you in another, and the result (unless the aircraft has been designed with this in mind) is undignified and usually expensive.

In the First World War, all airfields were broadly circular, meaning that you could take off and land in precise alignment with the wind, and avoid the crosswind problem, so aeroplanes were not designed to manage them. These days, virtually every airfield has one or two runways only, making the operation of these early aircraft much more problematic.

Ernie also said that a replica was only really useful as a display machine; even with a modern engine, it was usually too impractical to be used for sport flying, and it was not of interest to museums, since it was not historically accurate.

For us, the problem was fairly easily resolved. We wanted to build and fly my Granddad's aircraft, not something that looked a bit like it. We were not particularly interested in display flying and we were interested in being able to pass it on to a suitable museum once we had flown it a few times. Finally, we had the information to be able to say hand on heart that every part of the machine would be exactly as in 1915. So, the decision was taken: Bristol Scout 1264 would be a reproduction.

Different countries have different views on how much regulation to apply to a home-built aircraft such as this. In the USA, it would fit into the 'Experimental' category, and would receive more or less no supervision apart from a fairly rudimentary check by an inspector before its first flight.

In the UK, it would have to receive a Permit to Fly, a lower category document than a full Certificate of Airworthiness, and these are administered by an organisation called the Light Aircraft Association (LAA). It is a member association that looks after home-built aircraft on behalf of its members. I have been a member and an inspector for the LAA for more years than I care to remember, so I was pretty familiar with the normal procedures.

If you want to design your own aircraft, or import a kit that has not already been approved, you will need to provide a reasonably complete set of calculations to show that it meets an acceptable airworthiness standard. You will also generally need to carry out a number of load tests to demonstrate positively that the aircraft is sufficiently strong. The materials will need to be from approved sources to the correct standard, and the build will be overseen by an LAA inspector. Then the machine will undergo careful flight tests against an agreed programme to ensure its performance and handling do not hold any nasty surprises. This is all daunting stuff, and the cost of getting an aeronautical engineer to do the necessary calculations can be sufficient to put most people off, quite apart from the load and flight testing.

Yet for historic aircraft like ours, there are some concessions made in recognition of the fact that it was not designed to a modern airworthiness standard, that it is not likely to spawn a host of others, and that it is unlikely to be flown except by experienced pilots in ideal circumstances. The rule they generally apply in these cases is that provided it is an historically accurate reproduction of a production machine (not a one-off experimental sort), structural checks are not required. However, it still required the *imprimatur* of the LAA's chief engineer, Francis Donaldson. Therefore, in October 2007, Theo and I took a set of drawings for him to look at to see if he would be prepared to take it on as a project.

Francis is a very experienced aeronautical engineer and test pilot and takes a particular interest in early aviation (he flies a replica Sopwith Pup, for example) so while we clearly needed his approval to go ahead, his comments would also be constructive and helpful.

He spent a couple of hours going through the drawings with us, and he came up with a list of queries to be resolved. None of them was a show-stopper, however, and while we were going to have to do some investigation before coming up with solutions to the issues raised, we felt fully justified in carrying on with actually going ahead and starting manufacture.

7

Frank Barnwell:
X-Planes (1911–1913)

The offer Frank received was this: Sir George White had been approached by a naval lieutenant, Charles Dennistoun Burney (son of Admiral Sir Cecil Burney), who had flown as a passenger in a Boxkite fitted with floats in October. He was keen to develop the idea of naval aircraft capable of operating with the fleet independent of land bases, and had studied work by two Italians, Forlanini and Guidoni, on the use of hydrofoils. His father put him in touch with Sir George, and Burney Jr suggested developing patents for his ideas. The Whites were enthusiastic and, having been assured of Admiralty support, asked Frank to take charge of the project.

It was no wonder he decided to stay—here was a research project involving the newest ideas with the possibility of opening up a completely new use for aeroplanes. He would be working on it full time, with funding from the Admiralty. Also, if he managed to make it work, his path to greatness would be assured.

There is a typed document in the RAeS archives that purports to be Bristol hydro-aeroplane policy in 1914, but appears to me to be the original submission from Burney, in which case it would date from around November 1911. It sees two possible avenues for the use of aeroplanes at sea: machines capable of use with existing warships, and the use of more standard aeroplanes on specially developed ships.

It points out that the best option for an aeroplane manufacturer is the first—in other words, to design an aircraft capable of use from existing warships, and it then goes on to outline a long list of requirements for such a machine. It specifies wings that can rotate and fold back against the side of the fuselage, hydrofoils to enable it to lift clear of the water prior to take-off using waterscrews, and two engines, either of which can be used for water power, but both of which would be needed for the air propeller.

The plan was for the machine to be stowed in the davits of a warship like any of the other boats carried aboard, with the wings folded and air propeller horizontal. It would be hoisted out with the crew aboard, and they would presumably start the engine (in neutral, so to speak) and erect the wings.

They would then engage one or other engine to the waterscrews and taxi out to the take-off point, when they would accelerate until it lifted out on its hydrofoils far enough to be able to let the air propeller rotate in the breeze. In this state, they would have to keep her level and properly trimmed using the water or air control surfaces and simultaneously engage the clutch for the air propeller, then disconnect the drive to the water propellers and accelerate further to take off.

There does not seem to be any discussion about how to land it. Presumably, even if the air propeller clutch were disengaged, it would continue to freewheel like a windmill, and therefore it would come into contact with the water when one touched down. Alternatively, the crew would have to bring it to a complete stop at a sufficient height using a shaft brake, after which they would have no opportunity to adjust their landing approach. The document is not dated, but by 19 December 1911, Frank had written a report drawing up ideas for a pneumatic wing based on tests he had carried out the previous week.

The experiments started with a cylindrical rubber tube in order to establish its basic mechanical properties and how they vary with pressure. Next, he tried restraining it into a more aerofoil shape to see how the rubber tube deformed in between (and ended up breaking the formers), and with astonishing speed came up with a plan consisting of a rubber tube with internal ties restraining it to a more or less aerofoil shape, and external ribs based on the structure of a bicycle wheel rim distorted into the final aerofoil shape.

He recognised that this would not be strong enough on its own, so he introduced vertical spokes into the rib design. Of course, they could not go through the rubber envelope, so it was effectively divided into little independent cells between each of the ribs by pairs of vertical divisions. Frank also suggested the rear fuselage be pneumatic, and that the machine be controlled by bending the pneumatic fuselage.

In the meantime, Burney had come up with a suggestion for replacement of the monoplane wing with a series of tiny wings one behind the other, like the primary feathers of a bird wing.

All of Frank's ideas (and another for constant-speed water propellers) were written up into patent applications between late December 1911 and February 1912.

Clearly, however, the idea was too radical for the Whites, and they abandoned the idea of folding wings at least to start with. Burney's original proposal, a modification of the GE1 biplane then under construction, was designated X1 but was not proceeded with, although a well-known photograph of Burney shows a model of the proposed scheme.

In order to preserve the secrecy required by the Admiralty, Frank had been moved out of the main office at Filton into a private house, No. 4 Fairlawn Avenue, overlooking the school training ground, and in early January he was joined by a freshly recruited draughtsman, Clifford Tinson.

Frank produced a comprehensive set of calculations in February 1912 for the lift and drag of the hydroplanes (hydrofoils), wings, and propeller. They are dense and complex, and clearly demonstrate his talent as an engineer. The proposed layout was a large tractor monoplane of no less than 17-m (55-foot 9-inch) span with a watertight round-bowed boat as a fuselage and three long legs (known as hydropeds) replacing the normal undercarriage (chassis).

Each leg had a 'ladder' of hydrofoils capable of lifting the boat clear of the water. 'Hydroplanes' (aeroplanes that took off from water) were common at this time; in the absence of prepared landing fields, water was an attractive alternative. Virtually all of them were modifications of a land plane fitted with floats, but these had a number of disadvantages.

The floats were heavy and created a lot of drag in the air. They were generally flat-bottomed and could only be used in calm conditions, and on landing their high drag in the water tended to tip the aircraft on its nose. It was felt that the hydropeds would overcome many of these problems, but introduced a further complication in that they would not support the machine when it was stationary or moving slowly. Burney's solution was to use water propellers to get up to sufficient speed that the machine rose out of the water, and only then engage the air propeller to get into the air.

Frank drew up a wooden planked fuselage with a bluff bow covered in canvas. There were two hydropeds at the front angled outwards and a third at the tail. He and Burney had abandoned the idea of two engines and had an 80-hp Canton-Unné water-cooled radial engine at the front driving a conventional two-bladed air propeller and a pair of waterscrews at the bottom of the two front hydropeds via long shafts inside the legs and bevel gear drives at top and bottom.

Hele Shaw in Oldham had come up with purpose-designed clutches so that the engine could drive either or both systems. There were two seats side by side behind the large wings, which employed warping for roll control; the tail surfaces were conventional. It was called the X2, and, following checks of the centre of gravity on 6 May 1912, it was loaded on the lighter Sarah on 9 May and shipped to Dale in remote Milford Haven at the south western corner of Wales for secret trials.

Secret or not, the trials were frequently witnessed by the White family, and presumably Burney and Barnwell as well, since they had no other responsibilities at that time. There are photographs in the White family archive—many stereoscopic taken on glass slides—showing the family and the trials.

George Bentley Dacre had studied engineering at Bristol University and obtained his pilot's RAeC brevet the previous November. He was employed as assistant test pilot under Busteed and was at the controls of X2 throughout its test programme. His diary (which is kept at the National Aerospace Library) records all the details.

Initial flotation tests on 13 May showed that the hull (without the wings) was not watertight where it was penetrated by the hydropeds, and it was insufficiently stable. After some difficulty getting the engine started, initial water trials on 17 May showed up a number of problems. The trailing edges of the hydropeds came off more or less immediately; the clutch slipped, and it had a strong tendency to heel to the left. On 25 May, they mounted the X2 across the Sarah and tried the air propeller, and this caused a lot of vibration of the hydropeds.

It was clear there was a good deal of work to do on both power trains, so they waterproofed the hull and on 30 May engaged the services of a torpedo boat destroyer (TBD) from the Naval dockyard to tow the X2 to see if the hydropeds were satisfactory. At 8 knots (kt), there was no lift. The following day's tests showed a tendency for the X2 to roll to one side or the other as it started to lift above about 8 kt. On 3 June, Henri Coandă was present and suggested that the alignment of the hydrofoils might be to blame. The following day, the inner halves of the hydrofoils were removed.

This improved the stability a bit but not enough. By 10 June, they had fitted larger hydrofoils and steerable rudders on the front hydropeds. Testing in a 30-kt wind and a steep chop, the towrope broke, but stability was still found to be unsatisfactory. Larger rudders and hydrofoils were fitted, as were the wings (in the hope that they would improve the stability) but tests on 11 June showed that the wings needed to be waterproofed and have tip floats fitted.

Ten days later, when the wind was back up to 30 kt again, yet more towed tests with even larger (1 square foot) rudders proved more satisfactory, though a mysterious tendency for the bows to dip before they were lifted clear of the water was thought to be caused by downwash from the bows affecting the hydrofoils.

There was a three-week break from trials while modifications were carried out, but on 13 July 1912, they tested the static pull of the water propellers, finding that the pitch was too steep, causing the engine to stall. Burney wrote a letter to Phillips at the factory saying that the thrust from the propellers was much less than obtained by Forlanini and tried to identify reasons for this.

Full towed trials on the modified machine were not recommenced until 26 August and were undertaken, either behind an available TBD or the tender Medina. The TBDs were fast (more than 20 kt) but were steam powered and at 125 feet long must have been difficult to manoeuvre precisely; poor old Medina could only do 10 kt, and even less than that with the machine in tow.

By this time, the troublesome hydroped casings had been modified and a new tail hydroped incorporating vertical and horizontal control surfaces had been fitted. As before, trials were commenced without the wings being fitted. The 'elevator' proved effective at controlling the attitude of the machine on the water as the hull lifted clear, but the rudders were not effective as they were not securely mounted to their shafts. When one leg came out of the water, it suddenly flipped the other way. When this happened, it was incumbent on the towing team to slip the tow immediately in order to avoid further damage.

This was fixed, and the subsequent towed trials were more successful, though still suffering from stability problems. On 30 August, it was determined that this was because the tow was attached at the bottom of the hydropeds, making it unstable as the machine started to heel. On 2 September, they managed ten minutes continuously under tow and felt they were beginning to get somewhere, though the test was terminated by a bent elevator.

It is not clear precisely which of these trials were witnessed by Burney and Frank, but although it was clear they had a long way to go—it still had not proceeded under its own power, either on the water or in the air—they were starting to get confidence that the hydropeds were at least looking as if they might be practical. At any rate, ten days later, with the elevator fixed, they ran more towed trials with weights in to simulate the engine; on 20 September, they were confident enough to carry out runs with Burney and then Frank on board (Fig. 12).

How must he have felt? He had submitted a formal report to the Whites summarising the results of these tests on 7 September and the day before giving an upbeat assessment. This was very much uncharted territory and here they were on the verge of a breakthrough.

So it seems likely that he was there on the following day, 21 September, when they conducted another trial, this time with the wings fitted and no less than 500 lb of ballast in the bow to mimic the engine. The conditions were marginal for such a trial—30-mph wind and 4-foot waves increasing—but the tow behind TBD 049 was exactly into wind with the aerodynamic controls locked (presumably because the pilot, George Dacre, had his hands full with the water controls). Control seemed good and at 10 kt, she rose just clear of the water (Dacre could feel the water rudder control go limp in his hands); at 12 knots water speed (around 40-kt airspeed), she lifted a full 20 feet into the air in a *cabré* attitude (i.e. fully stalled with the nose very high).

The crew on the TBD slipped the tow. This must have seemed the instinctive reaction, but had they held on, it is likely the nose would have been pulled down by the tow and the situation might have been saved. As it was, Dacre was just a passenger since the air controls had been locked and could only sit and wait as she lost way, stalled, and dropped her right wing. The wing broke as it touched the water and she settled in the water on her right side with the left wing up in the air. Dacre rolled out of the cockpit and swam clear as the X2 rolled on to her back and quickly sank. They were able to get hold of the end of the towrope and recover the wreckage, but it was decided that it was not worth using and they would start again.

Frank started work on it right away, but it was not until March 1913 that construction was started and although this cannot have occupied Frank full time, what he did the rest of the time that winter seems a bit of a mystery. At any rate, the X3, when it finally appeared in August 1913, was slightly larger with a broader hull and larger wings of 17.6 m (57 feet 10 inches) with ailerons instead of wing warping and wingtip floats with small hydrofoils. The hull was still round-bilged and bluff-bowed, but was sent to Saunders at Cowes for covering with their special Consuta plywood system. One of the reasons identified for the instability on the hydrofoils was the fact that both propellers turned the same way, and it was felt that it might be a torque reaction. On the X3, two contra-rotating propellers were fitted in tandem (one pushing, the other pulling) on a separate central leg. It had a 200-hp water-cooled radial Canton-Unné engine amidships with two seats as before (Fig. 13).

I must admit to being slightly bemused by the use of the very bluff bowed hull shape, which is reminiscent of a galleon of the sixteenth century. By this time, it was standard practice on flying boats such as the Curtiss Model 'E' to use a hard chine planing hull, but it may be that since the machine rose out of the water at only 8 kt, a planing hull was not thought necessary.

The X3 was shipped to Dale again and Dacre recorded towed tests on four occasions in August. After that, he left the project and Busteed took over in the expectation that actual flight was possible, and Dacre was relatively inexperienced. Towed tests showed the hydroped control surfaces to be very effective, and initial self-powered trials using an 80-hp Gnome engine (according to C. H. Barnes, though how they managed an air-cooled rotary engine inside the hull, and presumably being regularly splashed with seawater I cannot imagine) and temporary structures to locate the tip floats showed that control was also good under her own water power. There are sketches in Frank's notebook in January 1914 for full-span ailerons for the X3, complete with construction details, but this idea was not pursued.

When the air propeller clutch was engaged, however, the high thrustline caused the nose to dip, so Frank designed an additional horizontal control surface between the propeller and wing at the front of the fuselage. It seems odd he did not simply enlarge the elevator at the back to give more control authority, but there was probably some good reason for this alternative scheme.

It was fitted, along with the 200-hp Canton-Unné engine in June 1914, but as Busteed taxied out, it hit a submerged sandbank and was substantially damaged. By this time, Frank was busy on other things and although his calculation book includes entries up to June 1914, it would seem unlikely that he was as closely involved with the X3 as with the X2.

In any case, the Admiralty refused to spend more money on the project and it was abandoned. Burney's active mind also cooked up an 'aerial torpedo'—essentially a guided glide bomb—on which some tests were carried out before it too was dropped as impractical; he ultimately found success with his paravane idea, which became the standard method of clearing mines for many decades.

Busteed had no sooner completed the X3 trials than war was declared and he volunteered for the newly formed RNAS, where he went on to transfer to the RAF in which he served with distinction for the rest of his career.

As a postscript to the whole affair, there is a letter in the National Aerospace Archives at Farnborough from Frank to B&CAC chairman Stanley White in December 1913 when the X3 machine had completed initial trials but before it was fitted with the larger 200-hp engine. It includes an exquisite sketch of a proposed alternative arrangement for the Burney concept—one that looks altogether more practical (Fig. 14). It was never built, of course, but he revived the idea in 1921 for another seaplane with retractable hydrofoils (the Type 66), though this too remained unrealised.

Myrus Deane, Combe Dingle, Westbury-on-Trym

17 Dec 1913.

Dear Mr. Stanley White

As I threatened a few days ago I herewith enclose small sketches of a suggested design for a hydro aeroplane.

I thought of this type of thing over a year ago when getting out drawings for Burney's first machine, when the patents were being got out.

I mentioned it to Phillips, asking whether he thought these swinging air propellers might be included in, or added as a substitute to, the patents, in case the idea might be of value.

But we concluded that they probably could not be patented & would also probably not be worth it if they could.

But I still rather like the idea. One retains in this scheme, the strong Boat Body fuselage unit & good disposition of weight & thrust in flight, as in Burney's machine, also the greater efficiency & sea-worthiness of Hydroplanes over floats (?) but I think also that the weight could be considerably less & the air propeller efficiency greater than in X3.

You will note that I've stuck the hydropeds more or less in a bunch, like Chassis struts—I think this would be all right for stability (with such short legs) & it would of course give good wing stay leads & make a decent rigid structure.

Of course I don't know if the thing would be of any use, but I do think the design has points & would I think be better than the present X3.

No clutches with their actuating gear is another score.

I'm sorry to bother you with this, but trust it may amuse you.

My main reason for sending this in is to get in first with my claim for the brain-wave of air propellers on swinging radius arms, in case there should be any wild competition for the patent rights!

Though as a matter of fact I'm rather taken with the design right now, having just drawn it.

F. S. Barnwell.

As a postscript, the concept of hydrofoils on a seaplane has been tried since; in 1929, the Piaggio P7 was built for the Schneider Trophy races, but never flew. In the 1950s, the Convair F2Y Seadart was intended to be a waterborne supersonic interceptor. Four were built, but it never went into production.

8

Harold Barnwell: Instructor (1911–1913)

Meanwhile, what had happened to Frank's brother Harold? If you read the press reports of the time, you will find no mention of the name Barnwell from early 1911 and the winning of the Laws prize until June 1912, and when the name recurs, it is not Frank, whose work was top secret, but Harold.

As we saw in an earlier chapter, he made a couple more flights on the prize-winning monoplane in the late summer of 1911, and there is no record of his activities during the winter of 1911–12, but in the last week of June 1912, his name appears in the list of those learning to fly at the Bristol School at Larkhill on Salisbury Plain under the tuition of Bristol's senior pilots Pizey and Busteed.[1] He was clearly a fast learner, because he was awarded his brevet by the Royal Aero Club on 3 September.

Harold's address is given as Lewisham, which possibly indicates that he had obtained employment by this time at Vickers, one of the largest conglomerates specialising in military hardware, having added shipyards, car makers, and gun and torpedo manufacturers to their original steel foundry business. In 1911, they had, like Sir George White, seen the military possibilities of aeroplanes, and set up an aviation department at Brooklands in Surrey which had become the *de facto* centre of aeroplane activity in the UK and acquired more or less all their design expertise by poaching it from B&CAC.

Certainly, by November, Harold was employed at the Vickers School at Brooklands as an instructor himself, making an excellent twenty-five-minute flight on Friday the 14th and another on Saturday 15 November, on No. 5 Farman with a student called Pollok.[2] On the Saturday, he went for a flight of twenty-five minutes in the same machine, reaching 4,000 feet.

Meanwhile, a bomb-dropping competition in which Tommy Sopwith and Harry Hawker competed was entertaining the crowds. It is interesting to note that even at this stage, aviation of any sort was a spectator event and in any sort of decent weather crowds would collect to watch the goings-on and magazines such as *Flight* would report each flight.

On the Sunday, Harold participated in a relay race, in which a baton was flown round a circuit then handed over to the second pilot on the ground before being flown round the circuit a second time. Harold teamed up with Merriam from the Bristol school and came second to Harry Hawker and a Mr Spencer. Unfortunately, he also walked into the tailplane of the Farman, breaking some teeth and injuring his upper jaw. It sounds extremely painful, and kept him out of the air for a while.

By the beginning of March 1913, Harold had taken over from Leslie MacDonald as chief instructor at the Vickers school at Brooklands, and started making a name for himself and for the school at a time when schools generally were in transition; the previous year five schools had shut down and nine had started up.[3] Then in June, he was very busy at the Brooklands Flying School, testing and instructing.

Among his distinguished passengers was Major Brancker, who had only obtained his brevet the week before, and who went on to have a very successful career in the RFC and RAF (where he became an air vice marshal in 1919), and then as Director of Civil Aviation from 1922, dying in the crash of the ill-fated R101 airship in 1930.

On 28 June, Harold participated in a handicap race at Brooklands on a Blériot monoplane; for the whole of the following week, he was very fully employed giving instruction.

In September, he was in the news again. In this report he participated in a wager placed by the colourful Noel Pemberton Billing. The report in the issue of *Flight* dated 27 September makes entertaining reading:

Mr Pemberton Billing Wins a Wager
    Last week, as most people know, Mr. Pemberton Billing made a most remarkable demonstration of how it is possible to learn to fly and secure a pilot's certificate within the space of a few hours. Subsequent to the feat we saw Mr. Pemberton Billing, whose account of his experiences was as follows:
    'The flight was the outcome of a wager made at Hendon when Handley Page stated that on his automatically stable machine anyone could learn to fly in a very short time—twenty-four hours, to use his own expression. I stated, in reply, I did not believe in automatic stability, but I did believe in the skilful handling of a machine, and that any man who had enough sense to come in out of the wet could learn to fly a known flying machine in one summer's day.
    The result was that I made a wager with Mr. Page that he, as the inventor and constructor of his own machine, could not learn to fly it

in the time he stated, and I made another wager that I would take any aeroplane that he could secure and would not only learn to fly but obtain the Royal Aero Club's certificate within twenty-four hours of sitting on the machine, the terms of the wager being £500.

This attempt was to start at dawn on Wednesday morning, and the ticket was to be completed before dawn on Thursday morning. As I found it impossible to hire a machine for the purpose, I had to buy a machine eventually, to be able to carry out the conditions.

At a quarter to six on Wednesday morning, in drizzling weather, I started at Brooklands on the Henry Farman biplane which I had acquired, which is a facsimile of the one that Paulhan flew to Manchester. Mr. Page was to make his try at Hendon. Mr. Barnwell, chief pilot of the Vickers school, volunteered to come up as passenger and verbally instruct me, I taking the pilot's seat and controls.

After four minutes taxying Mr. Barnwell gave the sign to shove her up in the air. I did so, and we attained a height of 200 ft flying steadily. Mr. Barnwell accompanied me for about 20 to 25 min in the passenger seat, during which time I succeeded in doing some dozen circuits of the aerodrome. Several figure eights, two or three *vol plané* landings and some landings under power were carried out, and as it was raining and the machine was sodden and sluggish in consequence of carrying two 13 stone men, this made the landing rather speedy and much more difficult in consequence. At the end of 25 mins Mr. Barnwell left me, and told me to get up and get on with it.

I immediately started away without any taxying, rose straight in the air at an exceedingly dangerous angle, amid the yells and shrieks of the spectators. I did a half circle and landed successfully, got up again immediately and did a circle and landed successfully, and then rose again and did five circuits. It was my intention to do twelve, but the petrol running out brought me down, the idea of coming trouble dawning upon me by the missing of the engine and the frantic waving of petrol cans by agitated spectators below.

The rain had then set in so heavily that I was obliged to put the machine away for half an hour, at the termination of which time the machine was brought out again, and Mr. Barnwell went once again a passenger for three or four minutes to test my right-hand turns before allowing me to essay the figure eight alone.

Immediately on descending, Mr. Barnwell jumped out of the machine, and I took her up at once, doing three successful eights. During the right hand turns of these I managed to execute the most alarming banks, and, from inexperience, startled by the angle at first hung on to the struts. When I had descended from this stunt, on Mr. Barnwell's orders I proceeded to practise *vol planéing* from an altitude of about 100 ft., with the engine cut off, which experience I found about the most arduous of all.

While I was performing my gyrations in the air Mr. Barnwell thought it about time to send for Mr. Rance, the Royal Aero Club official observer. There was some delay in finding him, as the weather, which was puffy and wet, never led him to believe anyone would want his services on such a morning.

Eventually he was found, and kindly consented to observe, notwithstanding the short notice given. Incidentally this entailed a loss of an hour or more in the time in which it would have been possible for me to have taken my ticket, because it stands to reason that if I was capable of doing the test at a quarter past nine I was quite as capable of doing it at a quarter to eight, so I was practically waiting during that time to go through the regulation tests.

Although Mr. Rance expressed himself as exceedingly dubious about the advisability of attempting, he consented to act in his official capacity. I then rose in a very steep climb to a height of about 250 ft., so as to make sure of the altitude test once and for all. Then I came round with a left hand bend, and proceeded on my first five figure eights.

The five, so I was told afterwards, were good sound flying of an experienced airman, although the fifth right-hand turn proved an alarming one. I was flying over the paddock, where my wife was watching very anxiously, and to give her confidence I waved my hand to her, taking my attention off the elevating plane for the moment. The machine, as machines will on right-hand turns, shot up, throwing me back on my seat.

The position was rendered more hopeless, undoubtedly, by my grabbing hold of the 'JOY stick' to recover myself, which caused her to stand on her tail. She stopped dead in the air, about 200 ft. up, and then fell about 100 ft. tail first. From the looseness of the control, caused by the machine being stationary, I jumped to the conclusion that the wires were broken, and tried to save the position by throwing all my weight forward, with the result that when about 50 ft. from the ground the machine righted itself and dived head first.

This, of course, was not attributable so much to my throwing my weight forward as to the fact that with me also came the joy stick, bringing the elevator down and causing the machine to dive, which immediately tightened up the controls.

I instantly realised that I had the control of the machine again, and, thinking I would be disqualified for this stunt, saved her from landing about 20 ft. from the ground, climbed up again to 60 ft. and did an extra figure eight to make sure.

Then followed a *vol plané* landing, and after listening with some impatience to Mr. Barnwell's illuminating and very forcible remarks on right-hand turns, I started off for the last half of the test, which was accomplished most successfully, finishing off with a *vol plané* from 100 ft. with the engine cut off, and brought the machine to rest without switching on again, with the elevating plane over the heads of the observers, thus succeeding in obtaining my pilot's certificate before breakfast on the morning when I had for the first time in my life sat in a flying machine that flew.'

Of course, it will be remembered by all those who were in aviation in its pioneer day that Mr. P.-B. built three machines of his own, and the last attempt he made, when he smashed the machine up, is a matter of record. He dug the engine out of the ground, and did his right arm and leg a lot of good at the time.

Afterwards the tracks of the wheels of the machine were examined with a magnifying glass and it was found that 60 ft immediately preceding the smash there were no wheel marks in the ground, which we believe constitutes a record for being the first all-British machine to get off the ground.

Brooklands in Surrey was where the Vickers school was located, and where most of the serious development work on aviation took place. Hendon in north London had been set up by Claude Graham-White as a centre of excellence for aviation, but was in practice much more given to entertaining the crowds; hardly surprising since it was within easy reach of much of the metropolis by public transport. On 8 November, Harold was an entrant in a race from Hendon to Brighton and back, flying a Martinsyde monoplane, but he retired on the return leg when it started to get dark.

By the end of 1913, Harold had established himself as one of the premier instructors in the country, having trained thirty-five pupils at the Vickers school. This was less than Bristols (seventy at Brooklands and forty-seven at Larkhill) and the military Central Flying School at Upavon, (fifty-six), but was very creditable and earned him seventh place in R. Dallas Brett's *History of British Aviation 1908–1914* list of top British pilots for 1913.

9

Bits and Pieces (2008–2012)

Having looked through all these drawings, it was time to decide whether we could actually build it, and the answer was that, compared to many later types, there were no serious challenges for a homebuilder.

Most of the research phase had involved myself and Theo Willford. For the actual building, the team increased to three, with my brother Rick as an essential part of the team. Although Theo and I were reasonably competent workmen, Rick is a craftsman, and there were going to be critical areas where his abilities would be sorely needed.

The Scout follows standard practice of the time: a frame made of wooden struts with metal brackets at the corners and wire bracing to hold it all together and keep it straight. There are two large metal frames at the front on which the engine is mounted, the lower wings are attached to the bottom just behind that, and the pilot sits just behind them. The wings are similar: wooden spars (the large bits running the length of the wing) with ribs made from plywood and metal brackets with wire bracing internally to keep it straight.

Most of the wood is spruce, which is still used for aircraft construction today, although the front part of the fuselage and some of the undercarriage was made from ash, because it is better for the heavy loads imposed by the engine and by the wheels. Although ash is not as commonly used for aircraft, it is still available. There are one or two more unusual pieces of timber. The tailskid, on which the tail rests on the ground, is made of hickory, and semicircular hoops underneath the wingtips (to stop them catching on the ground) are of Malacca cane. Yet these should not be too hard to find.

The metal sheet and tube are still available from stock in the original sizes, as are the nuts and bolts. There are no complicated forming processes, forgings, or castings to be made; pretty much everything was designed to be made with hand tools on the bench.

The wire bracing consists of cable where the loads are highest and piano wire elsewhere. In every case, they have a turnbuckle (a screw adjuster) to adjust the tension in each wire. These are specified on the parts list as coming from a specialist manufacturer; in other words, although the aviation industry was in its infancy (I do not suppose there were 1,000 aircraft in the world by 1915), there were already people going into business to manufacture specialist parts.

Of course, there would be difficulties, the main one being an original engine. Although the RNAS originally specified the Gnome 7 Lambda for its reliability, there are virtually none in existence today; just a couple on static display in museums. Thankfully, Granddad had fitted 1264 with an 80-hp le Rhône 9C of which there are a good number still in airworthy condition, and we were reasonably confident of being able to find one.

The other area that caused some concern was the instrument fit. Thankfully, there are very few: airspeed indicator, altimeter and engine tachometer, clinometer (spirit level) and watch in the panel, and a floor-mounted compass. The first thing was to get the airframe finished.

Establishing exactly what state an individual aircraft was in at any particular time can be a mammoth task. Thankfully in our case, however, things were a good deal easier. We had the drawings and parts list relating to exactly the right batch. It was the first batch, so we could ignore all the later modifications. We had a good photographic record to double check against.

One of the first things we did was to check the control column we had against the photographs in the parts list, and were delighted—and relieved—to note a perfect match. The design of the bottom lever changed fairly early on from machined aluminium to welded steel, and when we checked what we had got against the photograph, it was clear this was the earlier aluminium type.

The parts list proved the most spectacularly useful asset. Every last part is listed and cross referenced to the relevant drawing. Every split pin, piece of locking wire, every thread and leather patch are listed, together with what it is made from and sometimes the amount of raw material required to make it.

We spent a very long time going through its ninety-five pages, and so far, I think I have discovered three mistakes (apart from spelling inconsistencies). It is brilliant, and I wish I knew why they produced and published it.

All three of us had built aircraft before, and we knew that wood was a lot easier to work than metal.

Metal

Although the metal parts were relatively simple—they could be made from tube and sheet material that was easily available off the shelf—each little bracket is a complicated shape with all sorts of weird lightening holes, and making each of them by hand would probably double the build time. There was an awful lot of them—somewhere between 250 and 300—so we took the decision straight away to make use of modern metal-cutting facilities and have them transferred on to CAD, so that they could be cut by machine.

Until recently, that would have meant a plasma cutting machine: a tiny stream of incredibly hot 'gas' that melts the metal and cuts a path through it. It is a very good system, but there is one little snag: next to where it cuts the slot, the metal warms up and expands, and so the cut that you make does not go quite where you want it; it is therefore not really possible to predict how it is going to expand, or how to compensate for this movement.

However, technology has come up with an even more extraordinary solution: a water jet. It may seem incredible that you could actually cut metal with a stream of water, but this jet is very thin and contains fine abrasive powder, and it is at a pressure you cannot really imagine. It can cut a very, very narrow slot—1 mm or less—to levels of accuracy that leave one's imagination reeling. As it does not heat the metal up, there is no distortion and it leaves a perfectly clean cut. It will cut metal up to an inch thick.

In September 2008, we gave the task of putting the metal parts on to digital drawings to Derek Walton. We threw him in at the deep end with the undercarriage (i.e. the bits where the wheels are attached) because they were by far the most complicated part, and he did a superlative job. These days, it is pretty old hat to see a 'drawing' in three dimensions, and to be able to turn it round and look at it from every angle, but it was still pretty cool to us.

Yet in early 2009, we were approached by Dave Graham, who had just completed building—from scratch—a very fancy aircraft with a radial engine called a Great Lakes biplane. His enthusiasm won us over, and he took on the very tedious and time-consuming task of transferring the details of every bracket from the original 1915 drawings to the computer.

Eventually, we started to get a stack of bits back from the cutting process, and Rick and I started to fold them ready for welding in Dad's workshop at his smallholding in Worcestershire. Since the holes were already in position, getting the fold in exactly the right place was quite nerve-wracking, but we got better and more confident as time went on. Sometimes it involved more than one fold, and things got more complicated, since all the folds have to be in the right place, and you cannot grip the piece easily to fold it (Fig. 15).

One particular bit of forming was even more interesting. The horns are crescent-shaped pieces that bulge in the middle where they are attached to the rudder and elevators. They are made from two thin pieces of metal that have to be formed to this bulged shape before being welded together round the edges. For this, we had a rectangle of 25-mm thick steel from which we cut a crescent-shaped hole.

Then we glued a piece of plywood on to the crescent-shaped cut-out and sanded it to a nice smooth bulge in the middle. After that, we made up a press using some bolted-together angle iron on to which we fitted a 10-ton car bottle jack, and by sandwiching the workpiece between the male and female parts of the former and using the bottle jack to force the plywood bulge into the workpiece, we got perfectly formed parts every time.

When we had enough pieces made, we would drive into the Welsh hills to see Alan Haseldine. He lives in a remote village in the shadow of Hay Bluff, about 15 miles up single-track roads. There are no shops or mobile signal, and even my GPS could not pick up a location. Yet Alan has a well-appointed workshop and is a magician with a welding set, and every time we came away with more little brackets to the gradually expanding pile.

Of course, this was not the end of the work by any means. Each hole had to be drilled and reamed to the correct size and all the edges had to be dressed smooth. Some needed brazing, which required all the slag to be dressed off. Finally, everything had to be painted with etch primer to stop it going rusty.

One other technical problem we had to solve was the means of fastening the bracing wires inside the fuselage and wings. Many of them are made from wire that is about the thickness of a coat hanger but much stiffer and stronger, and the approved method of attaching them is with a little ferrule made of more of the wire. The idea is to wind the wire into a tight spiral and cut it into short lengths called ferrules. The bracing wire goes through the middle of the ferrule, through the attachment point, and back through the ferrule before being bent back to stop it all coming loose.

Yet the ferrules obviously have to be a good fit around both bits of the bracing wire, and this meant they have to be oval in cross section. If you try to wind the wire round an oval mandrel, as soon as you let go the end of the wire, the spiral tends to unwind, locking up on the mandrel and making it quite impossible to remove. So Rick came up with a cunning plan, so far as I know unused by anyone else.

He made a circular mandrel about halfway in diameter between the major and minor diameters of the oval, and wound the wire round that.

It came away nice and easily, and could be cut to the requisite lengths. He then made a metal 'box' to contain the ferrules, and put them in a press to squash them to an oval section. Goodness knows how many of these we needed, but they all worked a treat.

Wood

Meanwhile, Theo, who lives in Dorset and has a workshop attached to his house, had cleared it of his other aircraft and made a start on the Scout. He had inherited a large baulk of aircraft quality timber with another project. 'Aircraft quality' is a very high grade of timber. It is normally spruce, though Douglas fir is commonly used too, and you have to be very picky about which bits you use.

The first thing is to get it kiln-dried (this means cooking it in a very low oven for ages and ages until the moisture content all the way through is within tightly controlled limits). If you do not, the uneven moisture within the baulk may twist and split the timber when you slice it up and expose new bits to the air.

Next, you can only use timber from the right part of the log: too near the middle and the grain is circular not straight, and the relative lack of sap can make it weak or even rotten; yet the outside is not ideal either as it can have faults in it that have worked their way in from the outside, and there is too much sap flowing, making it less dense. For the bits (like the main wing spars) that take the most strain, it is critical that the grain is going in the right direction to give the wood strength in the direction you want it. Also, the grain must be straight down your cut piece and the correct number of grains to the inch too, or its strength will be hopelessly compromised. Finally, of course, it must have no faults in it; no cracks, splits, knots, or shakes.

The trouble is that although you have some control over the first of these requirements, much of the rest is a matter of pot luck. You take a piece of wood that looks perfect on the outside; you plan carefully how to cut it up with minimum waste and make sure that the grain direction is correctly oriented with the strain on the finished piece; and then you hold your breath and pop it on the bandsaw.

Then you take up the cut piece and examine it to see what it looks like, because until you have cut it to size, you will have little idea about the straightness of grain, the grain density, or the defects. It is not uncommon to have to cut two or three pieces before you get one that is good enough to go on an aircraft, and you end up with a lot of scrap wood that—if you are lucky—can be cut down for smaller parts. It may be possible to use it for less critical areas or it may end up on the fire. At any rate, what started off as a very large baulk of timber, which more or less took two of us to lift, became a very small pile of usable bits.

The wing ribs are made from plywood, and there are lots and lots of them. Thankfully, the wings are pretty much rectangular, so most of the ribs are the same. Theo made a master rib out of thicker material first and used it as a pattern to cut out all the others using a following router bit. They have to have a 'capstrip' (a little strip of ordinary wood) glued on to the edges, and that was done using a jig (a solid wooden baseboard with blocks on it to hold the rib in place) and lots of little wooden cams that rotate to hold the capstrips firmly against the rib until the glue dries.

The spars—the main timbers that run the full length of the wings and give it most of its strength—are the largest and most critical bits of wood in the aircraft. There are eight of them (two in each wing) and we had to wait for nine months until suitable material came through from our timber guru, Dudley Pattisson, known as 'Duds'. In fact, there was a bit of a scare with these rare and precious bits of timber when they were machined to size. A couple of resin inclusions came to light, and we wondered if they might have to be declared 'Duds', but thankfully they are considered okay.

All of this took a considerable time, as you can imagine, and it was not until 2012 that we were ready to start assembling the many components into subassemblies.

The Baby:
Conception (1913)

By August 1913, the X3 had been shipped to Dale, and while Frank Barnwell and Tinson clearly had to be available for any changes in design that might become necessary, the majority of the workload would fall on Harry Busteed and the test team at Milford Haven. What happened next is subject to some debate.

In his book *British Aviation: The Pioneer Years*, Harald Penrose quotes the late Harry Busteed as saying:

> The Bristol Scout was initiated by me while Barnwell and I were together at Dale getting the Burney hydroped ready ... I broached the idea of a single-seater to Stanley White. He agreed to let me have a cut at one, so while down at Dale Barnwell and I got together and produced a general arrangement drawing which we thought would fill the bill.
>
> Shortly after, when we had rounded off the Milford Haven business, we took part of a fuselage of a tractor monoplane, known as the SB5, construction of which had been brought to a halt owing to the War Office ban on monoplanes, and this we proposed to convert into a biplane.
> At 'X' Department, we started making constructional drawings in an ordinary carbon copy sketch book for issue to the works, but I was pulled out for some testing jobs, so the brunt of the work fell on Frank Barnwell and Clifford Tinson, who stuck to our original schemes, and the Scout came out.
>
> Certainly the origin of the idea had been generated by Harry Hawker, with whom I kept more less in touch after bringing him over with Harrison and Kauper.

Yet Clifford Tinson's recollection, recorded in a letter to J. M. Bruce, dated 12 November 1953 was rather different: 'SN183 was 100 per cent Barnwell in design and we did the job under the counter, as it were, presumably so that Coandă would not know what was going on until it was a *fait accompli*.'[1]

Looking at the notebooks and drawings, there is no evidence of any written contribution from Busteed; all of the notebook entries (with a couple of minor exceptions) are Frank's handiwork with Tinson doing most of the drawings and Frank doing the remainder; although it seems feasible Busteed was consulted about the configuration, his lack of engineering training would seem to exclude the possibility of his having been involved in the design process.

In any case, he was preoccupied for much of the time at Dale with assembling and testing the TB8 seaplane, while the design work is more likely to have been carried out at 4 Fairlawn Avenue.[2] It is on the cards that Busteed kept in touch with his friend Harry Hawker at Sopwiths, and had heard about their plan to develop what was to become the Tabloid, but even this was developed as a side-by-side two-seater, only becoming a single-seater later on.

It also seems unlikely that the managing director would approve such a major project without having a potential market in mind, so perhaps we have to find another explanation for the origin of the Scout.

Heavier-than-air flying had developed as part of a fascination with transport which can be seen to have started with the safety bicycle (1870s) and progressed through the motor cycle (1880s) and the motor car (1890s). Yet unlike these other modes of transport, the market for aeroplanes was always seen as military, and this was still held to be the case, even in 1913 (see much of *Flight* magazine and Fred Jane's introduction to his *All the World's Aircraft* for 1913).

Unlike the other modes of transport, which seem to have been absorbed into the military without too much fuss by ordering standard machines modified to military specifications, the aeroplane seems to have come under the gaze of the politicians and strategists at an early date, and rendered the organisation of military aviation unbelievably confusing.

This was partly because of the history of military ballooning, which was seen as the natural home for heavier than air flying, and partly due to the more or less simultaneous development of airships, but the result was a bewildering series of policy decisions that saw the purchasing, maintenance and operation of them combined, then split, then combined and then split again. In this, the major influence was Lord Haldane, Secretary of State for War, who decreed in 1909 that aircraft (i.e. airships and aeroplanes) should be designed scientifically, in a similar fashion to how the Germans worked.[3]

The Germans were no more scientific in their development of aviation than anybody else, and technology has always relied on visionary dreamers, with university research tending to follow in their wake, but Haldane decided this was the way to go, and in April 1912, this resulted in the setting up of the Royal Aeroplane Factory (RAF), who would specify and design aircraft in a scientific fashion, and of the Royal Flying Corps (RFC), who would train the pilots and operate the aeroplanes. In fact, the RAF's first designer was one of the greatest of relatively untrained visionaries, Geoffrey de Havilland, but the net effect of this policy in 1913 was that private firms were being flooded with orders for RAF-designed machines (in particular the BE2), leaving them less capacity to manufacture their own designs.

Weirdly, the Admiralty had their own separate purchasing department despite the fact that their flying training and operation now came under the newly formed RFC, and because they had no internal design capability were keen to order privately designed machines.

In February 1913, Major F. H. Sykes, commandant of the military wing of the RFC (which had been formed only a year before), had presented a paper on military aviation to the Royal Aero Club.[4] It is an excellent piece, detailed and thoughtful, yet delivered with a delightfully dry sense of humour, which shows clearly that the military were fully alive to the potentialities of aviation for the military and had carried out a careful analysis which, though it might be obviously flawed with the benefit of 20-20 hindsight, was probably about as good as they were likely to achieve with the aircraft available to them in 1912, when the major trials had been conducted.

He identified three types of heavier-than-air machines they would need.

The first was a two-seat reconnaissance aeroplane. Due to the limited power available in the aero engines of the time, a top speed of about 80 mph was all that could be expected of a two-seater, and it would be the main source of strategic information gathering, the observer being equipped with a notebook to make a detailed record of what he saw, a machine gun to provide some defensive capability, and a pilot to take care of the actual handling of the aeroplane. He would report back to the military command on his return. By this time, Geoffrey de Havilland at the Royal Aircraft Factory had designed the BE2, which met this specification admirably (Fig. 16).

The second type was the fighting aeroplane. The aeroplanes of 1912 were low-powered and very slow to manoeuvre. Turns were often accomplished using only the rudder and rapid changes of course or attitude were likely to lead to very unpredictable consequences. Accordingly, it was seen that the only way to provide offensive capability was in a two-seat pusher aeroplane, with the observer put in front with a machine gun mounted flexibly. Due to the weight of observer, armament, and light armour, it would only be capable of around 70 mph (Fig. 17).

The third type was the unarmed single-seat scout. Its function was to provide tactical information to the military command as quickly as possible so that they could be kept up to date with the situation on the ground during an action. It would not be possible for the pilot to gather detailed information in the same way as a two-seater, but because it was only a single-seater, it would be capable of around 90 mph and would therefore not need any defensive armament since it could easily outrun the lumbering two-seat fighters.

By summer 1913, the only British example of a single-seat scout was the BS1 (later renamed the SE2), designed (like the two-seater) by Geoffrey de Havilland for the Royal Aircraft Factory (Fig. 18). Design work started as early as 1912, following the military trials, and it was a radical development. By this time, the established wisdom was that biplanes were slow and reliable (and much favoured by British manufacturers) while the monoplane was faster and more manoeuvrable (and mostly built by the French, who were the acknowledged leaders in aeroplane design). De Havilland stuck with the tractor biplane layout that was regarded as superior, but designed a monocoque fuselage with a tiny rudder, and small wings of only 27.5-foot span that used wing warping for roll control.

It was first flown by de Havilland in early 1913 with a twin-row rotary engine of 100 hp from Gnome. The engine performance was disappointing and he was not happy with the rudder authority, but despite this it had a blistering rate of climb of 900 fpm (feet per minute) and a top speed in excess of 90 mph. These figures exceeded by a considerable margin the performance of the top French monoplanes. On 27 March, de Havilland was injured in a landing accident in it (the stall speed of 51 mph was very fast by the standards of the day), but it was rebuilt with the standard 80-hp Gnome rotary and larger tail surfaces. It seems likely that this was the machine that Sykes had in mind when he produced his specification.

Although the French Morane-Saulnier model 'H' had flown about this time, it was primarily designed as a sporting aeroplane, and although it was later ordered in small numbers by the RFC, it was too slow to meet Sykes's specification.

The two-seat reconnaissance type was already well served by the BE2s; indeed, they were already crowding the Filton factory, being built under licence. The two-seat fighter type was already being experimented with by Vickers with their EFB1 and 2 for the Admiralty, and was in any case a larger and more expensive design to build.

So for a private aeroplane company, looking for a new design project, the single-seat scout must have seemed a logical idea, in the absence of any significant possibility of regular orders outside the military sector. It was relatively cheap to build and did not involve any extreme design concepts (such as the X-planes).

The X3 was taken to Dale in August 1913 and trials, with Busteed in the cockpit, started soon afterwards. They were not there for long; the tests fairly quickly established that significant modifications were required, and by 20 September, the TB8 biplane arrived at Dale for trials involving Busteed.[5] In between, according to him, they had been back to Filton to look over the fuselage of the SB5 machine that was touted as capable of modification. So he might have been there for a couple of weeks. Busteed says that both Frank and Stanley White were there; this is confirmed by the White family archives.

It was during this short period that the idea of a single-seater may have come up. Maybe Harry Hawker had mentioned to Busteed that a high-speed single-seater would be a good project, and he brought this up in conversation. They discussed the justification for it, and Sykes's paper together with the RAF's BS1 prototype were mentioned. Stanley White could see the merit in it, and asked Busteed and Frank Barnwell to come up with some ideas.

They would have been able to come up with some basic principles for the design pretty quickly. By this time, the tractor biplane was the favoured layout; the faster you went, the more dangerous the early monoplanes were. The BS1 had demonstrated the possibility of reducing the size of the wings in order to maximise speed, and it is possible that Busteed, with his wide experience of different aircraft types, suggested that ailerons would be superior to wing warping for roll control. They may also have identified the potential weight reduction from simplifying the chassis and eliminating the nose skid that was more or less *de rigueur* at the time.

There are no surviving documents to substantiate any of this, but other likely points for discussion may have included the continuing need for secrecy in order to protect the work on the Bristol-Burney machines, its cost and a target date for completion.

How much was finalised in the relatively short period at Dale is not clear, but we must assume that at least the germ of an idea had been enthusiastically received by at least Stanley White, and possibly his father too, since he was often at Dale as well.

There is no record in the Board meeting minutes in respect of the project, but we can draw conclusions from the facts that are known. The design work was done at Fairlawn Avenue, and the prototype was built at the tramworks at Brislington, using the serial number SN183, which was officially allocated to a single-seat monoplane design (called the SB5) intended for the Italian government and designed by Coandă. The build location may have been for convenience, since the main Filton shop was busy on the government contract to build BE2s, but the fact that the design work was done at Fairlawn Avenue and the re-use of the serial number suggests strongly that it was considered important to maintain secrecy,

and the Admiralty contract for the Bristol-Burney machines would seem
to be the obvious reason for this.

The engine used on the prototype was the 80-hp Gnome engine that had
been recovered from No. 120, a floatplane that had crashed on landing,
throwing Busteed into the water. This is slightly curious for two reasons;
firstly, the Gnome, while in plentiful supply, was not the most powerful
engine available and might not have been the obvious choice for a high-
speed scouting machine. Secondly, dunking a rotary engine in the sea
will do a great deal of damage, some of which may not be immediately
apparent. The reasons for its choice remain obscure, but one can only
conjecture that this was not seen as a project of the first importance, and
the expenditure was kept as low as reasonably practical.

The rate of production of sketches in the December–January period was
enormous. Was this because the Olympia show in March 1914 had been
slated for its roll out? This is guesswork too, but it is certainly feasible.
What would Frank have thought of this new job? I think he must have
been delighted and somewhat relieved.

He had already demonstrated his ambition to get on in the aviation
business; as we have seen in Chapter 5, when Bristol were not keeping him
busy enough in the summer of 1911, he had a close encounter with A. V.
Roe, and even proposed investing his own inheritance with them.

By this time, it must have occurred to him that the X-plane was unlikely
to lead to the major breakthrough that had been hoped for. They had
already abandoned the inflatable wings; and the very complex gearboxes
required for the water propellers, plus the equally complex clutching
arrangement to allow the engine to drive them or the air propeller were
never likely to be practical.

The workload required of the pilot—or even two—to transfer the
power from water to air at the moment of take-off when they were fully
employed trying to keep the wings level and making sure there were not
any obstructions in the water ahead was more or less superhuman; also,
the ungainly hydropeds made the machine very difficult to stow safely on
the deck of a ship, even if one could somehow fold or remove the wings.

Finally, no one seems to have given any thought to the landing. It was
possible to lock the air propeller in the horizontal position for take-off,
but how would you return it to the horizontal position for landing?
Presumably, this would have to be done at, say, 1,000 feet altitude to
make sure it was securely locked in place before landing, and one was then
committed to a glide landing (*vol plané* in the terminology of the time)
with no possibility of changing one's mind.

The alternative—the use of floats—was well-tried and Burney's system
must have appeared to offer little or no advantage, other than the ability

to take off and land in rougher water. It must have seemed that it was not going to be the breakthrough project to launch his career.

He may also have realised that working in the isolation of Fairlawn Avenue meant that if and when the project was abandoned, his career might well be abandoned too. He had no contact with the rest of the design department, those who had been there in his first nine months having all left, and while he had more direct contact with the Whites, he may have considered that to be solely associated with a failed project such as this would mean that there was a greater risk of his being laid off when the Admiralty funding was terminated. So one imagines that wherever the impetus came from, the single-seat scout must have seemed an ideal opportunity for him.

I think Frank, for all his easy-going manner, was ambitious and determined. His father had been managing director of a large shipbuilding firm, his brother was chief test pilot for the only other sizable aeroplane manufacturer, Vickers, and he knew in his bones that he was a match for either of them. This was the perfect project to allow him to show the world his talent as a designer; the brief—make it go as fast as possible— was simple and easily achievable, and top speed would garner attention in the press and ensure the steady progress of his career with B&CAC. He valued continuity; he did not want to keep moving employers, and B&CAC were the best, the most business-like aeroplane manufacturers in the world.

I can imagine him returning to Fairlawn Avenue with a skip in his step, passing on the information to Clifford Tinson and popping down to the pub for a celebratory pint.

11

The Baby:
Gestation (1913–1914)

We do not know exactly when approval was given for the single-seater project, nor when it first appeared in Frank's sketchbooks, since the relevant one (numbered 400–500) is missing.

Nor do we know exactly when the design process started for the same reason. The only surviving book (500–600) was started on 12 December 1913 and is almost exclusively taken up with detail drawings of what was to become the new type; it is clear it was very much the focus of Frank's attention (Fig. 19).

So presumably by 27 November, the design process would have been pretty far down the road, and the first flight of the Sopwith Tabloid, which may or may not have spurred B&CAC into development of the new machine, would have occasioned intense interest; although they were unlikely to be able to adopt any of the Tabloid's features, they must have known the two would be closely compared, so they would have taken great interest in it and may have been slightly disappointed that it got into the air first.

The Tabloid was a tractor biplane as expected, with small equal span wings—smaller than the BS1 but slightly larger than those proposed by Frank—and used wing warping for roll control. The engine was the same 80-hp Gnome. The cowling was unusual, having only two small horizontal slots at the front to admit cooling air. There was an interesting variation on the specification since it had two seats that were side by side in a very narrow cockpit, making it necessary to stagger them slightly so that one's shoulders could cross over. Initial flight tests showed a considerably improved performance over the BS1, with a claimed (and frankly improbable) rate of climb of no less than 1,200 fpm with two people and a top speed of 92 mph. Although the BS1 was the real pioneer in reducing the span of a biplane to improve performance, it was the Tabloid that excited the press, who regarded it, not without justification, as ground-breaking. The War Office placed an order for forty early in 1914; this must have irritated Frank and B&CAC not a little.

The sketchbook itself is fascinating because it is original, preserved at the National Aeronautical Library, and when you open it up, you get so much more than the written information. It is 196 mm by 240 mm (somewhere between A4 and A5 size) squared on the right side, blank on the left, with a B&CAC sticker on the cover. Then there is that faint scent of old paper, which gives anyone with a sense of history a premonition of the possibility of exciting discoveries to be made.

Most of the entries in this book are by Frank himself, and the handwriting gives one a good insight into his character. The writing is large, round, and very neat. The drawings are clear and simple; he has an artist's instinctive feel for how much information to put on a page: not too much to leave the eye disconcerted and confused, and not too little so that you have to keep cross-referring to other drawings. Like Goldilocks, Frank gets it just right. On occasions—the one showing the engine cowlings, for example—his use of shading definitely indicates an artist's eye.

His is a sure hand, too; the number of corrections is astonishingly small. It is possible there was a very large waste paper basket at his side full to overflowing with screwed up rough sheets, which he used before committing himself to the sketchbook, but there are other reasons why I believe the basket was fairly small.

Each page has the date and the project number clearly marked on it. Frank was generally very methodical, and while there are some interesting anomalies, he must have had an orderly mind and been easy to work with. For all of the initial design phase, the reference is to GO2346, s/no. 183. Obviously, GO2346 is the works order number he booked his time to, but I think it is significant that there is no description following the SN183 serial number.

If we fast forward to the sketches done after the first flight, there was a new works order number (GO2447), but the serial number SN183 disappears, and suddenly it is the Scout Biplane. My theory is that SN183 was used as a disguise so that attention would not be drawn to the top-secret work going on in the X Department. Once the new aeroplane had flown, the deception was unnecessary, and the machine acquired its own serial number (SN206). At any rate, it became known as 'Barnwell's Baby' in the workshop, and that is what we will call it in this chapter.

The next thing that strikes you is the pace Frank worked at. There are seventy-seven drawings all relating to the Baby between 1 December 1913 and 3 February 1914; that is more than two for each working day. On occasions, he was in the office working on Saturdays, Sundays, and even Christmas Eve and New Year's Day. Clearly, it was work that inspired

him, and with that rate of output, he cannot have had time for lots of
rough work except for the weight calculations. Right from the beginning,
weight has been a critical factor in the design of aeroplanes, and on almost
every page, Frank has made a note of the weight of the individual item,
and using only a slide rule, this must have taken ages.

Tinson later recalled that they had been asked to re-use as much of the
original SN183 fuselage as possible (presumably to keep the cost down)
and Tinson said they had not managed to re-use anything. In fact, we have
discovered a single part that was used—the tiller (rudder) bar (on sketch
558)—and Tinson can be forgiven for having forgotten that. One might
have expected there to have been other small fittings and brackets and so
on that could have been re-used, but it is amazing how quickly one ends
up making other compromises to fit these pieces, and Frank clearly knew
he was better off starting from scratch.

There are no major surprises in the overall design. Frank would have
been aware of the BS1 at the Royal Aircraft Factory and may have had
some idea of the work going on at Sopwiths, but he does not seem to have
deliberately copied either.

By this time, the tractor biplane had become the standard layout, most
commonly with wheels at the front and a tailskid at the back. Construction
was of a spruce frame throughout with steel fittings at the corners and
wire or cable bracing, and most commonly steel tail surfaces. Aluminium
was becoming more available, but was typically only used for the engine
cowling. Doped linen fabric was used for the majority of the covering. The
new design more or less kept to all these conventions. It did not involve the
very experimental monocoque plywood fuselage adopted by de Havilland
on the BS1, or the radical cowling shape on the Sopwith Tabloid.

This may have been because Frank did not see the need, or it may have
been because it was part of his design brief to keep the cost of the prototype
down. I favour the latter since there is good evidence that he was always
keen to 'think outside the box' (in twenty-first century management-speak),
the X-plane pneumatic wing and his rotating propeller arms on the X-plane
project afterthought (Fig. 14) being perfect examples.

The wing is the trickiest part of any aeroplane design, and it is not clear
how much original design work Frank did on this. C. H. Barnes asserts
that the wings (or at least elements of the design) were taken from the PB8,
which was a pusher biplane intended as a replacement for the Boxkite that
never flew. It had four ailerons and the aerofoil section and profile looked
similar, but since it was a two-seater it would have needed scaling down.
Barnes says that the ailerons were taken direct from the PB8, and certainly
the ailerons on the prototype are enormous, which would indicate that he
had not scaled those down proportionately.

If this is true, it seems odd that he would go to all the time and effort of redrawing every part of wings and ailerons, particularly if the ailerons were actually identical. He did not bother to redraw the tiller bar from the SB8, so why would he not just refer to the aileron drawings for the PB8? There is also a problem with timing. The PB8 was being designed in November 1913, pretty much concurrently with the Baby. One wonders if this was a misprint by Barnes, and he had meant the SB5, which was the design number of the fuselage he was supposed to be reusing, but this was a monoplane, and it seems very unlikely they would have been of any use for a biplane.

I think it is more likely that Frank used the aerofoil section, the general profile, and four ailerons for roll control, but designed the wing from scratch.

Most aeroplanes up to that time had used wing warping for roll control, where the whole wing twisted. Instinctively, you would think this would be a very effective form of control, but it was not in practice, and the flexibility in the wing structure was becoming an increasing problem as airspeeds increased.

So Frank opted for the modern option of ailerons, where the majority of the wing was rigidly fixed, and small winglets (*aileron* is the French for 'little wing') hinged from the back of the wing. I am sure he will have consulted test pilot Harry Busteed over this feature. Harry had flown more types of aeroplane than most, and while there were some primitive theoretical calculations available to decide on the sizes necessary, I suspect there was no substitute for practical experience.

The size of the wings themselves was another crucial design consideration. As I said in the previous chapter, reducing their size is the easiest way to ensure the machine goes as fast as possible. The downside is that it also lands faster, and this puts huge responsibility on the pilot during the landing. They also decided to fit enormous ailerons, which would ensure plenty of roll control. This would make it easier to keep the wings level at low speed, but made it likely that the handling would be really exciting at higher speeds. It also raised the possibility of accidental spins if too much roll control was applied, though they may not have been aware of this at the time. Once again, I detect the influence of Harry Busteed here; he was a brash Australian who was a first-class instinctive pilot and knew it.

Another critical design decision to be made on the wings is the aerofoil section: the cross-sectional shape of the wings. The amount of lift generated depends on the square of the speed, but the amount actually needed stays pretty much the same since the weight remains more or less constant, so a wing has to generate lots of lift at low speed and much less at high speed. At all speeds, it should generate as little drag as possible. Also, it should

not do things unexpectedly; in particular the stall should be progressive
and predictable. Therefore, the choice of section is tricky.

Frank used an unusual section—one normally expects them to be curved
pretty progressively, but on this the top surface is more or less flat in the
middle. It is reasonably certain that Frank used one designed by Henri
Coandǎ that was used on a number of his contemporary designs, including
the TB8, and possibly itself derived from that used on Nieuport machines.[1]
It was reckoned to be a fairly low-drag section, and Frank simply scaled it
down from the larger wings on the two-seater. It is interesting to note that
when Frank was given a TB8 to modify into the GB75, he had decided to
revert to wing warping. It was not flown until after the Baby, so he would
not have had feedback on its performance during the design.

The Baby may have been as conventional as possible, but he could not
resist some unusual features. Firstly, the use of aluminium was generally
restricted to the cowling that fitted over the engine. Aluminium was still very
expensive and its properties were not well understood, and working and
welding it were pretty much black arts. It was used around the engine where
there was the greatest risk of fire, because aluminium was a good deal more
fireproof than wood or fabric. Yet Frank elected to use sheet aluminium
all the way back to the cockpit, perhaps influenced by the Coandǎ designs
being produced in the factory while he was working on the X-planes.

Secondly, almost all machines at the time had a skid (or skids) in
front to help protect them from the very frequent landing accidents
where they tipped on their nose. Typical contemporary examples include
the BS1, BE2C, the Sopwith Tabloid, and the Avro 504. Henri Coandǎ
almost exclusively used a four-wheel undercarriage with the main
wheels behind the centre of gravity and two small wheels at the end of
skids extending in front of the propeller. Yet Frank decided to go for the
simplest two-wheeled layout, relying on the skill of the pilot to keep the
tail down on landing, despite the faster than normal landing speeds due to
the small wings.

The final feature that is worth a mention is the engine cowling. A wide
variety of shapes were in use at this time, and Frank's adds to the variety.
The cowling does three jobs: it stops some of the oil being sprayed out
from the rotary engine from going all over the airframe and the pilot; it
lets in enough air to the engine to keep it cool; and it provides a clean
surface for the reminder of the air to flow over on its way past the engine.

The cowls for the Baby were designed very late in the process—at the
end of January 1914—and were frankly ugly and impractical; I suspect
Frank had run out of inspiration, put off designing them until the last
minute, and threw together a design that he was not happy with. Coandǎ's
designs used a similar half-cowled layout, but were altogether more

elegant. It seems strange that he did not choose to use one of these since they were certainly available for the 80-hp Gnome engine.

Perhaps he decided, particularly since they were using an engine with a short but very chequered history, to go for a design which at least ensured maximum cooling and was easy to manufacture, with the idea that it was something he could fairly easily modify later on. At any rate, the result is bluff fronted, causing lots of drag, with little or no cooling air going over the crankcase, relying on the completely exposed lower third, and accepting that there would be lots of oil flung about all over the place.

All of Charles Dickens's novels were published in serial form, either weekly or monthly. This required Dickens to work with huge discipline; not only was he working against the clock, but he could not go back and amend earlier parts of the book once they had been published. Frank was not under quite the same restriction but since one can account for every page in the sketchbook you can see where he has had to amend a design or cross a page out, and it is astonishing how few of these there are.

All design work was carried out at 4 Fairlawn Avenue. Barnwell and Tinson clearly got on very well together, and when Frank was eventually promoted to chief designer, he ensured that Tinson continued to work for him.

Carbon copies of the sketchbook pages were used by Tinson to make into proper working drawings, the numbers of which were occasionally recorded on the sketchbook pages as they were allocated. Unfortunately, very few of these early drawings survive, but they are numbered XD (for X Department) 659–714. Presumably the earlier drawings were for the X-planes, and they would have left a sensible sized gap in the numbering before allocating a sequence for the Baby.

Interestingly, the XD numbering sequence was continued when the design was updated (roughly, the 'C' Scout) after receipt of the first production orders from the War Office in November 1914, even though the X Department had been wound up in the previous July. They are numbered roughly 750–800, so it seems likely that the prototype drawings would have been from around XD650 to around XD750, but the highest drawing number referenced on the sketches is XD716.

The detail design shows that Frank, with a few exceptions, had a good grasp of engineering; both the stresses involved and the means of manufacture. Glasgow University and the shipyard design office would have given him a good grounding in engineering generally and stress analysis in particular, but it is amazing that the safety factors he uses are identical to those used today for light aircraft. There is no doubt his time with brother Harold in Scotland, then in the B&CAC design office, and finally on the X-planes gave him a good sense of what can be manufactured with the facilities available.

Yet there are exceptions. Perhaps the most glaring is the access to the seat. Frank would have positioned the pilot as close to the centre of gravity as practical, thus ensuring that trim was affected as little as possible by the pilot's weight. In order to save weight, he made the supports for the pilot's feet (the heel troughs) as short as possible. Once you were installed in the cockpit, it would have been snug but reasonably comfortable—for someone of Frank or Busteed's stature at any rate—but getting there must have required advice from Harry Houdini. The trailing edge of the top wing got in the way badly, and while you could stand on the seat, there was then nowhere to rest your feet as you slid down into place.

It is particularly important to save weight at the tail of the aeroplane, and the ribs for the tail surfaces are very light. Yet the struts, which go from the tailplane to the bottom of the fuselage and are only there to stop it wobbling from side to side too much, weigh almost the same as the tailplane itself.

The attachment of the wings and the wing struts seems a little odd too. When you design an aeroplane from scratch, there is a small but significant element of guesswork involved, so it would seem sensible to design the prototype to be adjustable. In particular, this applies to the precise layout of the wings, where dihedral, stagger, and washout may all benefit from adjustment. Yet the fittings on the Scout more or less preclude any such adjustment; in fact, when the dihedral was increased from 3 to 5 per cent later on, it required a small but critical change in the inboard ends of the wing spars that was not immediately obvious to the naked eye, requiring a stamp to indicate which type it was. The wing strut fittings are a nightmare to manufacture, with all sorts of strange angles and dimensions that have to be very carefully checked before welding or machining. If only he had used pinned joints, they would have self-aligned and could have been altered later.

There is a fitting in the roll control system (sketch 577) that must have had the welder scratching his head. Interestingly enough, this was intended to replace something called a warp lever on an earlier drawing (554), and by the time we get to the big redesign in November 1914, the warp lever has been restored; you wonder if Frank drew this up and then abandoned it after complaints from the welder. In fact, there is another curious anomaly here, since the roll control adopted was ailerons, not wing warping, and yet the part is called a warp lever. Is this because it is another part rescued from the original SN183? We would need sketch 469 to find out.

While we are on curious naming conventions, here are some others. We must not forget this is only five years after flying became practical, and the language was still settling down. Today, the wheels an aeroplane lands on are called the undercarriage. In 1913, it was universally known as the chassis. Perhaps more strangely, they had not decided what to call the wings. Frank uses 'wing' in the sketchbook, but it was not universal, and on the later drawings, the word 'plane' is still in common use.

The terms used for the rear flying surfaces look unfamiliar to our eyes too. Today, we would use the French word *'empennage'* to include all the tail surfaces. Typically, the individual parts would be the tailplane (or horizontal stabiliser to Americans), which is the fixed horizontal surface, with the elevator hinged off the back. In 1913, the fixed horizontal surface was the empennage, and the hinged part was the 'air elevator flap'.

Similarly, in the cockpit, the main control is generally called the control column today. In 1913, it was a hand lever or joystick, and the bit you put your feet on was a foot lever or tiller bar (we would call it a rudder bar these days). The whole machine was universally called an aeroplane; the term aircraft, which is used today, actually means any type of flying machine: balloon, airship, fixed wing, or rotary wing.

The order in which Frank drew things up was largely determined by the lead time. Thus, the first items that appear in the 500–600 book on 12 December are the engine mountings. These were made in a large hydraulic press and the special dies would have been made in the toolmaker's shop from steel and took a long time. Of course, you could not start to assemble the fuselage without them.

The stern post is the fitting right at the back of the fuselage and although it did not need special dies, fabricating needed a fair amount of time, and was needed for fuselage assembly.

After that, he drew up half size wing spars, which were used for load testing. Although he had done detailed calculations on the sizing of the spars (laid out in drawing XD659), they were of such critical importance it was felt that a load test gave one additional confidence. Obviously, these were done early in case there was a problem that would require the wings to be redesigned.

After that, he concentrated on the tail surfaces, and had those pretty much completed by Christmas Eve. He was back in the office on 29, 30, and 31 December 1913, working on wing and fuselage parts; from then on, there was scarcely a weekday when he did not produce one or more drawings through to 3 February 1914.

There is one sketch signed by Tinson, but everything else is drawn and signed by Frank. It was an enormous workload and a huge responsibility for one man, especially when he presumably must have been popping into the works at Brislington at regular intervals to check on progress, as well as keeping on top of the X-plane project. We have already seen that he came up with a radical idea for it in December, and just as the design work on the Baby was coming to a conclusion, there are half a dozen sketches for revised ailerons for the X3—Frank was on fire. The wings and ailerons occupied him for the first week of January 1914.

The wing spars were made of spruce and of rectangular cross-section (sketch 535), except that the top and bottom surfaces were cut with a slope to match the aerofoil section, with ribs consisting of 4-mm ash ply ribs with spruce capstrips. The ribs have lozenge-shaped cut-outs to reduce weight. Internal wire bracing runs diagonally inside the wing to keep it rectangular. They are supposed to run through the lozenge-shaped holes in the ribs, but fail to do so in a number of places and require some additional holes to be cut. Weirdly, this is something that seems never to have been fed back to the drawing office for revision throughout the life of the Scout and its many upgrades.

The tips slope outwards towards the back in order to reduce the drag, and the ailerons are more than half the span: 1.8 m of the wing panel's 3-m length. They are controlled by a closed circuit of cables running from the warp lever down the back of the front wing spar, round pulleys and out to the aileron. They are attached to a 'horn' on the underside of the front of the aileron, with a couple of wires leading to the trailing edge; a couple of lightweight cables from here lead up to the trailing edge of the upper aileron, and then a similar route in the upper wing but with the two upper cables joined together under the centre section. The aileron has ribs but no other internal structure, and the cables to the trailing edge look rather too close together; one can see the possibility of the inner and outer ends of the ailerons flexing dangerously.

One oddity I have been unable to resolve is that the drawings of the original wing layout dated 1 and 7 January 1913 show a dihedral angle (the slope of the wings upwards towards the tips) of 1 in 50, and yet the photographs of the prototype clearly show that they were rigged with no dihedral. Dihedral helps to make the aeroplane fly straight automatically and many aeroplanes incorporate it, so it is hard to know why the prototype did not follow the drawings. It is an important feature, and not one that would have been omitted by mistake; I can only suppose that Frank agreed to make the change but did not get around to updating the drawings in the rush to get the prototype in the air.

A good design feature that was commented on positively in the Olympia Show of February 1914 was the doubled-up flying wires (the cables that do most of the work in the air), so that failure of one would not be critical, but their attachments are slightly odd. Frank had determined that they needed to be 10- standard wire gauge (swg) (3-mm) thick, but actually made them from two pieces of 16 swg (1.5 mm) welded together along their edges. Today, we would turn our noses up at such a plan since the welding would introduce the possibility of microscopic defects that could cause early metal fatigue and because water could get in through the bolt holes and cause invisible corrosion in between the two plates.

Why would he choose such an option that was more expensive to make and introduced additional possibilities of failure? Was it because the method of cutting them out could not produce a nice clean edge with material this thick? Or was it because they were concerned that the bending process might introduce faults? We will never know, but our reproduction opted for the single thickness of 3 mm, using modern material and modern cutting techniques.

The chassis occupied him for the next three days after that. As we have already seen, he had kept it as simple and as narrow as possible in order to keep weight and drag to a minimum. The rear legs are of ash and the front legs and horizontal member behind the axle are of spruce with wire diagonal bracing. There is a single axle that only just extends beyond the width of the fuselage with standard motorcycle wheels at each end. Even an uneducated eye can see that the narrow track is going to cause it to tip on to a wingtip at the slightest excuse. The axle sits in the vee between the front and rear struts, and is attached to the chassis by many loops of bungee cord. By this time, it was pretty much the standard way of providing suspension, and indeed it is still used on many modern light aeroplanes. One needs to stop the axle from moving sideways, and Frank adopted a cunning plan involving a pair of lightweight cables from the port axle just inboard of the wheel to the bottom of the starboard chassis strut and vice versa. It is a neat system that allows the axle to travel vertically but not horizontally.

Then he sketches out the control mechanism in the fuselage. By then, the method of control was pretty much standardised; the use of a stick and rudder bar had been pioneered by Blériot in 1908 and pilots took to it immediately since it was so instinctive, as the aeroplane follows the stick. If you move the stick to the left, the machine rolls to the left. If you pull it back, the machine tips back, and vice versa. There were alternatives: Coandă favoured a 'steering wheel' mounted on arms so that it could be pulled backwards and forwards as well as turned; however, the stick was certainly the lighter of the two.

The seat may have come from the Coandă machine; it is an aluminium bucket type with lots of holes in it and was difficult to get into, but once there, it looks extremely uncomfortable if you did not have a cushion. It is also said to have been adjustable, and indeed there are some cables shown on the general arrangement drawing XD700, which may have supported the seat and allowed for adjustment of height.

The stick is forward of the instrument panel (which would put it out of sight) and has the 'blip' switch (to control the engine by momentarily cutting the ignition); the quadrant throttle lever (like that on a motor mower) is very far back, making it very difficult to get at easily in flight. Rotary engines have a separate mixture control. Later, it would become standard to have two quadrant levers mounted side by side, but at this early stage, the mixture is controlled by a rotary knob, which would add to the awkwardness of the controls.

There is no floor to stand on, and only tiny heel troughs a long way forward to rest your heels on in flight. It was not at all clear how you would get your feet all that way forward without putting one or both through the aluminium skin. All in all, it does not seem to have been designed with the comfort of the pilot in mind.

The petrol tank is right forward and made of riveted steel. It has no gauge on it, so you have to rely on your watch to know how much longer you can stay in the air. The oil tank is of riveted brass and is behind the pilot with a long rubber tube leading to the oil pump just behind the engine. With the controls detailed, he spent 17 January 1914 sorting out the tail skid.

There is another oddity of design here. It obviously makes sense to line up the empennage (tailplane) leading edge and main spar with fuselage stations so that it is mounted as rigidly as possible, but for some reason this did not happen. One wonders if he had designed the fuselage based on a preliminary layout and then decided to increase the size of the tailplane, by which time it was too late to sort the fuselage out.

Both 19 and 20 January were spent on the engine cowling and aluminium forward fuselage coverings, and that was pretty much it for the design process.

After this, Frank had to address modifications to the X3 ailerons while the workshop got on with building the Baby. No doubt Frank was called over to Brislington to settle minor design details, and this would have occupied him more and more once the design work was complete.

There is no record of Harold's activities in this period, but it seems likely that he was back in the Vickers office at Brooklands, emulating his brother and helping to design a Scout biplane. The Vickers machine was a two-seat tractor biplane powered by the 100-hp Gnome Monosoupape and looked (apart from the extra seat) similar in many ways to the one being developed by his brother at the same time. It is intriguing, but fruitless, to speculate on how much—if any—information they exchanged in this process, but they shared the simple chassis layout, extensive use of aluminium on the forward fuselage, and balanced rudder of Frank's Baby.

However, the Vickers chassis was from steel, not wood, and the aerofoil section looks almost like a flat plate. Both occupants were seated fairly low in the deep fuselage, making it difficult to carry out careful observation, and impossible to use any form of defensive armament, but it was claimed to have a remarkable top speed of 100 mph, due no doubt in large part to the small wingspan of 25 feet—larger than Frank's Baby but smaller than most single-seaters, let alone the two-seaters.

12

Wings and Things (2012–2014)

So it was not until 2012 that we had enough parts to start assembling them together. We had decided Theo's workshop was the ideal place, since it was dry and could be made reasonably warm.

This was not something you would want to do all on your own, so we agreed we would arrange for concentrated weeks with two or three of us working on it together. The first of these was at the end of May 2012, and in that year, we met five times, by which time we had the wings and tail surfaces pretty much finished. These were tiring but hugely satisfying times. People tend to think that once you have the drawings and the parts, it is simply a question of putting them together, but in practice, about 90 per cent of the time is spent making decisions about how to do the job; actually doing it (provided you have made the right decisions) is pretty much an afterthought.

That is why it is so important to have more than one person on the job, but of course they have to get on well together, and that was where we scored in spades. I have been cobbling things together with Rick since he was old enough to hold a saw. Theo is the relative newcomer to the team, but we have both known and worked with Theo for the past thirty years, and by now we know each other's strengths and weaknesses to a 'T'. There are disagreements, but never any arguments, and our skills are a pretty good blend. If Theo told me I was doing something wrong, there was no hubris; we discussed it and picked the best solution.

By far the most nerve-wracking part of the process was shaping and drilling the wing spars. It had taken nine months to get eight aircraft-quality bits of timber, and we absolutely could not afford any mistakes. So we fretted for ages; the sides were routed out in places to save weight; the drawing showed where these were supposed to be, but what if the drawings were wrong? It is not uncommon to find drawing errors that were sorted out on the shop floor but never reported back to the drawing office to have the drawings corrected.

The spars taper off at the outboard ends. Would they match the shape of the ailerons? Would all the holes for the aileron hinge bolts and so on still have enough wood around them to be strong enough? Would the other holes—for wire bracing, aileron control cables, and so on—fit with the placement of the ribs? Most basic of all, but one of the easiest of things to get wrong, are they all the right way around and right way up? It was so easy to end up with two starboard spars instead of one port and one starboard. We spent at least a day going over this time and again, each of us double checking the other's work, and trying to think of other possible problems down the line.

Most of the routing, shaping and drilling was pretty straightforward, but the inboard ends, where they are mounted on to the fuselage, was complicated and required Rick's special woodworking skills.

There was one point on the wing that had caught the eye of Francis Donaldson at the LAA, and that was where the flying wires attach to the wings; to explain why, we will need to indulge in a little theory.

When an aeroplane is flying normally, the lift of the wings and the weight of the fuselage will try to bend the wings upwards. On a biplane, there are wires running from the bottom of the fuselage to the fittings on the top wing that stop that happening; these are called the flying wires (the ones in the opposite direction, from the top of the fuselage to the bottom wing are called the landing wires, of course).

On the Scout, the wires are attached to fittings that also hold the end of the vertical struts between the wings, and these fittings are clamped to the spar by four bolts. Yet the bolts do not go through the spar because that would weaken it at the point where it is doing the most work, so you can imagine that when the load comes on the flying wires, they might drag the fittings along the spar towards the fuselage, which would definitely spoil your day if you happened to be flying it when that happened.

Yet Frank Barnwell had thought this through carefully; there was another plate sandwiched between the fitting and the spar, which led outboard to a bolt that went through the spar at a point, which was less highly stressed.

However, Francis Donaldson at the LAA had looked at this and was not confident that the bolt going through the spar was strong enough and asked us to make up a test rig, and sure enough, when we tried this, the bolt started to pull through the spar timber at about three times the normal load, instead of the six times that is considered acceptable.

We had to come up with a solution, and Francis suggested gluing hardwood blocks to the softwood spars through which the clamp bolts could go. It was a simple solution that avoided making more holes in the spars and would be virtually invisible on completion.

The drawings were astonishingly accurate and we found few problems with the assembly as shown on the drawings. The only place where there did seem to be a problem was with the internal bracing wires, which did not seem to fit through the lightening holes in the ribs; we therefore had to widen the holes or make new ones so that the cable could run straight without touching anything.

We have been blessed with serendipity throughout the project, and one particular piece of luck involved Theo's living room. Theo lives on his own, which means that he does not need permission from anyone else to use particular parts of the house for aeronautical purposes. We found that the completed wings fitted in the wall behind his sofa in the living room to within 10 mm (Fig. 20).

The cut-out for the aileron fitted exactly around a picture hanging on the wall, and the only downside was that each time we completed assembly of another wing, the sofa moved a few inches closer to the TV, so he had to find another pair of glasses to be able to see it clearly.

One new skill we were going to have to learn was wire splicing. This is pretty much the same as rope splicing, but more painful, and since every cable on the aeroplane would need an eye splice at each end, there would be around 200 needed in all. Each of us had a go, and Theo's was clearly the best, so he was promoted to splicer-in-chief, on double his previous pay (Fig. 21).

It is a requirement that finished splices are tested to 67 per cent of their proof strength; for this, we devised a rig that looked a bit like a medieval trebuchet, with 3-m lengths of timber giving sufficient leverage to apply the necessary force. It also doubled as the test rig for the wing spar fittings. By Christmas 2012, the wings were substantially complete and were comfortably stacked behind the sofa watching television, so in February 2013, it was time to start on the fuselage.

If the central parts of the wings are the spars, the central parts of the fuselage are the longerons—the four long wooden strakes that run from front to back. These are not quite as straightforward as they look as the front part is made of ash (to withstand the vibration of the engine) and the back is of spruce (for lightness); also, the spruce tapers down from 30 mm square at the front to 19 mm at the back.

The first job was to cut the taper. We had been debating for most of 2012 how best to do this, without having come to any very sensible conclusion. Faced with having to make a start, therefore, Theo and I decided simply to very carefully scribe a pencil line all the way down and post it very carefully through the bandsaw, in the sure and certain knowledge that—as with the spars—if we made a mess of it, getting replacement timber would be very difficult. Thankfully, with Theo and I watching that bandsaw blade and the pencil line like gambling addicts, they came out perfectly.

So the next stage was to join the front ash part to the spruce. In 1915, this was done by means of a long-tapered joint, which was glued. But since the animal glues used in those days were not very good, they also used copper boat nails and then bound the whole thing together with twine.

These days, modern glues are as strong as the wood, so there is no need for the boat nails and twine, but we added them anyway to make it as realistic as possible.

Finally, the bottom longerons curve up at the front. This had to be done by steaming them. It is fairly easy to rig up a wallpaper stripper to a long piece of plastic downpipe, but we could not work out what to do with all the condensation; in the end, we poked the longeron out of the bathroom window with the front end inside the plastic downpipe, the bottom end resting in the toilet pan.

Getting it from there on to the worktable so that it can be cramped into position has to be done as quickly as possible before the wood cools off. It was not easy, but it worked fine, and the ash formed a perfectly even curve that stayed in place once it had cooled overnight.

One particular concern was the length of the bracing cables. There are about thirty on the fuselage alone, and they are spliced permanently on to the relevant fitting at one end, with a strainer on the other. Although the strainers would allow some adjustment of length, it is not a great deal, so we had to calculate the length of each one from the drawings so that Theo could get on with splicing them in time for the fuselage frame assembly. Since I had done the calculations, there was a good deal of nervousness when we marked one side of the fuselage out on the table and offered up the longerons, struts and fittings with their cables attached. Thankfully they were all within limits and I did not have to ask Theo to remake any.

Thereafter, forming the basic structure of the fuselage was relatively straightforward; starting from the front, you post the longerons into the big plate engine mounts, and work aft, adding the relevant metal brackets and spruce struts and connecting the cables.

Aviation (particularly sport aviation) has more aphorisms per square metre than any other occupation. For those who build their own aeroplane, the favourite is '90 per cent complete, 90 per cent to go'. This was the case for us. The basic fuselage frame was complete in a couple of weeks, and we were deluded into thinking it was only a question of filling in the remaining bits—if only.

Of course, it was an important step to fit the seat and controls, partly to enable us to dream about actually going flying, but it was clearly of very great practical importance to see if we could fit, particularly since the Scout had always been noted for the cramped cockpit, and my Granddad, who was my height, could only get sufficient room for his knees by removing the seat cushion. It was an important moment when the original stick and rudder bar were fitted into the fuselage for the first time, and to find that they actually fitted as intended.

We have been pretty fierce about sticking to the original build standard. However, when I looked at the transverse seat supports I became a little concerned that modern supersize pilots might be a bit much for them, and after doing some calculations that confirmed they were a bit marginal ended up making them half an inch deeper. This would, of course, make further inroads into the available space for my knees.

It was not until July 2014 that we were able to have a first go, and even then, the fuselage was propped up on trestles, not on its own undercarriage. Nevertheless, it was possible to get a preliminary idea of the room available, and it was clear that it would be pretty tight for me, though Theo was having to stretch to reach the rudder bar at full lock. Would we end up having to make yet more modifications?

Later that summer, we came across another wonderful bit of history. The top of the brass control column has a plastic grip, and the plastic was cracking with age and coming away from the cork interior. A little googling showed that it was in fact taken from a 1913 motor cycle, and that a small outfit in Kent called Dial Patterns had moulds from which replacements could be made.

I took it down and proprietor Dick Pettit thought it might be possible to put the original in his mould and recast it. So we carefully removed the original bolt securing the grip and eased it off the stick for the first time in ninety eight years. Underneath was an amazing revelation. The stick had been extended by 50 mm. Pretty obviously, this was at the instigation of my 6-foot 3-inch (1.905-m) Granddad, so that his fist would clear his knees (Fig. 22). This did two things; it established beyond reasonable doubt that the parts were from the original 1264, and our reproduction was even more personal than we had thought at the outset.

Yet before we could establish the final seating position, there was another decision to be taken. There is an important cable called a carry-through which seemed to have been left out on the drawings, apparently because it got in the way of the heel troughs on which the pilot's heels slide as he operates the rudder. We felt a bit nervous about leaving it off, but what would we do with the heel troughs? If we ran them underneath this cable, there was the possibility that your heels would catch on it as you were operating the rudder, which did not seem ideal. However, if we raised the heel troughs to go over the top of the cable, it might be the final straw that made it impossible for me to fit my knees under the instrument panel, with or without the cushion, bearing in mind that the seat was already half an inch higher.

In the end, we came up with a satisfactory compromise; the heel trough was raised by the tiniest amount so that the cable almost went through it, and I found that by wearing pumps with the thinnest of soles I could get full movement of the rudder bar, which was a considerable relief, I can tell you. Yet our troubles were not entirely over yet.

The elevator cables run from the control column under the seat and back to the tail. The original drawings show four little brass pulleys under the seat to guide the cables and make sure they run freely. Yet when we tried the whole thing out, it was clearly a non-starter. The problem was the cables connected to the bottom of the stick; when it was moved from side to side, so did the cables and they jammed up in the little pulleys. There was no way this had ever worked satisfactorily. When I looked among the drawings, we found that later Scouts had used a roller instead of pulleys, allowing the cables the necessary lateral movement. Had 1264 been modified thus? We will never know, but this was at least a factory-approved arrangement, and it seemed likely that an unofficial fix sorted out in the workshop had eventually found its way back up to the drawing office.

By this time, we had started to connect all the main parts together; the rudder, tailplane, and elevators were permanently attached to the fuselage; temporary wooden struts enabled the centre section of the top wing to be mounted above with the wheels underneath. It only required four more temporary struts to allow the wings to be attached as well, so that we could at last get an idea of the overall sit of the thing. We were very proud to be able to show Granddad's son, my uncle Christopher, around and he took great interest in it (Fig. 23).

At this stage, the external woodwork—cabane, wing struts, and the undercarriage legs—were temporary only, designed to ensure that we knew exactly what length they had to be and what angles they should be cut at. In fact, this was tricky work since there were no right angles or parallels anywhere; they involved many careful measurements and modifications before we were happy that everything was exactly correct. The actual struts were waiting in the wings, having been made by Rupert Wasey of Hercules propellers, based on 3D drawings made from the original drawings. They were very beautiful and very expensive; we could not afford to make any mistakes with them.

With those done, it made sense to remove the fuselage to Milson in Worcestershire, since the next stage was the fitting of the oil and petrol tanks, instrument panel, and the ply cover between the petrol tank and the cockpit, so we hired a 7.5-tonner, and it was just possible to fit it in. For the first time for a couple of years, Theo had nothing in his workshop, though the wings were still watching telly from behind the sofa in his living room.

13

The Baby is Born (1914)

The last sketch for the original Baby is dated 3 February 1914. There is a final one on 18 February drawn by Tinson, detailing some additional formers for the rear fuselage, and one is tempted to conclude that somebody in the workshop must have handled the fuselage too roughly and broken some of the relatively delicate stringers that formed the nice rounded shape.

At any rate, this was a Thursday, and the first flight is recorded as being at Larkhill (about 100 miles away on Salisbury Plain) the following Monday. In order to fit these formers, the fabric covering, if it had been applied, would have to have been removed to get access. The only way I can see all this fitting in is that the machine had already been moved to the B&CAC hangars at Larkhill (which are still standing, incidentally) before the 18th, and perhaps the damage occurred when they were getting it off the lorry. Even so, it is quite a tight schedule to get the fabric removed, the frames fitted, and the fabric repaired and doped (it would take at least three coats, each of which had to dry before the next was applied), unless they were working over the weekend.

They would also have wanted time to check the machine thoroughly before flying it. The alignment of the wings would need to be rechecked after reassembly, and the entire airframe inspected to make sure everything was correctly tensioned, aligned, and wirelocked. The engine would need to be test run and all the controls checked for correct operation. This is not something that can be rushed, and would take at least a day or two.

All of the histories of the Baby state that the first flight was on 23 February (which was a Monday). Yet the Larkhill logbook indicates that there was no flying on that day, owing to poor conditions (strong blustery wind), and Wednesday the 25th is the first date on which test flying of the new biplane is recorded.

There is no doubt the pilot was Harry Busteed, however, and the photographs show that Frank was at Larkhill at more or less the same time. It would seem cruel and unusual punishment to insist that he be in the office on this occasion (Figs 24 and 25).

As for Busteed, he seems to have been possessed of a robust self-confidence and one cannot imagine him being so concerned, even if it was his neck on the line. He may also have been thinking about the engine, which had been dunked, with him, into the Solent. He himself was in the water for twenty minutes and in fear of his life, and he may have wondered how much invisible damage had been done to the engine.

The aeroplane itself looks neat and compact; to a modern eye, the wings look very small and the ailerons look positively enormous, reminiscent of a modern top-of-the-range aerobatic machine. The cowling looks awkward and ugly, but the reminder of the airframe seems well-proportioned.

Whether the first flight was on the Monday or the Wednesday, it clearly seems to have gone off okay, and I am sure there were a few celebratory pints downed in the evening.

We do not have detailed information about the flight tests, but Busteed was pleased with it and was able to achieve a top speed of 95 mph, which outstripped both the BS1 and the Tabloid that may have been thought to be its nearest rivals, and this was with the rather underpowered Gnome. In fact, he liked it so much that it came to be known as 'Busteed's machine'. It also met the War Office requirements published in *Flight* magazine the same week (21 February) for a light Scout: 50 to 80 mph speed range, and a rate of climb of 3,500 feet in five minutes.[1] Whether it met the requirement to be capable of being started by the pilot unaided is a moot point.

This must have marked a major highlight in Frank's life. He had spent the first twenty-five years of his life being prepared for a career in shipbuilding. He had rejected that and spent a year or so trying, and failing, to run the Grampian Motor and Engineering business with brother Harold. At the age of thirty-one, he started a third career in one of the least secure professions: aviation. By the summer before, it looked as if he had become disillusioned with that choice, and decided to move things forward by suggesting this project to the Board. So a good deal was riding on the success of this project, and although rapid progress was being made in aeroplane design, there was still a good deal of the black arts about it, and there was no guarantee of success.

In fact, it is likely that Frank had been developing ideas during the creation of the Baby on the way in which aeroplane design should be carried out; they were published as a paper read to Glasgow University Engineering Society in 1914 and subsequently published as a book the following year.[2] That book is still recognised as breaking new ground by establishing the seven consecutive pivot points of aeroplane design. Those steps, and the order in which they are carried out, are still in use today.

Although it flew well, and faster than its competitors, it was capable of improvement. Busteed presumably reported that it was a bit of a handful and landed a bit faster at 44 mph than was desirable. It seems likely that he also mentioned the difficulty of getting in and out.

So a new works order was made out to carry out the necessary modifications. Presumably, they must have been satisfied that the project was worth pursuing, and authorised a new set of wings. The restricted access would have involved a major redesign and they balked at that; they were quite possibly eyeing up the upcoming racing season and wanted to make sure it was available for that.

From now on, the work came under works order GO2447 instead of GO2347, and this is the first time the word Scout is applied to the design; previous sketches only referred to SN183, with no description. From here on in, it is called the Scout Biplane, with a new serial number, SN206. Only a week later, on 5 March, he was drawing up enlarged wings—150 mm wider and increasing the span from 6.7 m to 7.5 m—to improve the low speed handling. There is a beautiful drawing, XD659A dated 1 April by Frank himself, showing the load distribution for the new wing. The calculations are very similar to those we would do today.

Yet before testing could be completed, it was dismantled and shipped off unmodified to the Olympia Exhibition on 16–25 March, where it was exhibited on the B&CAC stand along with the two-seat GB75.[3] According to C. H. Barnes, the GB75 was a major reworking of Coandă's TB8 design by Frank, the most unusual feature of which was a louvered spinner intended to force cooling air over the rotary engine while reducing the drag.[4] Yet much of the fuselage had been redesigned, and—given the pace at which the Scout had been designed, and the fact that Frank was working at 4 Fairlawn Avenue with only Clifford Tinson to help—it is hard to see how the two could have been achieved at the same time.

The Scout caused something of a stir at the show, although the similar Avro 511 Scout was much more radical in design, featuring heavily swept back wings, single broad interplane struts, and flaps to reduce the landing speed to only 35 mph—a feature that would not become standard on aeroplanes until the 1930s. If Frank did get to Olympia (and he certainly was not there on the Wednesday 18 March because several sketches have this date), one would imagine he had a good look at this, as well as several other new designs in the single-seat scout market.

Blériot had a monoplane with the wing mounted above the fuselage at eye level in order to give the pilot as good a view as possible. Clément Bayard had a monoplane Scout with the forward fuselage from the engine to the back of the seat in nickel steel to act as armour plating. Both of these used 80-hp engines. The Nieuport monoplane only had 60 hp, and the downward view was very poor, as the pilot was seated in the centre of the wing. Sopwith were not exhibiting, but on the Vickers stand was the tandem biplane designed by brother Harold, and I am sure he would have taken a great interest in that.

Although Frank had designed both machines on the B&CAC stand and they were well received, it is remarkable that his name does not appear in any reports of the time. Was this something to do with the secrecy agreement with the Admiralty, or related to the fact that Coandă was the official chief designer? It is unlikely we will ever know.

With the show over, the Scout went back to Larkhill to continue testing with Busteed, while Frank worked on design changes based on Busteed's tests. Sketches are dated 5 to 18 March, but drawings date from 1 April to mid-June. In addition to the longer, wider wings, the dihedral was returned to the 1 in 50 (2 per cent) originally planned and the ailerons were shortened.

The construction of the control surfaces—rudder, tailplanes, and ailerons—was beefed up and the rudder size was increased. The odd-looking cowl with the lower part cut off, reminiscent perhaps of the Coandă two-seat machines, was replaced with one of annular form of the type that was to become standard for all rotary-engined machines from then on. Its construction was unusual; it had six external stiffeners made from plate, which was folded into a tee section and rolled to the curve of the cowling. They must have been tricky to make.

One of the drawings, XD710A, shows a substantial redesign of the fuselage structure and controls in order to move the seat aft, presumably to make access easier and to correct the wrongly placed fuselage stations at the tailplane. Frank would have realised that making the wings wider had made access to the cockpit even harder, and we can see his thoughts developing at this stage. It includes pencil corrections and erasures and is overwritten with 'Cancelled', but the ideas were resuscitated later on, as we shall see.

In April 1914, an event occurred that took the aviation world by the ears, and while it did not directly involve the Scout, it certainly did it no harm. This was the Schneider Cup trophy event, which had been instituted in 1911 by French financier Jacques Schneider and would become one of the most sought-after and famous trophies in the aviation world. In 1914, the event was held in Monaco, and the surprise entry, among all the purpose-built French racing monoplanes, was a Sopwith Tabloid that had been modified with a single seat, floats, and a 100-hp engine.

The whole story is fascinating, but the end result was that the Tabloid was so much faster than any of the other machines there that several of the much-fancied competitors simply did not bother to compete, so great was its superiority. Up to this time, it had been taken for granted that France led the world in the design and manufacture of aeroplanes. This was the first time a British design had wiped the floor with them, and marked the point at which British aeroplane design became a global force to be reckoned with. Although the Scout did not compete, its performance was very similar to the Tabloid, and the resultant publicity certainly did it no harm.

Frank also designed a special racing biplane design at this time, intended for the Gordon Bennett aeroplane trophy race in September. Called the GB1, there are very few details, but it seems to borrow heavily from the Scout. The drawings date from May and early June, and are all Barnwell or Tinson, indicating that they were still working from Fairlawn Avenue. At any rate, the GB1 was not pursued, and the race itself was cancelled on the outbreak of the First World War.

Around the middle of June 1914, the X Department was wound up, and Frank and Tinson returned to the main office at Filton. The X-plane project was not formally closed until July, but it must have become clear to everybody that it was going nowhere and the need for secrecy had evaporated. Certainly, by 1 July, Scout drawings were being created by draughtsmen other than Frank and Tinson.

While the Sopwith Tabloid was out in Monaco garnering the world's attention, the Baby, now officially called the Scout, was back at Filton having the larger wings and an altogether more elegant-looking annular cowling fitted. Busteed took her to Farnborough for further official trials and was delighted to find that the stall speed had reduced to 40 mph but the top speed was the same as before and the handling had improved.

He then flew on to Brooklands, the cockpit of British aeronautical development, and gave a spectacular demonstration, competing for the first time directly against the Sopwith machine, which, despite having the more powerful 100-hp Gnome engine, only beat the Scout in the handicap race by a few seconds. Bear in mind that the Scout would have been handicapped according to its nominal horsepower, whereas in fact the 80-hp Gnome only delivered about 65 hp, which makes the closeness of the race even more remarkable. Incidentally, the Sopwith was piloted by Frank's brother Harold; one wonders whether there was an element of sibling rivalry involved.

One of the other competitors in that race was Lord Carbery, who was competing in a Morane monoplane. His eye was caught by the Scout's sparkling performance and he bought it for £400 and arranged to have the more powerful le Rhône engine transferred from the Morane. B&CAC were happy to sell the machine as they had two more under construction.

Carbery was tall and thin, and must have had an interesting time trying to fold himself into the cockpit, but was an enthusiastic aeronaut who had his eye on the upcoming racing season. He took delivery of the modified machine only three days before the first of these races, a London to Manchester return, scheduled for 20 June. In practice, the more powerful engine gave him a top speed in excess of 100 mph, and he must have felt that he had an excellent chance of victory, but landing at Castle Bromwich on the outward leg, a gust of wind tipped the machine on its nose and it had to go back to the factory for repairs. The definitive head-to-head between Scout and Tabloid would have to wait another day.

The second race was more challenging: from London to Paris and back. Repairs (which included an additional tank for the long distance needed) were finished in time for the published start date on 7 July 1914. Elsewhere in Europe, Austria-Hungary, Germany, and Russia were considering their options following the assassination of Archduke Ferdinand of Austria in Sarajevo the previous week.

The weather was foggy and Carbery's engine was not delivering full power, so the climb rate with enough fuel for the five-hour trip to Buc, near Paris, was so marginal that he had to circle Hendon three times before gaining enough height to get away. Navigation in the poor visibility was tricky, but he eventually made it there and left the aeroplane in the hands of the French mechanics to refuel it.

Unfortunately, they had not clocked the additional tank and only filled the normal one. Carbery failed to check both before he took off, so that when he got to mid-Channel and the main tank emptied, he switched to the extra tank and it was also empty. He landed near a tramp steamer and was picked up without getting his feet wet, but the aeroplane was wrecked when they tried to lift it on board and was beyond repair.

14

Harold Barnwell: Test Pilot and Designer (1913–1915)

No correspondence between brothers Frank and Harold seems to have survived, which is a pity. It would have been fascinating to see how the relationship between the two of them developed. They appear to have been very contrasting characters: Harold outgoing and somewhat showy; Frank quiet, reflective, modest, and generous. So how much Harold knew of Frank's work on the X-planes or the Baby is unknown, but it is hard to imagine he was totally unaware of what his young brother was up to.

At any rate, in the autumn of 1913, while Frank was beavering away on his Baby, Harold had teamed up with Frank's old boss George Challenger—who had started off as the chief engineer for Bristol Tramways, transferred to B&CAC at its inception, and been headhunted by Vickers when they started their own aeroplane manufacturing arm—to design a two-seat scouting aeroplane.

It was a tractor biplane with the two cockpits well separated. No provision for armament was fitted, but the 100-hp Gnome Monosoupape engine was cleanly faired in. It is not known if it ever flew, though the projected performance figures (a speed range of 45–100 mph) was pretty fast. It was shown alongside the EFB3 Gunbus and was dropped in favour of development of the Gunbus fighting aeroplane.[1]

Harold became the chief test pilot for the Gunbus about this time, spending more and more time testing various versions of the type. *Flight* records many of his exploits, in which the word 'fearless' seems to feature much of the time. In April 1914, they report the following from Brooklands:

... the flights of the afternoon were made by Mr. Barnwell on the Sopwith 'tabloid' biplane, on which he achieved the distinction of being the first Brooklands airman to 'loop the loop', after having quickly climbed to

4,000 ft. In the strong sunshine and at the height the evolution was carried out it was difficult to follow every detail of movement, but to most it seemed that the machine, after turning vertically upwards, fell to one side, and then, turning over, completed the loop prior to planing down.

Mr. Tom Sopwith ran out to greet Mr. Barnwell and to ask him what he had done, to which question the aviator called out: 'That's just what I've come down to ask you!' His idea of movements, however, coincided with the above opinion, so, apparently quite satisfied as to what he had to do next time, he immediately restarted, and at his second attempt made three very good loops at a height of about 3,000 feet.

On his return to terra firma he had a warm reception by the crowd near the 'Blue Bird'. It is worthy of note that nobody has attempted the feat on a machine approaching the speed of the Sopwith 'tabloid'. Mr. Barnwell seemed to think nothing of the feat he had accomplished, merely remarking after his second attempt: 'I began rather to wonder where the world had got to that last time!'

The following month, he was slated to take part in the third Aerial Derby around London in the two-seat Vickers tractor, which he had helped design, but it was postponed due to poor weather; by the time it took place in June, he started in the 100-hp Schneider Trophy-winning Sopwith Tabloid but retired due to the continuing poor weather (Fig. 26).

However, his routine work throughout this period was testing of the Vickers Gunbus, though this did not preclude having some fun. On 31 July 1914, just as the world was bracing itself for war, *Flight* reported:

Under the clever piloting of Mr. Barnwell, the new gun-carrier flies exceedingly well, and although it is comparatively new it has already been put through all manner of tests. The first day this machine was in the air Mr. Barnwell, on his arrival at Brooklands, did some fancy flying before coming down, including spirals, most alarming banks, that is to say, banks which would have been alarming had the pilot been less experienced.

This was the first flight of the prototype FB5, which became a mainstay of the RFC (Fig. 17). By this time, Harold clearly decided he had learned enough to have another go at designing his own aeroplane, and set about doing so in his spare time, at his own expense (but using a 'spare' 100-hp Gnome Monosoupape engine from Vickers' Erith works).[2]

It was a tubby tractor biplane with short unstaggered wings and four ailerons, and soon acquired the nickname 'Barnwell's Bullet'. Had it been a success, it might have caused some confusion with the Bristol Scout which was at that time also becoming known as the Bullet. Yet Harold had likely got his centre of gravity calculations wrong, and on its first flight in early 1915, there was insufficient control in pitch and it crashed and was wrecked. Harold seems to have escaped unscathed, both physically and in his career, because Vickers, instead of sacking him for theft of one of their engines, instructed a junior designer, Rex Pierson, to redesign it.

It emerged in August as the E.S.1 looking not dissimilar to Harold's original concept, and was found to be very fast (118 mph) and capable of gaining height in a loop, as established by Harold.[3] He looped the loop in it overhead Hendon aerodrome in November 1915 to the consternation of onlookers, and thus ensured maximum publicity for the machine and himself with a full-page photograph in *Flight*.[4]

There were two flaws, however. The first was that fuel and oil thrown out from the engine tended to collect in the cowling, causing a fire when the throttle was opened, and the view from the cockpit was poor, owing to its position under the top wing and the very wide fuselage.

Nevertheless, it was fitted with a modified cowling and a synchronised Vickers machine gun. Yet it got a reputation for being tiring to fly and difficult to land, and although a couple of examples of a Mark II were built, it never went into production.

In fact, the author of the 'Eddies' column in the same issue of *Flight* gives a good account of an earlier encounter with Harold:

Talking about Mr. Barnwell and his wonderful loops on his equally wonderful machine calls to mind an occasion, way back in the dark ages of aviation when looping had never even been thought of, much less attempted, I was paying one of my usual visits to the aerodrome and as one of the Vickers School's buses was just being brought out Mr. Barnwell invited me to come for a 'joy ride'.

I was unaware of the fact that he had been practicing some horrible side-slipping spiral *vol plané*, and in my innocence I gladly accepted the invitation. When we had reached a height of a few hundred feet Barnwell switched off the engine and began the glide without, it seemed to me, getting the nose of the machine down. The turns became shorter and shorter and the bank steeper and steeper, until I felt perfectly certain that something had gone amiss. While clutching firmly at the nearest strut I looked around to see if I could discover any reason for the bus's unseemly behaviour, but the planes, ailerons and rudders were all there, as far as I could make out under the bewildering conditions of having the wings and elevators vertical and the rudders horizontal.

I happened to look down, or rather across, as we were by now on the same horizontal level, at the pilot, and was somewhat reassured to find him grinning. I have always been glad that he didn't have a camera! However, just as it looked as if we were going to try Helen's trick of landing on a wing tip, the machine flattened out and we landed without the engine—not literally, of course.

Since then I have had a great admiration—not to say respectful awe— for Barnwell's piloting, mingled with a little nervousness when going up with him; not that you do not feel perfectly safe with him, but you never know quite what new stunt he is going to put up against you.

Harold's career as designer had come to an end, but his work as test pilot continued unabated. His knowledge and instinctive feel for an aeroplane were clearly of the highest order.

15

Granddad Goes to War
(1914–1915)

In July 1914, my grandfather, Francis Donald Holden Bremner (known as 'Bunnie' because of the way he twitched his nose) graduated from Cambridge University. His father was the assistant commissioner of the City of London Police, and both he and his younger brother Bill led relatively privileged lives. Both boys were highly intelligent. Bunnie had obtained an exhibition scholarship to study mathematics at Cambridge and was, he said, the first exhibitioner to obtain only a second-class degree, owing to his enthusiasm for rowing.

At the outbreak of war, he was on a yachting trip to Norway with university friends (he claimed that the best cure for seasickness was to tie a piece of string round a rasher of raw bacon, swallow it, and pull it up again) and they hurried back. One of his friends, Stuart Garnett, obtained the use of a luxury steam yacht, the *Zarefah*, and volunteered it, complete with a crew of graduate friends, for use by the Royal Navy.

Bunnie considered learning to fly with Tommy Sopwith, whom he knew slightly (he had been interested in flying since it became practical in 1908) but was not quite happy with the set up at the Sopwith school, and joined Stuart and the *Zarefah* instead. For a year, first on HMSY *Zarefah*, and then from January 1915 on HMSY *Sagitta*, they hunted mines, liaised with the fishing fleets and acted as messenger ship for the Admiral in the North Sea, and carried him on board when they became the Admiral's flagship (Fig. 27).

Bunnie, by now an able seaman, happily shovelled coal and carried out general seaman's duties with this thoroughly over-qualified crew. Checking the records, it seems that these were two of no less than 190 such steam yachts conscripted into the Royal Navy at this time; clearly, it was not such an exceptional form of service as it now appears.

Her Majesty's Steam Yacht *Zarefah* was sometimes treated with disdain by the 'proper' Navy, and destroyers would cut close in front of her during manoeuvres. On one such occasion, the Admiral was on board but not flying his flag. When a destroyer was heading for another close encounter, he ordered his flag to be broken out as she crossed *Zarefah*'s bows. This got the destroyer captain's immediate attention, and it did not happen again. HMSY *Zarefah* was sunk in 1917 with the loss of all hands.

After a year, the Admiral decided a crew composed entirely of Cambridge graduates was probably not the best use of resources, and he offered to get the graduates into whichever branch of the Navy they preferred, and for Bunnie, the choice was obvious: he chose the RNAS.

Initial training was at Chingford in Essex (the site of the airfield is now submerged under a reservoir) and started in September 1915. Bunnie, by now promoted to probationary flight sub lieutenant, did his first circuits in Maurice Farman Longhorn No. 146 with Flight Sub Lieutenant (FSL) Fowler. Most of his later instruction was under Lt F. Warren Merriam, who was regarded as the most successful flight instructor in Great Britain and ran the Bristol school at Brooklands before the war. Merriam had joined the RNAS at the outbreak of war a year earlier.

They flew a variety of different machines with a confusing variety of different seating positions and control methods. Within the first month, he had flown a Maurice Farman Longhorn and Shorthorn, a Graham White Type XV, and a Bristol Boxkite; it was the latter on which he carried out his first solo on 3 October, having never flown in one before, and after only one-and-a-half hour's flying experience, most of it as an observer.

One of the most revered (and best) accounts of Great War aviation is *Sagittarius Rising* by Cecil Lewis. It is interesting to compare notes since they both learned at the same time, although Lewis trained under the RFC at Brooklands in Surrey. Both learned on the Maurice Farman Longhorn and Shorthorn and the Bristol Boxkite.

Lewis describes the Longhorn as having dual controls and being well-behaved and reasonably robust. In an accident, you were reasonably safe, being so far from the ground and surrounded by wires and spars. The Shorthorn was more capable and was used at the front in France for artillery observation for some time afterwards. The Boxkite, on the other hand, having been the first machine to be produced in any quantity in the UK, was by now thoroughly outdated, even as a training machine.

It is clear Bunnie was a natural, and he completed the flying tests for his licence only ten days later, being awarded brevet No. 1884 by the Royal Aero Club (there were no government pilot licences at that time) (Fig. 28).

Four days after that, he was put on to the Avro 500, a 'tractor' machine with the engine in front for the first time. He loved the Avros—he flew the 500, 503 and 504, all variants of the same basic concept—and found them delightful machines with no vices. He says of his first flight in the 504:

Right: Figure 1: F. D. H. Bremner *c.* 1970. (See page 10).

Below: Figure 2: In this composite picture, F. D. H. Bremner is on the right at Thassos in 1916, with Theo Willford on the tail and David Bremner in the cockpit in 2015. (See page 12).

Figure 3: Fairfields Shipyard on Clydeside at the time Richard Barnwell was managing director. (See page 15).

Figure 4: Leo Opdyke with his part-completed Scout in around 1980. (See page 18).
(*Leo Opdyke*)

Figure 5: Leo's moment of triumph in the skies above Old Rhinebeck, New York. (See page 20). (*Leo Opdyke*)

Above: Figure 6: The first Barnwell machine was a canard biplane. Construction looks very flimsy, and the downward curvature of the top wing is very unconventional, so it is probably just as well that it was only powered by a 7-hp Peugeot engine, which would have been unlikely to have persuaded those tiny wheels to have moved at all, never mind fly. (See page 22). (*P. Lewis, British Aircraft 1809–1914*)

Below: Figure 7: By the end of 1908, the Barnwells had put together an even more unusual design, which seems to prefigure the microlights of the 1980s. Notice the leather armchair for the pilot and the long propeller shaft running from the 40-hp engine to the rear propeller. Even this was insufficient to reach flying speed. (See page 22). (*SCRAN.ac.uk*)

Figure 8: The Barnwells' 1909 machine was very different, copying the original Wright Flyer's layout of 1903 with a canard biplane and twin propellers powered by a single engine. Like the Wright Flyer, it took off from a rail to reduce rolling resistance. It flew only two or three times before it was too badly damaged to be repaired. (See page 24). (*SCRAN.ac.uk*)

Figure 9: It was not until January 1911 that they produced their next machine but this was a huge step forward and would not look out of place on the flight line 100 years later. It flew a couple of times that month in the hands of Harold (who had never had any form of instruction) and they won the J. R. K. Law prize for the first flight by a Scottish aeroplane of a mile in length. (See page 25). (*SCRAN.ac.uk*)

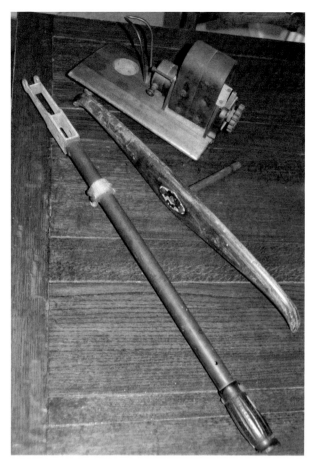

Right: Figure 10: The stick, rudder bar, and magneto as found in Granddad's workshop in 1983. The magneto has been mounted on a piece of propeller blade so that one can turn the gear wheel to produce a spark that will light a candle. (See page 28).

Below: Figure 11: B&CAC managing director Stanley White about to take to the air perched on the leading edge of the wing of a Bristol Boxkite piloted by the Bristol school instructor, Henri Jullerot. (See page 35). (*Sir George White Bt.*)

M. Jullerot Preparing for Flight with Mr. Stanley. White.

Above: Figure 12: Frank Barnwell (in the felt hat) aboard the X2 machine. In the background is the *Sarah*, the boat used by the White family to witness the testing. (See page 46). (*Sir George White Bt.*)

Below: Figure 13: The Bristol-Burney X3 under its own power at speed in Milford Haven. Note the bluff-bowed fuselage and the three 'hydropeds' with hydrofoils lifting it out of the water. Counter-rotating waterscrews are mounted front and back on the central column under the bows. Curiously, the hydrofoils seem only to be fitted to the starboard side of each hydroped. (See page 47). (*Sir George White Bt.*)

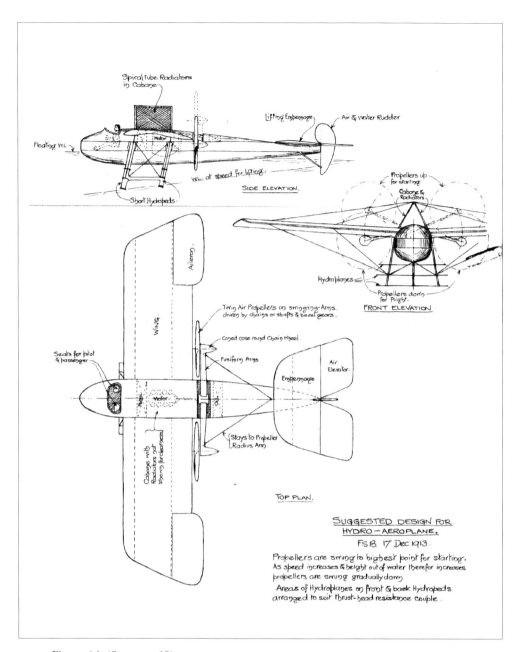

Figure 14: (See page 48).

Figure 15: Rick Bremner surveys progress on making the large collection of metal parts needed to assemble a Bristol Scout. (See page 58).

Figure 16: The two-seat observation machine is personified by the BE2; the BE2e was the final development. The pilot sat in the rear seat with the observer in front. His ability to observe was considerably impeded by the presence of the lower wing which severely restricted his view. He also had a Lewis machine gun with which to defend against enemy fighting aircraft, but it had to be moved from mounting to mounting, and there was a significant risk of hitting your own machine. (See page 63).

Figure 17: The Vickers FB5 first flew in July 1914 and met the requirement for a fighting aeroplane. The pilot sat in the rear seat so that the gunner had a clear field of fire in front. This arrangement was vulnerable to attack from the rear, as Granddad found when he was attacked in a Voisin with a similar arrangement and could not defend himself, having to make an emergency landing when his engine was shot up. (See page 63). (*Wikimedia*)

Figure 18: The Royal Aircraft Factory BS1 was designed and flown by Geoffrey de Havilland and was the first example of a single-seat reconnaissance machine. (See page 64). (*Royal Aircraft Establishment—RAE 71197; Crown Copyright*)

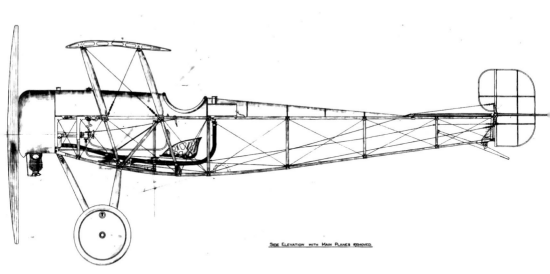

SIDE ELEVATION WITH MAIN PLANES REMOVED.

Figure 19: Bristol Scout Type 'A'. (See page 68). (*Bristol Aero Collection*)

Figure 20: The wings were a perfect fit in Theo's living room behind the sofa. Theo claims that when they were finally moved away, he had to buy another pair of glasses to be able to see the television. (See page 81).

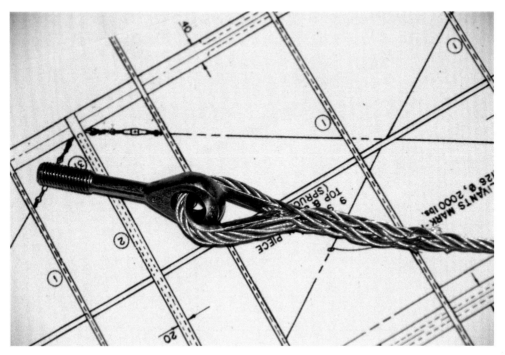

Figure 21: An eye splice in wire cable. Theo can do one in about twenty minutes, and the result is possibly more reliable than the modern equivalent, which is to use a metal ferrule compressed into the weave of the cables. (See page 81).

Left: Figure 22: The stick grip has been removed from the stick in this picture and placed in the mould ready for repair. Granddad's extension to the stick can clearly be seen at the bottom of the picture. (See page 83).

Below: Figure 23: The part-completed airframe, with my uncle Christopher (in the hat) surveying his father's machine. (See page 84).

Figure 24: The Baby on its first outing at Larkhill in February 1913. Test pilot Harry Busteed is in the cockpit, and Sir George's wife, Lady Kate, is looking on, dressed for the February weather. Note the very narrow undercarriage, wings lacking any dihedral and the tiny rudder. (See page 86). (*Sir George White Bt.*)

BRISTOL (British). Side view of the *Bristol* "Bullet." One of the most successful fighters of the early days of the war. Mr. Harry Busteed (now Lt.-Col. and Wing-Comm. R.A.F.) is seen in the pilot's seat. Mr. F. S. Barnwell (now Capt. R.F.C.) the designer, is seen in front of the machine, and Mr. W. Stutt, the Chief Instructor of the New South Wales training school, is holding the fuselage.

Figure 25: The photograph shows Busteed in the cockpit, with Frank alongside. We can only guess at their feelings, but for Frank, this must have been a supreme moment in his career, and there would have been a powerful mixture of pride and worry. The top-secret nature of his work meant that he did not know many people well in the company, but as a result, he got particularly close to Busteed and Tinson. There was also the risk to his career as well. If anything went wrong—even if it was Busteed's fault—he might be seen as having designed two failures, which would certainly seriously scar his career prospects. (See page 86). (*Sir George White Bt.*)

Figure 26: Harold Barnwell in 1914 with the Sopwith Tabloid. (See page 92).

Right: Figure 27: F. D. H. Bremner (Bunnie), able seaman, RN 1914. (See page 95).

Below: Figure 28: Royal Aero Club Brevet No. 1884, issued to F. D. H. Bremner on 13 October 1915. (See page 96).

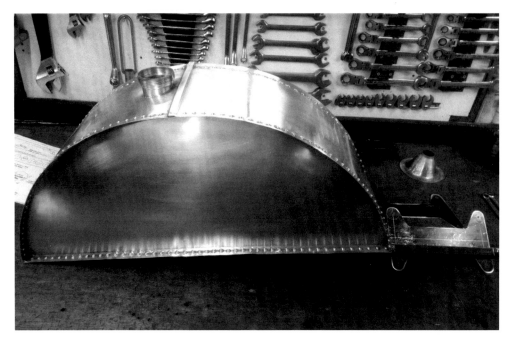

Figure 29: The oil tank buried under the plywood cover so that Ian Harris's magnificent craftsmanship is almost entirely hidden from view. (See page 100).

Figure 30: All the instruments (with the exception of the airspeed indicator) are original period instruments of the type that were issued to the RNAS in the early part of the war. (See page 100). (*Darren Harbar*)

Figure 31: The picture shows how the rim of the wheel hub had fractured, releasing the inner ends of all the spokes and coming within a whisker of causing a very expensive accident. (See page 103).

Figure 32: At the LAA Rally in September 2014 with a severely damaged wheel and a brand-new propeller on the front of the engine. (See page 104).

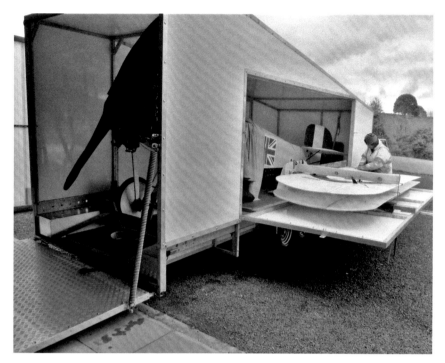

Figure 33: The bespoke trailer which has transformed the viability of the project and enabled us to bring 1264 to so many places she would never otherwise have been. (See page 105).

Figure 34: Our engine on the test bed at Masterton with TVAL's production manager, Gene DeMarco. (See page 113).

Figure 35: Bristol Scout 1264 before her first flight, looking utterly pristine. By the end of the first flight, she was thoroughly oil-soaked, and has remained that way ever since. Barnwell's artistic eye is evident in the classic elegance of the design. (See page 117).

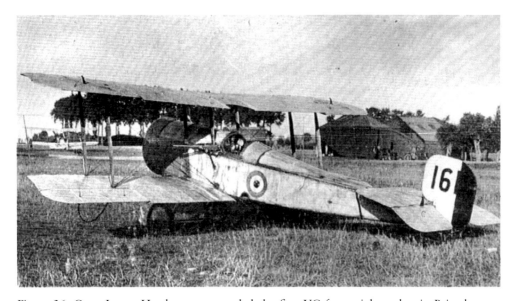

Figure 36: Capt. Lanoe Hawker was awarded the first VC for aerial combat in Bristol Scout Type 'C' serial number 1611. Note the Lewis gun angled outward to miss the propeller, and the oil tank behind the pilot, as fitted to the majority of the first batches of Scouts delivered to the RFC and RNAS. (See pages 128 and 165). (*Scanned from inside front cover of Windsock Datafile No. 44 by Albatros Publications*)

Figure 37: Flt Lt Towler in Bristol Scout Type 'C' s/no. 1255 taking off from HMS *Vindex* on 3 November 1915. (See page 129). (*IWM*)

Figure 38: Bristol Scout Type 'C' s/no. 3028 mounted on the top wing of the Porte Baby seaplane. On 17 May 1916, Flt Lt Day successfully launched the Bristol Scout from the seaplane in the air. (See page 129). (*Wikimedia*)

Figure 39: Sir George White, great grandson of the founder of the B&CAC, signs 1264's propeller prior to her first flight. (See page 133).

Figure 40: Gene DeMarco completes 1264's first flight at Bicester on 7 July 2015 with an absolutely perfect landing. (See page 134).

Figure 41: Dodge Bailey, chief test pilot of the Shuttleworth Collection. (See page 134).

Figure 42: This superb 35-per cent flying scale model of Bristol Scout Type 'D', s/no. 5570 in her post-war civil registration G-EAGR, was pictured at Old Rhinebeck airfield with her builder Brian Perkins on the right talking to no less than Leo Opdyke, builder of the only other post-war Bristol Scout at the place of its only flight in 1986. (See pages 18 and 143).

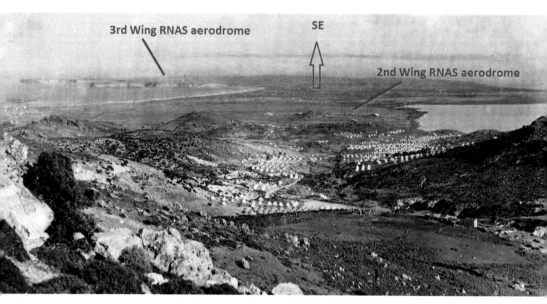

3rd Wing RNAS aerodrome

SE

2nd Wing RNAS aerodrome

Figure 43: Imbros airfield, 1915. (See page 144). (*Paschalis Palavouzis*)

Figure 44: This astonishing picture was taken by one of Bremner's colleagues and shows the Voisin pushed into the revetment at the emergency strip on Cape Helles, with the shell holes caused by the Turkish bombardment that Bremner had to dodge. (See page 147).

Figure 45: Bremner tipped 1264 on her nose immediately after exchanging the original 80-hp Gnome Lambda engine, which weighed 96 kg (212 lb) and replaced it with the 25.5-kg (56-lb) heavier 80-hp le Rhône 9C. Three days later, she was back in the air, much to his relief. Image taken 20 March 1916. (See page 150).

Figure 46: This painting shows Bremner chasing the Fokker Eindecker at about 4,000 feet over the Gallipoli peninsula on 25 March 1916, with the Dardanelles and Chanak, the Eindecker's home airfield on the far side. Flt Lt Savory has made a pass at the enemy and Bremner, having dropped behind in the dive, is catching up on the level to empty his ammunition drum. (See page 152). (*Ivan Berryman*)

Figure 47: Bremner running up the engine of 1264 prior to take-off at Imbros. (See page 152).

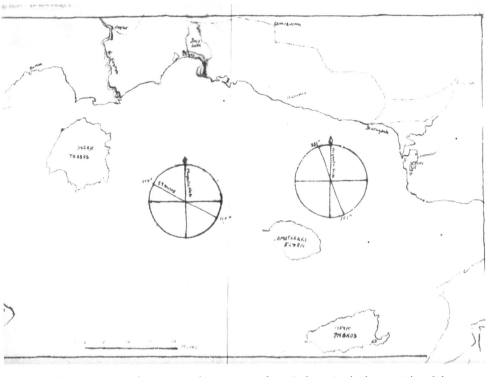

Figure 48: Bremner's map that was used to navigate from Imbros, in the lower right of the picture, to Thassos in the top left. The airfield is identified by a small red dot. There was no other information available to him before he took off on 30 May 1916. (See page 154).

Right: Figure 49: Bremner (with the solar topee) on Thassos with an unidentified French pilot and a Nieuport 12 Gunbus behind. The picture was taken by Sam Kinkead. (*Fleet Air Arm Museum*)

Below: Figure 50: This wonderful watercolour sketch painted by noted watercolourist Lt René Prejelan who commanded the French detachment on Thassos in June 1916 shows the response to an attack by a German aircraft on the aerodrome at Thassos. We like to think that the figure wearing the solar topee is Granddad. (See page 154).

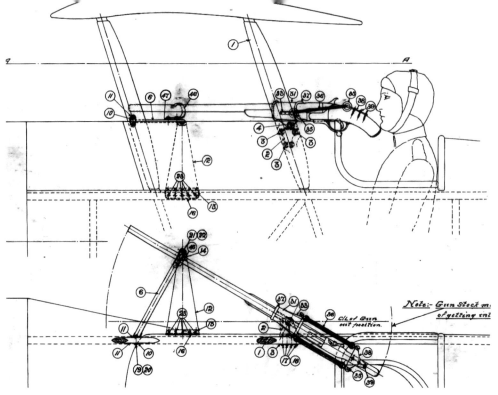

Above: Figure 51: This factory drawing shows a large-bore shotgun, known as a duck gun, mounted on the rear cabane strut. The recoil would be quite sufficient to break the strut, so the dark lines are bungee loops allowing the gun to move rearwards, presumably delivering a knockout blow to the pilot. (See page 164).

Below: Figure 52: A Scout Type 'D' on Thassos with unsynchronised guns on the starboard fuselage and top wing. The fabric doped to the propeller can be seen together with a deflector plate underneath the fuselage between the wings, apparently intended to keep the worst of the oil from the underside of the rear fuselage. It seems to have been fitted to some machines, both Type Cs and Type Ds. (See page 166). (*RAF Museum, Jack Bruce collection*)

Figure 53: Downward-firing Lewis gun fitted to a Bristol Scout Type 'D', presumably for attacking Zeppelins with incendiary ammunition. The photograph appears to have been taken on board HMS *Vindex*. (See page 167). (*IWM*)

Figure 54: David Bremner and Theo Willford accepting the Transport Trust's Preservationist of the Year Award from Prince Michael of Kent. (See page 172).

Figure 55: Prinos Airstrip from the air, showing the original strip consisting of crushed and rolled marble at the far end, with the extension done by grader nearer the camera. (See page 173).

Figure 56: Dawn on 23 June 2016. David Bremner takes off from the same spot as his grandfather, holding the same stick and with his feet on the same rudder pedals, 100 years to the day later. (See page 175). (*Paschalis Palavouzis*)

Above: Figure 57: The landing, ten minutes later. (See page 176). (*Vasilis Tziatas, www. billytzphotography.com*)

Right: Figure 58: 2Lt David Bremner, First Battalion, Border Regiment (1889–1916). (See page 184).

Above: Figure 59: The Newfoundland Park, where David was fatally injured on 1 July 1916, taken on 2 July 2016 from the Bristol Scout flown by his namesake. The front line trench can be seen in front of the two white marquees, with the support trench roughly where the tarmac road is disappearing into the shadow of the trees. The German lines were at the bottom of the picture. The solitary tree in the middle of the picture marks the farthest advance by any Allied troops. David watched the slaughter for thirty-five minutes before having to order his own men over the top from the support trench, knowing exactly what was in store for them. (See page 185).

Left: Figure 60: Theo Willford, who started the ball rolling in 2002, and achieved his ambition to fly over the Somme in a Great War aeroplane on 2 July 2016. (See page 187). (*Ron Saunders*).

'Far the most pleasant flight I have had.' Lewis was of the same opinion, and the 504 was produced in enormous numbers and remained the main British primary trainer right through until the 1920s.

He also got to try the Curtiss JN-4 (universally known as the Jenny). Knowledge of aeronautics was pretty thin on the ground, and aeroplanes could acquire a reputation that spread like wildfire, even though it may have been undeserved. The Jenny was one such craft as it was supposed to be incapable of recovery from a spin, but an expert pilot was sent to Chingford to demonstrate that it was perfectly capable of recovery from stalls and spins, and the rumour was put to bed. Bunnie certainly found it to be a very pleasant machine.

He also flew the BE2a and BE2c, and it was on the latter machine that he did his first cross-country flight to Ruislip in West London, a straight-line distance of about 20 miles. He had been about to leave on 19 November 1915, but the engine packed in before he left the aerodrome, so it was the following day before he actually got away.

At this time, he had twenty-four hours in his logbook, and had never been out of sight of Chingford aerodrome. The clouds were at about 1,500 feet, so he elected to go above them and fly by compass. When he came down through them, he could not recognise his location and carried out a long detour south to the Thames, and from there to Hampton Court, then to Greenford, which he recognised by the name on a factory roof before following the railway and finally spotting Ruislip. The whole trip out took an hour and three quarters. On his way back, he kept low and in sight of the ground, and was back in half an hour.

He also attempted to fly a Blériot XI that was at Chingford, but sticking inlet valves meant that he never achieved more than a straight hop from one end of the airfield to the other. The Blériot XI had achieved eternal fame when, six years previously, it had crossed the Channel in the hands of its designer; by now, it was a museum piece of no practical use at all.

In late November, with twenty-eight hours in his logbook, he came to the end of his training. He was clearly regarded as a good pilot because he was asked to try out the Bristol Scout, which was the hottest aeroplane in the RNAS. Bunnie was 6 feet 3 inches (1.905 m), and found that although he could get into the cockpit, his knees were contacting the bottom of the instrument panel and he could not operate the rudder bar.

It was a common problem. Cecil Lewis, who was 6 feet 4 inches (1.93 m) mentions that he was allowed to try out the Bristol Scout (both men refer to it as the Bullet) kept at the maintenance depot at St Omer. It was regarded as the ultimate pilot's machine and they were very rare, so he was very privileged to be allowed a go in it with less than twenty hours in his logbook. His knees also jammed under the instrument panel, and lack of rudder control led to his turning it over on landing and writing it off.

Bunnie was very disappointed and requested that he be posted to a seaplane wing. Yet in the way of these things, the wheels of bureaucracy were not to be deflected and he was posted to No. 2 Wing, which mostly operated the Bristol Scout. Eventually, he found that he could—just—fit into the Scout cockpit by removing the seat cushion.

He was sent to Dover for the last week in November, but managed to get in several flights in the Avro 504 there before travelling to Imbros to join No. 2 Wing in support of the Dardanelles campaign.

16

Final Touches (2014)

One of the few things we could not do ourselves was to make the oil and petrol tanks. They are made using riveted and soldered joints, which was standard practice 100 years ago, but is more or less a forgotten art today. Happily, however, we found a local craftsman, Ian Harris, whose full-time occupation is the restoration and maintenance of vintage and veteran cars.

Ian operates out of a Nissen hut in a farmyard. He has never had to advertise and is fully occupied. His workshop is an Aladdin's cave, and each time you go there, a new marvel meets your eyes, such as a 1915 Sunbeam, a chain drive Frazer Nash, a 1904 Franklin, or an 1893 Benz.

He started with the oil tank, which is brass (easier to work) and constant cross section (easier to mark out). The ends are roughly semicircular and the edges are bent over (flanged) and then dished, or slightly bulged outwards. We had no idea how to do this, but Ian formed the flanges first by gently tapping the brass over a former using a sort of small cricket bat (as he did not want any little hammer marks on it) and then took a blowtorch to the middle.

As the heat expanded it, the gentle bulge formed and he played the torch all over the surface until he was happy that the bulge was the right amount and nice and even all over. Yet miraculously, it did not all shrink back when it cooled. Any slight unevenness was taken out using an English wheel, and Bob's your uncle.

Riveting the joints took a lot longer and involved all sorts of expertise that I understood at the time but have subsequently forgotten. I have not mentioned making the outlet connection, which involved yet more arcane mysteries that I would love to master and know I never will.

The thing that really touched me was the filler cap. I had found a steel filler cap, which was more or less the right size and seemed pretty practical. Yet Ian read the drawing, which specified a Rotherham's No. 3;

he checked around his contacts and came up with an actual Rotherham's No. 3 cap. Since the tank is entirely hidden on the finished machine, it is a small comfort that this wonderful piece of care and attention to detail can be seen (Fig. 29).

We were persuaded to make another minor change to the design. Scout 1264 was one of the first Scouts to be fitted with the tank under the plywood between the wings; earlier ones had been behind the pilot and did not provide enough head to keep the oil pump suction flooded reliably. The design change was made in a bit of a rush and so they always developed leaks due to the vibration of the engine, which you can see on many contemporary pictures of Scouts. Removing the tank to effect repairs is very difficult so we took the opportunity to change the mounting method to obviate this risk, which worked fine.

Yet the oil tank was as nothing to the petrol tank, which was a fiendish piece of work. First of all, it is made in steel, which is harder to work, harder to solder, and quite capable of rusting. Yet hardest of all was the shape, which starts out as broadly similar to the oil tank, except that the rear face is sloping forwards and the bottom gets wider at the front; there are also a couple of baffle plates inside. I will not attempt to go into the complications of manufacture here, but you can be sure that it involved many hours of head-scratching; the end result, when it finally arrived, was perfect and has not leaked at all, despite many hours of flying and being hauled across Europe in a trailer.

Working our way back, the next interesting bit is the instrument panel. Great War aeroplanes tended to have personalised instrument fits, depending on the preferences of the pilots and what was available at the time. We had no photographs of 1264's panel, so we used the factory drawing, and by searching for much of the build period, we ended up with a very representative collection of instruments; watch, magneto switch, altimeter, tachometer, inclinometer, and pulsometer are all as they would have been at the time and laid out as shown on the factory drawing, which also includes a map holder and fuel sight glass. We had to make these ourselves; both are in brass and give the cockpit a very vintage feel (Fig. 30).

It was not until all of the above were fitted to the fuselage that we could start on the plywood cover that tops off the fuselage between the back of the petrol tank and the back of the cockpit. It was just a flat bit of ply, bent to match the curvature of the top of the petrol tank, but it gave us some problems.

It was reinforced front and back by ply bows, which were really difficult to form. It was pierced by any number of holes for the cabane struts, bracing cables, and oil tank filler cap; locating those precisely was unquestionably a job for craftsman Rick. The end result looks perfect, but it hides many hours of head-scratching and swearing. The last job was to cut the opening for the cockpit; by the time that was done and the leather padding fitted, it was really starting to look like a Bristol Scout.

All of this took place in and around Milson in Worcestershire. Meanwhile, Theo was working on the last bit of woodwork required. These were the ailerons, which fit into the cut-outs in the wings. They need to be a good fit in those cut-outs so that they can move perfectly freely. This was more complex than we thought and a couple had to be dismantled for another go. We brought the wings up to Milson to connect up the aileron circuit and the airspeed indicator tubes, aware that this would be the last time the whole of the beautiful spruce airframe would be visible.

The next stage was to apply the fabric covering to the wings and tail surfaces. We waited until the warmer weather to make a start on this. The most common covering for Great War aeroplanes was Irish linen or Grade 'A' Cotton, which was then painted with dope (a compound developed in Germany in 1911 specifically for aeronautical use).

We bought two rolls of linen made to the original specification. The instructions tell you that the fabric must then be sewn into a 'sock' that is slipped over the wing using a 'balloon' or French seam. It is then sprayed with demineralised water to remove all the creases and shrink it on to the frame, four coats of dope applied, and then sewn to the ribs using a long needle and a special locking knot for each stitch. Finally strips of fabric with frayed edges are doped round the edges of the wing and across all the ribs to cover up the stitching. Needless to say, it was not as simple as that.

First of all, the balloon seams consist of two edges folded over and the folded edges interlocked before being sewn down each side of the joint. Yet getting the seams exactly in the right place is critical to getting the sock the right size. We went through much head scratching to work out how to do it best. In the end, we found it was best to overlap the two edges and sew them together before folding, then do the folding; the first sewing ended up invisible inside the folds, but made sure the seam ended up in exactly the right place.

Of course, that was fine on straight lines, but the curved parts generally had to be done by hand, which was very time-consuming. Yet by the time we got to the wings, Theo, who rightly considers himself a bit of a dab hand with the sewing machine, had come up with a cunning plan to machine sew the curves; that saved us loads of time, patience, and skewered fingers. They also looked much neater.

The next exercise was the tapes for covering the seams and ribs. These should have frayed edges; in other words, a cut seam should have about half a dozen warp threads removed all the way down, to leave the ends of the weft threads exposed. These ends add enormously to the strength of the attachment of the tape to the fabric. We had some pre-cut tapes, but they were not the correct width and had to be slit. We had been told that fraying tapes was another very time-consuming business, but I found a technique to do the slitting and fraying that was relatively painless. Later on, when we ran out of the rolls of tape, we made our own from leftover fabric, and found that much the simplest way was to just tear off a strip (which automatically did the fraying and tore in a perfectly straight line down the weave), and then iron it.

Third, and perhaps the most challenging of the lot, was the business of applying the dope. Amazingly, the original dope formulation is still available; even the newer ones act in much the same way. The main difference is that modern fabrics are heat-shrink, so that the dope does not have to do the shrinking, so you can buy dopes in two varieties: tautening and non-tautening, which leaves out whatever it is that shrinks the fabric. The unnerving bit with linen is that even if the fabric is perfectly smooth and wrinkle-free after you have sprayed it with water, applying the dope initially makes it stretch, so your beautiful surface goes all saggy.

We had started on the rudder, being the smallest surface and the easiest to test our techniques on. It all went remarkably smoothly and we were very proud of the result, even after applying the initial coats of tautening dope. It went saggy, but by the next morning, it had tightened up perfectly. Rib stitching was easy, and we tied each loop off with a fisherman's bend in the approved manner. We were worried about getting the tape to form smoothly around the curved edges, but we rang one expert who does this, who said 'Just keep on pulling, and it will go'. We had to pull very hard, but indeed it went, and we were very happy with the result.

From there on in, however, the results started to deteriorate. The next item on the agenda was the tailplane. Due to its tapered shape, we had to hand sew the whole of the trailing edge, and that certainly tested our patience; even with two of us sat on the sofa working on it, we were thoroughly bored by the time we joined up. Then we applied the dope; this time, there was little sign of tautening. At this point, we started to panic. The linen is not cheap, and if the tailplane was bad, how much worse would the wings be? We decided to phone a friend. In fact, we decided to phone anyone we could think of that had ever used linen covering. Here is a selection of their suggestions:

'It's a bit of a black art. Sometimes it works and sometimes it doesn't.'

'We use a large curing oven to get them to go reliably.'

'Try pouring boiling water on it.'

'Use a hairdryer.'

'Stick it out in the sun.'

'Be careful, because the dope will continue to shrink the fabric for its entire life. Ultraviolet is the culprit.'

We tried all of the above, and after a week, it looked no different. The bags for the wings were all sewn and ready to attach. Before finally slipping the fabric over a frame, it goes without saying that you have to make sure that everything inside is perfect: all the joints are properly glued, the wood protected (we used Danish Oil, which soaks in well), all the bracing wires correctly tensioned and wire locked, nuts fully tightened, pulleys running freely with the control cables trapped so they cannot come off, metal parts all etch primed, and no bits sticking out that will snag the fabric. As we had done all of that, we then had to decide whether to go ahead.

We could not think of any alternative, so we went ahead, but it was not a comfortable decision, which was not made any easier when we took one of the wings outside and realised a small wooden block used to clamp the frame while we glued the fabric had been left inside.

They sagged, but by now, we had become resigned to this and decided that eventually they would tauten, so we carried on as if they were perfectly okay. Rib stitching such a large surface was a two-man job, with one of us posting the needle through from one side of the wing and the other directing the point to make sure it broke through in the right place and pulling it tight.

The first weekend in September 2014 was reserved for the Light Aircraft Association's annual rally at Sywell, and we were booked to appear there with our part-completed airframe. It was to prove eventful.

We loaded the fuselage on to a flatbed trailer and the wings into a smaller covered trailer and set off in convoy. About 10 miles down the road, I happened to glance behind me and noticed that the fuselage was swaying from side to side, while the trailer was not. I stopped immediately and we trickled to a nearby lay-by to see what the problem might be. It was immediately apparent (Fig. 31).

The wheels consisted of a tyre and rim from a vintage motor cycle, with a purpose-made hub; the loads had simply snapped the hub flange where the spokes went through. We did not know what to do. Going home was likely to be almost as risky as carrying on. Yet the flange was only broken on the bottom half, so we decided that if we removed both wheels and made a cradle for the axle, it would be safe to travel, and when we got to the Rally, we could carefully lift it off, put the wheels back on when it was *in situ*, and leave the broken wheel rotated so that the good half of the flange was doing the work.

Accordingly, Theo and I set off for the nearest DIY superstore and topped up on timber and screws. The axle stand took surprisingly little time to knock up, and we were pleased with the result. The rest of the journey went smoothly, and there were plenty of volunteers at the other end to manhandle the fuselage into the marquee.

We rigged up our wrinkled wings and had a wonderful weekend at which we were the centre of attention, even coming away with the Albert Codling Trophy for the best part-completed home-built aircraft. We had been concerned at the condensation that tended to form inside the marquee over the weekend, but when we dismantled her on the Sunday afternoon, we were amazed to see that many of the wrinkles had gone—about a month after they had been doped (Fig. 32).

The final miracle occurred shortly after this, when we had the wings back at Milson. The wings were better than they had been but still not fully satisfactory. Nevertheless, I picked a sunny weekend and applied the final two coats, which were non-tautening. The wrinkles finally disappeared and we had positively airworthy wings. We do not know why this happened, but by this stage, we were in no condition to look a gift horse in the mouth.

The fuselage also needed to be covered, but this was done at the last minute because of all the work inside. It was a sock secured at the front by lots of bootlace hooks, which were laced to corresponding hooks on the frame. The drawings appear to show that the RNAS wanted a sock much like those for the wings, which would be applied permanently. Yet looking at contemporary photographs of the machines with No. 2 Wing, we were convinced that there was a laced seam all the way along the bottom centre line, and we felt that was desirable so that we could work on stuff in the tail of the aeroplane if need be.

With the covering in place, it was time to apply the markings; clearly, it was very important that they were as accurate as we could get them. We only had one photograph of 1264, but luckily, it showed us that she was clear doped, and the location of all the markings except on the lower wing. It also became apparent that all the other Scouts in that batch—1259, 1262, and 1263—were marked quite individually: 1262 had no roundels on the top wing, while 1259 and 1263 had Union flags on the fuselage sides instead of roundels.

One question we often get asked is the apparently French markings, with the red on the outside and blue in the middle, so here is the story. In the first few weeks of the war, there were no national markings, and ground troops took great delight in loosing off at anything that flew.

As a result, national markings were quickly adopted: the Germans used the Iron Cross, the French their cockade, and the British the Union flag. Unfortunately, they found that the Union flag was easily confused with the German cross at a distance, and so the RNAS adopted a red circle with a white or clear centre. Later, they acquired some Nieuport 11 aircraft that had originally been intended for the French Air Arm and were already painted with their cockade, so many RNAS machines acquired the blue centre for consistency with the French markings. This is why 1264 has French cockades; in fact, the fuselage ones are painted over the top of the Union flag. It was only later that the RFC reversed the colours of the cockade to become the familiar roundel that has remained ever since.

It is not as difficult as you might think to see the difference between red and blue colours on monochrome pictures; check the pictures of the Union flag and you will see that the red always comes out darker.

So the next question is what shades of red and blue to use; this is much less straightforward. Talking to all the experts, it became apparent that there was no way of verifying colours used; there was almost no original fabric, and although there are a very few original colour photos of Great War aeroplanes, the Paget process used is not particularly accurate. Of course, the paints used were unlikely to be standard, so the red on one aeroplane would not necessarily be the same as on another. One thing we could be sure of, however; masking tape is definitely out of the question, so the markings were all applied by hand.

As ours is a civil aircraft, it would need registration letters. The CAA allows you to apply for personalised letters, and having checked that it was available we applied for, and were given, G-FDHB, which were Granddad's initials. Yet the law requires that civilian aircraft must display registration in letters of a particular size and shape. Exceptions to this need special permission, and for military markings, you will need the permission of the relevant service. So in our case, we had to apply to the Royal Navy so that they could confirm that it was not likely to be confused with a current RN machine. With that in place, we were all set.

One other bit of kit deserves mention since it was such an integral part of the project. This was the fully enclosed trailer in which 1264 lives. We had discovered that the wings were short enough to fit between the wheels and the tailplane, and if we removed the elevators, the whole thing would fit inside a road-legal trailer, so I came up with a configuration in which the fuselage travelled tail first, with a rear door that doubled as a ramp (Fig. 33).

The wings would fit in racks on bottom-hinged side doors. These would have to be lowered before the fuselage could be rolled down the ramp, but would present the wings at hip level for rigging. It was a bit of a beast, 7.5 m long, and 3 m high at the back to clear the cabane and propeller, but there seemed to be no reason why it would not work; it was built for us by the Edwards twins from Clee Hill overlooking the Milson airstrip where final assembly took place.

Frank Barnwell:
Outbreak of War (1914)

Europeans had been preparing for war for at least a decade prior to 1914, but the end of peace, when it came, happened astonishingly quickly. The assassination in Sarajevo on 28 June was not seen as a particularly significant event at the time, and the possibility of Great Britain declaring war was only seriously considered about a week before it actually happened a month later.

So where did it leave B&CAC? This was the event Sir George White had anticipated four years before when he set up the company. Indeed, they had contributed significantly to the war effort by training more than half the country's pilots and in building many of the BE2 aeroplanes under licence from the Royal Aircraft Factory. In addition, a dozen two-seat Bristol-designed TB8s were ordered by the RFC and RNAS, a few of which saw action in France and the North Sea, the majority being used as training aeroplanes.

The prototype Scout crashed mid-Channel, thanks to Lord Carbery's lack of pre-flight checks, and it might have become a footnote in history if the Board had not approved the building of a couple more examples in June, which were given to the RFC at the outbreak of war. These two were later dubbed the Scout Type 'B', the prototype being known retrospectively as the Scout Type 'A'. They joined approximately 200 other aeroplanes in the British military: 113 with the RFC and ninety-three with the newly formed RNAS. Of these, the majority were BE2s, but with a significant minority from other manufacturers: B&CAC, Sopwith, Blériot, and Farman for example.

They were sent to France, and immediately, the Bristol Scouts became the favourite mount of two lucky pilots—Lt Cholmondeley of No. 3 Squadron and Major Higgins of No. 5 Squadron—who nicknamed them Bristol Bullets on account of their vastly superior rate of climb and manoeuvrability over anything else available at the time.

Cholmondeley mounted a couple of rifles, one each side of the cockpit firing outside the propeller arc, although the only victory was by Capt.

Vesey Holt, who managed to shoot down a German plane using his revolver. These, together with the thirty-six Sopwith Tabloids that had been delivered to the RNAS before the war, were so popular, and so obviously useful, that the RFC decided, despite the policy of only ordering Royal Aircraft Factory designs, to order more unarmed Scouts. Therefore, in the first few months of the war, orders were placed for more Tabloids and the Martinsyde S.1.

Meanwhile, back at the Filton works of B&CAC, the first to leave was the chief test pilot, Harry Busteed. He, along with other senior pilots Merriam, Dacre, and Sippe, joined the newly formed RNAS within a week of the declaration of war. Busteed had a distinguished service career, both in the RNAS and the RAF, ultimately becoming an Air Commodore. Their loss must have been a severe blow to B&CAC, who would struggle to find replacements, since all the best pilots were at the front. Indeed, the same was true throughout the works, and although it employed 200 at the start of the war, it struggled to recruit skilled manpower.

Next to go was Henri Coandă, who left for France (without giving any notice) on 21 November 1914. He was, by all accounts, difficult and temperamental, and his decision to leave without giving notice seems to confirm this.[1] Now B&CAC were without a Chief Designer and a Chief Test Pilot.

The history books will tell you that Frank Barnwell and his good friend Clifford Tinson left about the same time, depressed at the lack of interest by the military in private designs. Frank joined the RFC as a pilot, where he served at the front for the first half of 1915; Tinson went to the Air Board at the Admiralty.[2] However, the facts seem to tell a rather different story.

We do not have Barnwell's flying logbook, but we know that he obtained his Royal Aero Club brevet on 9 December 1914, and it would seem likely that his flying training started in September or October.

The Brooklands school had been owned by B&CAC until August, when it, along with the Larkhill school, was taken over by the military, so it would have been staffed by personnel who would until very recently have been B&CAC employees. At that time, one could not become a pilot unless you had already obtained your brevet privately, so presumably he, or someone, would have to have had paid for his training.

Another possibility that seems more practical is that he did his initial training at the Bristol flying ground behind the main works, and he went to Brooklands only for his final test. The works at this time was fully committed to manufacturing Royal Aircraft Factory BE2c machines, and the drawing office apparently spent much time correcting the errors in the drawings. Then, things really started hotting up.

On 5 November, the RFC ordered twelve modified Bristol Scouts and suddenly he had to produce a complete new set of drawings incorporating a

significant number of changes to the fuselage. His signature is on many of the
drawings issued at this time. Also in November, the RFC ordered fifty more
BE2s in addition to the twenty two ordered in August (no fewer than 1,150
of various types would come out of the Filton works in total).

It must have been a very stressful time for him. Flying training was (and
still is) very weather-dependent. One wonders how he managed his time
and how this squared with production priorities in the drawing office,
which was already very short-staffed.

A couple of weeks later, on 21 November, Henri Coandă left the
office for France without any prior notice. There was some acrimonious
correspondence between himself and Sir George White, from which it
appears that he was expecting to continue to be paid a salary without
actually being present or doing any work.

A week later, on 30 November, there was a meeting of the B&CAC
Board, at which Coandă's departure was noted, together with Barnwell's
resignation, though Barnwell's was regarded as 'temporary'.[3]

This seems very odd. Barnwell was the obvious candidate to replace
Coandă, and he was in the middle of the critical re-design of the Scout for
its first production order. Even if he had a patriotic notion of joining up
and doing his bit, it must have been quite obvious that he was far more
use to the country at Filton, not at the front. Some sources have suggested
that he was frustrated at not being permitted to design aircraft because of
the government's policy of only ordering Royal Aircraft Factory's designs.

Certainly, there was a strong feeling at B&CAC that the War Office
policy of favouring Royal Aircraft Factory designs was wrong, and they
were heavily committed to producing twenty-two BE2cs. Yet the war on
the ground was still fluid and had not settled down to the weary grind of
trench warfare, the war in the air was still very much in its infancy, and
it was only the War Office who had this policy; the Admiralty favoured
privately designed aeroplanes, so for Barnwell to come to the conclusion
that there was no future for private designs would seem very hasty.

At any rate the Admiralty placed an order for twenty-four Scouts on 7
December and two days later, Barnwell obtained his brevet, flying a Maurice
Farman biplane at the Military School Brooklands and he immediately
joined the RFC, his RAF records showing that on the same day he was
'Appt'd gtd leave to assist B&CAC A'plane Co'. There are six drawings
dated December 1914 to show that he was employed at Filton at that time.[4]

On 6 January 1915, he reported for duty at Farnborough and was ordered
'To proceed to Bristol once a week to assist British and Colonial Aeroplane
Co.'. On 22 January, he was appointed to No. 4 Wing, 1 Sqn; three days
later, he was appointed to 12 Sqn, which at that time was forming up at
Netheravon and did not go to France until September that year.

During the first three months of 1915, only one drawing was produced, indicating that he probably spent a good deal of his time at Netheravon but by 19 April, he was back at 'A'plane Co.' until 7 May, when he was back at 12 Sqn at Netheravon. On 2 July, he was back at Bristol again; he stayed there, being more or less permanently transferred back to B&CAC on 1 September before 12 Sqn went to France.

So why was he not appointed chief designer immediately after the departure of Coandă? Why did he spend so much time shuttling between Filton and the RFC at Netheravon, when it must surely have affected delivery of the first batch of Scouts that were so urgently needed by the RFC, the Admiralty, and indeed by B&CAC themselves?

None of the explanations put forward to date seem totally satisfactory, but one suggestion by Sir George White seems at least plausible. Clearly Coandă's departure was contentious and might have led to legal action. Coandă's father was a senior government minister in the Romanian government, and a public dispute would not have been in the public interest or that of B&CAC. Was this some sort of smokescreen to allow the dispute to be settled in private while Barnwell continued his work at Filton without arousing the ire of the irascible Coandă? It is unlikely we will ever know, but it is possible.

His military record does not finish there. He was made lieutenant on 21 April 1915, captain on 7 September 1915 (presumably coincident with his return to the drawing office at B&CAC), and flight commander on 20 May 1916, despite never having flown an active mission. In fact, he was always referred to thereafter as Captain Barnwell; he never used the flight commander rank in private life.

On his record, it states that he was injured in a flying accident on 10 May 1918, sent to 24 General Hospital, and thence to Eaton Square hospital. This was not incurred as a result of active service. It was on one of Frank's visits to the squadrons to obtain feedback on the performance of the Bristol F2B Fighter in service, injuries from which left him with a permanent limp. He was awarded the OBE on 7 June 1918 and the Air Force Cross on 1 January 1919. His record shows that he flew the following types: Blériot, Avro, BE2c/d/e, Bristol Scout, Monoplane, and Fighter. All of this seems to indicate that his military service was unconventional. There is no doubt that the design of the Scout Type 'C' was directly in Barnwell's hands, which is not always acknowledged. Also, if Clifford Tinson had left the company in late 1914, how is it that his initials (CWT) appear on drawing XD780 as late as 29 May 1915?

The real story does not detract from Barnwell's enormous achievements, and there is no doubt that he merited the OBE and Air Force Cross for the design of the Bristol Fighter (the Brisfit) alone, but although he undoubtedly paid visits to the front at some stages in the war, these seem only to have been as a guest, rather than in the line of duty.

At a personal level, the start of his flying training must have been an important moment for Frank. His brother Harold was often in the news with his flying exploits, both as an instructor and as test pilot for Vickers. He had obtained his brevet two years before, and had famously taught Noel Pemberton Billing to fly in a day the previous year. Frank had not appeared in the news at all; he must have felt at least the stirrings of sibling rivalry.

Professionally, being able to pilot an aeroplane was clearly a great benefit; Frank had a truly excellent grasp of the theory, but there was no substitute for practical experience, and all the top designers—de Havilland, Prier, England, and others—were experienced aviators. Indeed, it seems a little surprising that he had not taken lessons earlier; his inheritance would have provided more than sufficient funds to pay for himself if B&CAC were not prepared to.

One's first flight in a light aircraft, even today, is something that one never forgets. It is an overwhelming sensory experience, particularly if it is in an unenclosed machine, such as a hang glider or weightshift microlight. So that first flight—probably in a Maurice Farman Longhorn, Shorthorn, or Boxkite where the instructor and student were sat on the leading edge of the wing with nothing surrounding them—must have been an unforgettable experience for him, both emotionally and intellectually.

He would have been trying to match his exceptional grasp of the theory of flight to what he actually saw, while struggling to come to terms with the overpowering physical and emotional experience of seeing the earth from above, of feeling the forces of flight through the seat of one's pants, and of hearing the wind in the myriad wires. When the instructor made a turn, no amount of theoretical knowledge would have prepared him for the feeling in the pit of your stomach as the machine banks and the world tilts and spins on its axis.

As he settled into his training, what sort of pilot did he make? Clearly, Harold had taken to it like a duck to water, and he must have hoped that he would do the same. Yet it became clear over the years that Frank, while retaining his enthusiasm for flying throughout his life, would never acquire the instinctive feel for an aeroplane that marks out a great pilot. It is a common occurrence even today: a mastery of the theory of aviation can inhibit the truly instinctive feel for flying that one needs to become at one with the aeroplane.

Frank loved flying all his life, flew whenever he could, and put many hours in his logbook on a wide variety of types. Yet in so doing, he built up an impressive record of accidents that ultimately blighted his career and his life, as we shall see.

18

Engine (2014–2015)

We have not mentioned the engine as it deserves a chapter on its own.

Way back in 2007, we had decided that we were not going to compromise on the originality of the project, so we always knew we were going to have to get hold of an original rotary engine. Scout 1264 had originally been fitted with an 80-hp Gnome 7 Lambda. A little research showed that very few exist and none were flying. They were also difficult to service and prone to crankcase explosion, which did not endear them to us. Yet thankfully, Granddad had switched 1264's engine for an 80-hp le Rhône 9C, which had identical engine mounts. The le Rhône is regarded as the best and most reliable of the rotaries, and a considerable number exist, so that ticked both boxes: historically accurate and easy to use.

That said, it is a small market and you are unlikely to get hold of one in airworthy condition by checking on eBay. Most of them are in the hands of museums and wealthy collectors, and they are unlikely to be persuaded to part with their collections in exchange for cash alone. One collector in the USA has a dozen of them in his facility, but an initial enquiry produced a polite but firm negative. Nevertheless, we carried on building in the hope that one would turn up. We put out feelers and had several false starts, but we felt that the provenance of the airframe and its uniqueness would encourage someone to come forward eventually.

It was not until we were starting to assemble the wings in the spring of 2012 that Jean-Michel Munn at the Shuttleworth Collection said that although they had a spare, they could not let us have it, but suggested we try TVAL. The Vintage Aviator Limited (TVAL) is an extraordinary organisation. Set up by Sir Peter Jackson (director of *The Lord of the Rings* and *The Hobbit* films) in New Zealand it sets out to recreate and preserve Great War aviation history by means of a simply magnificent static museum at Omaka, a collection of around thirty machines in airworthy condition at the airfield at Masterton and their factory in Wellington, which builds new Great War aeroplanes to a standard of accuracy not achieved since 1918. These they distribute round the world. Three are in the RAF Museum at Hendon, and various others are operated by the World War I Aviation Heritage Trust based in Stow Maries in Essex.

For the first time, it seemed like a suggestion that might lead somewhere, and I emailed TVAL's operations manager, Gene DeMarco, to see if there was any possibility of doing a deal. Gene is something of a legend in the world of early aviation. Brought up in New York State, he spent his formative years rebuilding and flying the unique collection of early aeroplanes at the Old Rhinebeck Museum operated by Cole Palen. As a result, he is the most experienced pilot of Great War aeroplanes in history, with more than 800 hours on rotary-engined aeroplanes alone. At that time, he was the chief test pilot at TVAL and flew every one of their machines. So it was a big step forward when he replied to my email with a single word: 'Maybe'.

The next opportunity to move things forward was at the Shuttleworth show in September of that year, when Gene would be flying the RE8 they had recently delivered to the RAF Museum. Jean-Michel introduced us to Gene, and he spent a long time discussing our project and some of the technical issues we were coming across. I do not think we were particularly aware of it, but this was a sort of interview at which we were being tested to see if we met TVAL's exacting standards. Gene was satisfied, and by the end of that year, we had arranged a deal that was satisfactory to both parties. Nothing was ever signed, but I understood this was pretty much standard practice and that things generally worked satisfactorily. Of course, there was no rush, and we left them to prepare the engine while we looked to our side of the bargain.

It was not until late 2013 that Gene asked if we would like to come and have a look at our engine and see it being run. So in February 2014, I travelled to Wellington with my wife Sue and Theo. We drove to the airfield at Masterton and found Gene there together with other legendary pilots all sat down having a cup of tea. Among them were John Lanham, retired senior New Zealand Air Force officer and display pilot, and Keith Skilling, who (among many other things) had carried out the test flying of the new-built Second World War DH Mosquito a couple of years before. We were welcomed without ceremony as part of the family and shown round their amazing collection.

Over the next couple of days, we watched them practice for the weekend display, then the display itself. For anyone even remotely interested in early aviation, this has to be very high on the bucket list. That weekend, they flew four SE5As with their original Hispano-Suiza engines, the Sopwith

Camel with its rock 'n' roll 160-hp Gnome engine, and the cathedral-like FE2B with its Beardmore engine. Its performance is so marginal it had to have two goes at taking off; it is astonishing to think that it was regarded as a very capable performer in its day. The only artefact in the collection that is not related to the Great War is the car used in the film *Chitty Chitty Bang Bang*, which John Lanham and Keith Skilling drove around the field before offering Sue a lift, so that she could become 'Truly Scrumptious'.

Yet this was not all. We were given a guided tour of the factory in Wellington and met the guys who had restored our engine. To see racks full of spare parts for the 80-hp le Rhône engine was very comforting. We also talked to the experts on fabric covering and learned all sorts of useful stuff from them.

Then, the day after the show, we went back up to Masterton and walked across the field to the ancient truck that serves as a test bed for rotary engines. Gene introduced us to our engine, then primed the cylinders, asking Theo to turn it over. This he did, receiving an armful of castor oil for his troubles—the first of many.

Gene set the controls and pulled it over. It started without any hesitation and ran absolutely sweetly. The le Rhône is a rotary engine (so the whole engine rotates, helping to keep the cylinders cool). It delivers 90 hp, much like a modern small car, but it is 11 litres in capacity, with each of the nine cylinders displacing more than a litre. Top speed is only 1,250 rpm; although the exhaust valves are open to the atmosphere, the sound is quite soft because the compression ratio is so low. What does grab your attention, even at half throttle, is the sheer visceral power. Somehow, that enormous propeller and the fact that the whole engine is spinning exudes a majesty and might that no modern engine can hope to match. If you want to find out more about how a rotary engine operates, the Wikipedia page covers the basic types fairly accurately.

I found myself filling up. Here was the beating heart of the project. We had persuaded someone on the other side of the world to do all of this for us. It was pretty overwhelming (Fig. 34).

'Would you like to try the controls?' said Gene. 'Just don't open the throttle fully, or you'll turn the lorry over.' We may have touched the controls, but I do not think we actually moved them.

We came home buzzing. By now, the airframe was nearly finished and it was easy to visualise it complete with that glorious beast up front. Gene promised it would be on their next container to England—probably in June or July. We could not wait.

Of course, the engine was only the start of the propulsion unit. Several other bits were needed to make the system airworthy. Thankfully, the Bosch magneto had been thoughtfully provided by Granddad, and we knew that it still produced a big fat spark. Yet it would clearly need to be overhauled, and in the UK, everyone goes to Tony Stairs, who is 'Mr. Magneto'.

I do not know what we had been expecting in the way of a workshop, but to find a 1930s semi in suburban Hendon was not it, nor was the shack at the bottom of the garden labelled 'Granddad's Shed'. Yet do not be fooled. It is a bit of a TARDIS, partly because he manages to fit in so much stuff—bench, electrical and mechanical testing equipment and tools, and magnetos from any number of iconic and legendary planes, trains, and automobiles—and partly because you are transported back in time when you enter to the era when mechanical stuff was at its most romantic.

Tony stripped our magneto and clucked appreciatively over the platinum points, while explaining why he would have to strip out all the perfectly good wiring because of the deterioration of the insulation and how it would end up better than new by the time he had finished. On the day we came to collect the finished article, there were others there collecting magnetos for a 1923 racing car and a Griffon-engined Spitfire. The mags for the Bentley, the Hawker Typhoon and the DC-3 were still sat on the shelf. Ours looked immaculate and has behaved faultlessly ever since. Tony is the archetypical English craftsman—self-effacing, dedicated, and thorough—and one only hopes someone will be able to replace him when he decides to hang up his screwdriver.

The magneto is mounted on the back of the firewall with a gear at the front that engages with a gear ring on the back of the crankcase. The gear ratio ensures there is one spark per combustion, and the HT output is taken to a carbon brush that contacts a fibre disc also mounted on the back of the crankcase. There are brass pads set into the disc that are connected to the piano wire HT leads leading up to the plugs.

The oil pump works in a similar fashion with a similar gear ratio, which was thoughtfully provided by TVAL. The tachometer cable runs off the back of the oil pump, and we could not work out how, since the oil pump is running at a completely different speed to the engine. So you need yet another little gearbox on the back of the oil pump to bring the speed back to whatever is needed for the tachometer; that depends on which tacho you are fitting because the different tachos are calibrated differently. Eventually, we got the gearbox, but the tachometer read exactly half what it should. It was reliable and accurate enough and we knew what numbers to expect when we were flying.

So much for the back of the engine; on the front is the propeller. If manners makyth man, propellers makyth aeroplanes, so this had to be just right. The propellers made by B&CAC were a very beautiful shape—in fact, Frank Barnwell acquired a considerable reputation as a propeller designer—and it was important we get the right thing. Over the years, we had come across a few Great War propellers hanging on walls, but it was the Shuttleworth Collection's hangar wall on which we found one labelled 'Bristol Scout, 80-hp le Rhône'.

It was not the iconic Bristol shape, but it was clearly essential that it matched the engine or it might not fly, so we decided with a good deal of heart-searching to go with it. We arranged to borrow it and (with some difficulty as it was 2.5 m long) took it to Hercules propellers, where proprietor Rupert Wasey carefully measured it with their special jig and put the numbers into a 3D CAD programme, from which the whole thing could be recreated in cyberspace.

The next problem was sourcing the wood. Most of the original Great War propellers are mahogany, but it is so scarce these days that more or less the only way to acquire some in big enough sizes is to buy up old church pews. Thankfully, the parts list specified walnut, and Rupert could get hold of that a good deal more easily. Propellers have never been made from a single piece as they would warp very quickly, so they are laminated from a number of layers. For a big propeller like this, each layer is made up of planks glued edge to edge, then the layers are glued one on top of the other to make a blank, which is then machined to the final propeller shape.

On the day we were at the Shuttleworth Collection to take delivery of our engine, Rupert was all set to start the machining of our propeller. We still were not happy with the shape but did not know what else we could do. As I walked through the collection's hangars, my eye was caught by a propeller boss stamped 'Scout'. I stepped back to take a closer look, and, lo and behold, it was for a Bristol Scout—not only that, but it was the exact model we needed, type P3001, complete with Bristol logo transfer on one blade. Once I was absolutely sure of what I had found, I ran outside to try and get a decent mobile signal and phoned Rupert.

'Have you started machining yet?' I stammered breathlessly.

'No' came the answer. I sighed with relief.

'We've found the proper propeller. Do you think the blank will be good enough?'

'We'll need to check, but I should think it would be fine.'

I spoke to Jean-Michel Munn, who very kindly allowed us to take the precious object home with us in the car, and by the following day, it was safely at the Hercules workshop being measured up. Rupert confirmed there would be no problem making it from the blank. It was yet another of those serendipitous moments that have marked this project from start to finish.

The finished propeller is, frankly, a piece of art. Its size is imposing, the shape has a timeless beauty, the colour and grain of the wood are bewitching, and the Bristol logo (we found some unused ones for sale) sets it off to perfection. Rupert was so taken with it he threatened not to let us have it, and I must admit I had some sneaking sympathy for his point of view.

The final touch was to see that Rupert had managed to source some hard stamps with which to mark the propeller boss that were the exact typeface and size used on the original. I do not know how he did this, but we felt this was above and beyond the call of mere professionalism, as it gave the whole thing an air of complete authenticity. We would have to wait a month or so to see if it performed as well as it looked.

The engine arrived in June 2014 in a container along with two BE2es, both finished to TVAL's superlative standards, including the original RAF1A engines manufactured from scratch. We took it back to Milson, and, full of trepidation, set about seeing if it would fit into the engine mounts on the airframe. It might have been light for its day, but it still required a chain hoist attached to a pretty substantial roof beam in the hangar. It slid gracefully into place and we started to connect up all the various systems.

A brief explanation of the fuel system is probably in order at this point. The petrol system was designed and manufactured by a French firm, Tampier, and starts from a stopcock on the outlet of the tank through a needle valve, which controls the mixture. It is generally called the fine control. From there, it runs into the carburettor made by Tampier, usually known as the bloc-tube, fitted to the back of the hollow crankshaft. It is a horizontal T-shape, with the cross of the tee forming the air intake connected by short lengths of aluminium tube to each side of the fuselage and the crankshaft forming the third stroke.

In the body of the bloc-tube, there is a horizontal air slide that controls the air flow. On the end of the slide is a needle valve, which is connected to the output of the fine control valve. There is no float chamber, so if you open all three valves in the system, the fuel flows into the bloc-tube and down the drains to the underside of the fuselage. The mixture is drawn through the crankshaft into the crankcase and out along the distinctive curved copper tubes on the front of the engine to the inlet valves in the cylinder head.

We had a drawing showing the layout of the controls for the Gnome engine, but it became clear that the le Rhône would need to be laid out differently. The Gnome carburettor was operated by a Bowden cable; the le Rhône needed a pushrod system. Having accepted that, how would we modify it and retain historical accuracy? We decided to go with the system used by every other rotary-engined aeroplane we know of: twin quadrant levers as supplied by Tampier. It would be easy to install, easy to operate, and was most probably the solution adopted by Granddad's mechanics.

One added benefit for the pilot was that the controls would be in the normal place, whereas the factory drawing showed the control lever on the starboard side and above the top longeron—a position that meant that Granddad had to reach it with his left hand because of the cramped cockpit space. Getting all that lot installed and operating satisfactorily took a while and some experiments to establish the best place for the fine control valve. Eventually, we and the experts at the Shuttleworth Collection were satisfied.

The oil system is simpler. From the tank containing castor oil, there is a large pipe to the oil pump, which has an isolating cock in it so that it does not leak when not in use. The pump is a flooded piston pump delivering 5 litres per hour via a connection through the crankshaft to a gallery inside, which feeds the main bearings. Most of the system is splash lubricated, and there is no return; all 5 litres per hour goes out of the exhaust valves and lubricates the rocker gear first, then the inside of the cowling and most of the airframe, and eventually the pilot as well. That is why pilots had a silk scarf—it was the best thing for keeping your goggles clean.

The final pieces to be fitted were the cowling and the side shields: the aluminium covers below the petrol tank. Once again, we were directed to a craftsman with unique skills who is employed on aeroplanes and racing cars—namely, anywhere that requires aluminium panel beating to the highest standard. His name is Steve Moon and we had to wait a long time for him to get started on our job because of the long queue of jobs in front of ours and because the poor chap had a heart attack. Thankfully, he recovered to good health, and the finished job is quite stunning. His chief challenge was to make the joint between the bowl at the front and the cylindrical section, which was a bit like a balloon seam in metal. The result is perfect, and with it fitted to the firewall, Ian Harris could fit the side shields. The aeroplane was now complete (Fig. 35).

It was thirteen years since we had started looking in detail at the Bristol Scout, and as we had studied photos of all the different variants from every conceivable angle, I thought I knew what she would look like. Nothing could prepare me for that moment when she was first rolled out with everything in place. She (and from this point on, she was quite definitely feminine) had a harmony of line that had not quite been apparent in all those photographs. You can see from Frank Barnwell's drawings and sketches that he had an artist's eye, and the Scout, the only production machine he designed on his own, demonstrates that perfectly. Today, eighteen months on, those harmonious lines strike me every time I see her. She is a thing of beauty.

It was then time to see if the engine started. In early summer 2015, we rolled her out on to the grass at Milson to see what would happen. Starting a rotary engine is a good game played slow.

First, check the contents of the petrol and oil tanks. There is petrol capacity for about three hours and oil for six. If you are going to fly, you need to move the aeroplane to where you are going to take off, since it is not a good idea to do too much taxiing. You will need two ground crew, an oil can, a petrol syringe, several rags, two chocks, and a good fire extinguisher.

Place the chocks in front of the wheels and confirm the magneto is disconnected or switched off. Then, sit on the axle with the oil can and rags. Get your assistant to slowly turn the engine while you lubricate the rocker gear on each cylinder. There are five points on each cylinder. Also check each spark plug is screwed tight and in good condition and the HT lead is securely connected. At some point in this process, one of the cylinders will leak about half a litre of black castor oil on to your knees, but it is not possible to tell which one.

Next, get a clean rag and hold it on the back of the commutator ring while the assistant turns the engine a couple of turns. A film of oil forms there, which will act as an insulator and stop the spark getting to the plug. Now get out from under the aeroplane, trying to avoid scalping yourself on the valve gear of the lower cylinders. During this process, the pilot will have been getting into the cockpit.

When he is ready, ask him to open all three fuel valves: stopcock, fine, and bloc-tube (throttle). Watch under the fuselage until fuel comes out of the drains and ask the pilot to shut the throttle and check that the flow stops.

Then take the petrol syringe, which may need to be filled up from the petrol drains, and balance on the port wheel. For this, we actually use a modified oil can with an outlet that goes downwards. There is a little brass cover plate near the top of the cowling that you swing open. Then ask your assistant to rotate the engine until one of the exhaust valves is directly under the opening. Press it in with the tip of the syringe and squirt ten times. Repeat for all nine cylinders. Step down and get the assistant to turn the engine over a couple of times to distribute the petrol.

Go around to the starboard side and open the inspection flap. Ask the pilot to check that the magnetos are switched off, turn on the oil valve to the pump suction, and connect the HT lead to the magneto. Get your assistant to stand on the starboard side holding the fire extinguisher (any flames that come out of the open exhaust valves may set light to the undercarriage). Move the propeller until it is just coming to a compression at around the ten o'clock position. Reach up and hold it firmly with two hands, and shout 'Contact' to the pilot, who will switch the magneto on and move his hand to the throttle lever before shouting 'Contact' back at you.

Swing the propeller. It is not too difficult to get it over the compression, but you must pull it enthusiastically through half a turn to make sure it gets over two compressions, and normally, she will fire on the priming. The pilot smartly moves the throttle lever to about halfway open, and she should continue to run.

The assistant now holds the tail of the aeroplane down so that the pilot can try running her up to full speed and adjusting the fine control for optimum running. When they have done that, they will normally throttle back and indicate to remove the chocks. Both should be removed together using the strings, after which the pilot will open the throttle and fly, while you try and remove some of the castor oil from your face, hands, and knees and go for a cup of tea.

There was no question of flying at this stage, of course, but it was still a nervous moment. Had we connected everything up properly? Was the timing set correctly? Would the oil pump work? Was there enough head of petrol?

For this first test, Rick was in the cockpit and I pulled her over. We were amazed and delighted when she started first pull, and we spent maybe five minutes experimenting with the throttle and mixture controls to see what effect they had. Everything worked perfectly and we were getting over 1,000 rpm, which provided the most visceral experience I have had in any cockpit; the noise and wind rush overwhelm the senses and leave you feeling elated.

Milson airfield owners Chris and Pat Jones brought out the champagne, and we toasted 1264 and all those who had worked so hard to get her to this stage, before setting to with rags to clean the oil off. We had run the engine without the cowling to ensure there was sufficient cooling, and it ended up absolutely everywhere. Yet in our exhilaration, we did not mind a bit.

19

Scout 'C' (1914–1915)

As we have seen, the popularity of the two Type 'B' Scouts led to orders being placed for more in November and December 1914 by the RFC (twelve) and RNAS (twenty-four).

The wings and undercarriage had been substantially modified after the first flights of the prototype, and now Frank Barnwell used this as an opportunity to incorporate a substantial modification of the fuselage, which he had initially drawn up in June. It having now become a production order, Frank decided to call this the Scout Type 'C', applying 'A' and 'B' to the prototype and the two currently serving in France respectively.

So all of the drawings at this stage are clearly labelled Scout Type 'C'. They are also numbered XD, following on from the drawings for the prototype that were drawn up in the X Department, since they were using or revising a number of the original drawings. By now, the X Department had closed down and Frank and the other draughtsmen were housed in the main office at Filton. Although each one had a space for the GO (internal works order) number, it was not filled in once.

Forty-two drawings have survived, numbered from XD752 to XD830, and they seem to have been produced in a strange random order. One—XD766—dates from as early as June 1914, along with XD710, which outlines Frank's first thoughts on the revision of the fuselage structure. Then there are twenty others during November and December 1914. From then on, the remainder appear to relate to modifications during the production run, though the apparently random allocation of drawing numbers makes it difficult to be certain. Yet Frank had also decided on a significant number of changes to the fuselage and tail surfaces, some of which seem hard to explain so long after the event.

The most fundamental changes are in the basic fuselage. The fuselage consists of four long timbers running from front to back (longerons), with square frames at regular intervals. Obviously, the strongest points are at each of these frames, and one should make sure that frames are placed where there are any attachments: chassis, wings, seat, and tail.

For some reason, on the Types 'A' and 'B', the tailplane leading edge and spar had been in between frames, so Frank took the opportunity to correct this by adding an extra frame and juggling the positions of the others to suit. He also improved the attachment of the tailskid to make it stronger and lighter.

He also reduced the amount of aluminium at the front. The original had an aluminium sheet extending all the way to the back of the cockpit; this was replaced by ply on the top from the back of the petrol tank to the back of the cockpit. The side panels were reduced in size and the fabric run further forward. It is not clear at this stage why this would be done, though it is possible the large aluminium panels drummed in flight.

However, the biggest change was because getting in and out required a degree of agility and care that was unlikely to be found in the average pilot. If you look at the drawing (Fig. 19), you have to imagine that the cockpit surround is too fragile to put any weight on, so you have to grasp the tops of the two rear cabane struts and put your left foot in the step just behind the seat. As you raise yourself up, your forearms are restricted by the trailing edge of the top wing forcing you to crouch down, and it is very difficult to swing your right foot over the rear fuselage (again, too fragile to rest your foot on). Now, move your left foot on to the seat. You have now got both feet on the seat and are crouched down with the trailing edge of the top wing in your throat because the wing's in the way of your lower arms, and there is nothing on top of the wing to grip.

That is the easy bit. Now you have to slide your feet under the instrument panel on to the footrests without your bottom touching the cockpit surround. This means keeping your knees perfectly straight (otherwise they will not fit under the instrument panel), but there is nowhere to rest your feet until they are right up at the rudder bar itself, and I do not see how anyone other than Harry Houdini could have done it. Once in, the instrument panel is right in your face and obscuring the control column, which you have to reach for blindly.

Furthermore, increasing the chord (width) of the wing had moved the trailing edge about 100 mm further back, and Frank had also felt it necessary to reduce the stagger from 460 mm to 420 mm, bringing the trailing edge 140 mm further back in total.

At any rate, Busteed had obviously identified the problem during the initial trials, and Frank had sketched out ideas for a solution back in June, which involved moving the seat back about 150 mm (6 inches)—together with all the relevant fuselage frames, and the stick and rudder bar. The footrests were extended back as far as the seat, so that you could stand on them while getting in and then slide your feet along them forward to the rudder bar.

In service, the common solution to the access problem was to take a 'bite' out of the centre section trailing edge. It had minimal effect on the total lift generated, and removed the access problem completely. There is plenty of photographic evidence of this happening in the field from the outset, though not, unfortunately for us, on 1264.

He also introduced a lifting tailplane. The tails on most aeroplanes, both then and now, pull slightly downwards since this helps to promote stability, and as a result are flat on both top and bottom, and this was how the Types 'A' and 'B' were arranged. For the Type 'C', Frank made the top surface curved, as if he was expecting it to generate lift in flight. No one I have spoken to has been able to suggest a reason for this, but it does not seem to have any noticeable effect in practice.

Another oddity is that the tailplane on the Types 'A' and 'B' had been fixed, but Frank decided to introduce a change so that it could be adjusted, perhaps to suit different weights of pilot or engine. The trailing edge was the pivot and needed no modification. The little clip that secured the leading edge to the fuselage was extended with additional holes and the front stay tubes were made telescopic, increasing their weight. Yet the spar in the middle of the tailplane was fixed, making any adjustment impossible. Maybe it was something that was modified in the workshop and no one ever informed the drawing office of the problem, but generally, B&CAC seem to have been excellent at updating drawings. As the Scout had another major redesign a year later, it seems odd that nothing was done about it then.

The original seat had been suspended on cables so that its height could be altered—something of a first according to the reports from the Olympia Exhibition. This was a good idea, but I suspect the seat would have moved from side to side in flight, which would have been a bit distracting. The revised version was a conventional wicker seat fixed to wooden crossbeams.

They fitted a primitive seat belt, which was not there before. It does not come anywhere near modern standards, consisting of a 150-mm (6-inch) wide chest strap secured by two 25-mm (1-inch) leather belts to the top of the fuselage. The health and safety brigade would choke in their Ovaltine today but pilots in 1915 were happy to fly the Scout inverted with just this to hold them in, and Granddad turned a couple of Scouts over on landing with not a mark on him, so it certainly did some good.

Other changes in this area are harder to understand. The control column is mounted on the torque tube, a piece of steel tube mounted in bushes so that it can rotate. The torque tube in the Types 'A' and 'B' was mounted inside the fuselage as you would expect. The revised version brings the whole thing back behind the instrument panel so you can see it, which is great, but for some reason, the torque tube ended up underneath the fuselage and needed a separate aluminium 'bathtub' to cover it. Maybe it was for ease of access for greasing or maintenance or to stop the stick contacting the instrument panel, or to ensure a straight run of cable from the warp lever at the front of the torque tube to the aileron pulleys to minimise friction; nevertheless, it looks odd.

There are two cables connecting the stick to the elevators; one goes straight to the elevator as you would expect; on the Types 'A' and 'B', the other goes forward from the same attachment, round a pulley, and back to the elevator. It is an excellent system: compact, applying minimum stress to the components, and keeping constant tension on the cables throughout its range of movement.

Yet Frank decided to change it for an extension of the stick below the torque tube that sticks right down into the airflow, will get covered in mud from the wheels, increases the loads on the stick, and makes the cables go slack at full up or full down (though, having built it, this effect is not nearly as bad as I feared it might be). There must have been a reason for this, but we have not worked out what it is yet.

The flying wires—the ones that lead from the bottom of the fuselage to the top wing—are the most important ones in the whole structure, and we were a little unhappy about the way in which they were attached to the wing. When it came to the bottom end, there was another strange decision. Normally, the bottom ends of the two wires are connected together by something that stops the two ends flying apart under load. It is called a 'carry-through' and is nearly as important as the flying wires themselves. There are flying wires (and therefore carry-throughs) for both front and rear wing spars on the Types 'A' and 'B'. However, the revised footrests went exactly through the same point as the front carry-through, and yet rather than altering the footrests, Frank simply removed the carry-through. Here is another point at which we decided that discretion was the better part of historical accuracy and replaced the carry-through as it was on the prototype and raised the footrest a little bit.

The majority of the drawings for this modification work were completed in November and December 1915, only the rudder drawing, XD776, being completed the following year on 16 January 1916.

There are about twenty drawings produced in these two months; many of them were actually drawn by Frank, and his initials appear on all of them. Eight other initials appear on the drawings, indicating the number of draughtsmen he was working with.

Yet it is a sobering thought that he was making regular visits at the same time to Fairlawn Avenue or Brooklands for his flying training, and also found time to deliver a paper to his *alma mater*, Glasgow University, on aeroplane design, which was published in serial form in *The Aeroplane* magazine early in 1915, and then in book form, where it became a standard work and was reprinted several times. It had been written before the war, presumably immediately after the design of the Type 'A' was complete, and is both authoritative and approachable. Non-engineers will be turned off by the graphs and tables, but anyone with an interest in any branch of engineering will find it accessible.

It was remarkable in bringing intellectual rigour to a process that had hitherto been plagued by 'people who pose as "aeronautical experts" on the strength of being able to turn out strings of incomprehensible calculations resulting from empirical formulae based on debatable figures acquired from inconclusive experiments carried out by persons of doubtful reliability on instruments of problematic accuracy' to quote the iconic editor of *The Aeroplane*, C. G. Grey, in his introduction to the 1915 book. Incidentally, the same introduction implies that it was Frank Barnwell, not Harold, who designed their prize-winning monoplane in 1910—something I suspected but was never publicly acknowledged at the time. From it, we can understand clearly what a remarkable intellect Frank was, as also his openness and modesty. If this was the way in which he dealt with his work colleagues, no wonder they treated him with such reverence.

This may have been his first foray into the delights of military bureaucracy. It is interesting to note that even at this early stage, the different departments had sufficient 'expertise' to need to interfere with the design process. The RNAS insisted on the Gnome engine because of its supposed reliability, but the Army was happy with either the Gnome or le Rhône. Happily, the two engines had identical mountings, so this did not create any particular design issues.

The Admiralty wanted the hand control (control column) made in aluminium, while the Army wanted it made of brass. Ours is of brass, which presumably indicates that the parts were not always allocated to the right service. The Army insisted on laced seams in the fabric covering all the way down the rear fuselage for ease of access, but the Admiralty wanted none. The wheel hubs on the Army machines were wider than the Admiralty ones. At a fairly early stage in the production run, both of them agreed that it was possible to starve the engine of oil on the ground because the oil tank, which was behind the pilot, was too far back. Yet they wanted it moved to slightly different positions.

There was a long-heated discussion about which should get theirs delivered first. This was solved by letting the Admiralty have the very first machine off the line, and then completing the Army's twelve machines before completing the Admiralty's remaining twenty-three.

Production of the new machines started in the New Year, the first (factory serial number 450), being delivered to the Admiralty at Grain Naval Air Station on 16 February 1915 where it acquired its RNAS number (1243) on the rear fuselage. One of the first to get hold of it was Flt Sub Lt Geoffrey Moore, who described it in his book *Early Bird,* p. 12 (Putnam, 1963) thus:

> A Bristol Scout, No. 1243, known as the Bristol Bullet, which really belonged to the Naval Research and Experimental Station at Port Victoria, using the same aerodrome, was my favourite mount. I could loop it, do a half roll off the top of a loop, a stall turn, a slow roll and that most impressive of manoeuvres, a flick roll, which cannot be done with modern aircraft. Flying horizontally you could roll three times in about as many seconds, and also do the very sensational spinning nosedive not possible in modern machines. With the nose pointing to earth you could spin slowly looking completely out of control, and pull out only a few hundred feet above ground level.
>
> I would also glide this machine upside down, hanging in my harness. The engine would not run upside down as it was gravity fed.

The first thing that strikes me is the extent of Moore's knowledge of advanced aerobatics. The spin was considered fatal until eighteen months previously (in August 1912), when Lt Wilfred Parke discovered a technique by accident. At the beginning of the war, only about four pilots had undertaken even the most basic of aerobatics, such as the loop and the stall turn (one of these was Harold Barnwell).

Spin recovery techniques were not taught until the beginning of the war, and Moore must have been very confident to be able to do so under control down to a few hundred feet and recover. Yet a flick roll, which he describes quite accurately, is a very complex manoeuvre that involves sudden movements of the controls in both pitch and roll, and induces a sort of spin in a horizontal plane. That he should have known enough to try it and be able to recover from it, and that the Scout stood up to it, is truly remarkable.

Our experience with the attachment of the flying wires indicates that he was probably very lucky to get away with it; spinning of any sort puts very high stresses on the airframe, and flick rolls are particularly tough; many modern aeroplanes cleared for aerobatics are not allowed to do flick rolls. The thought of his hanging upside down held in only by that chest strap with 25-mm leather straps at each end sends shivers down my spine.

One wonders how or whether he kept his feet on the rudder bar. If he was very tall, he would have been able to jam his knees against the bottom of the instrument panel, but even the most adrenaline-fuelled pilot doing any of those manoeuvres today would expect to have one five-point harness and another backup strap.

After delivery of the first machine in February 1915, there was a two-month delay before B&CAC were able to start delivering the RFC order, but on 1 March, although none had yet been delivered, they received another RFC order for sixty-four. Things were really starting to look up. The drawing office seems to have been quiet at this time, but Frank Barnwell was at Netheravon from 25 January to 19 April, so this probably explains why. The first RFC machines were given service serials 1602–1613, and deliveries started as Frank returned, from 16 April through to 12 June.

There was a minor amendment to the elevator general arrangement in April, but it was not until May that the problem with the oil tank was addressed. As has already been said, the difficulty was that the oil tank, which was immediately behind the pilot's seat, was fine in level flight, but when the aeroplane was on the ground or climbing steeply, there was not enough head to keep the oil flowing into the pump inlet and it was possible to starve the engine of oil.

If you look at photographs of the early aeroplanes produced during this period, you will see that the top line of the rear fuselage is not straight; this is because the tank had a steeper slope than the rest.

There was vacant space available under the plywood cover between the cabane struts and Frank positioned the tank here, though he knew that it would make access for maintenance or repair more difficult underneath the plywood which was hard to remove. It also had an effect on the aeroplane's centre of gravity, particularly when the tank was full, and would go some way towards counteracting the movement of the seat which had been part of the changes in December. For some reason, the RNAS machines had the tank positioned slightly further forward; this may have been because each was anticipating the fitment of different engines, and the lighter Gnome engine would have justified a more forward position, but it is hard to be sure.

This tank acquired a reputation for leaking in service; you can see many contemporary photographs with oil streaks at this point, and while some of them may have been due to overflow because of careless refilling, some are undoubtedly down to leaks in the tank itself. The problem was that mounted so much nearer to the engine, it was subject to more vibration, and the very lightweight brass (24 swg, 0.6 mm, or 0.022 in), with its riveted joints would have been very susceptible to metal fatigue. Frank did what he could by fitting soft rubber blocks on the tops and insides of the fuselage longerons on which it was mounted, but there was not any room on the outside because of the ply cover, and so the vibration got transmitted anyway.

The change was not implemented immediately; by studying the individual photographs, it is possible to be confident that the whole of that first RFC delivery had the tank in the rear position. I imagine this was because these airframes were completed in March and April, and delivery was delayed by lack of engines—something that was to remain a problem throughout the war.

Indeed, most of the remainder of the RNAS order, serials 1244–1266, had the tank in the rear position, though the last of these was not delivered until August. It seems likely that 1262 was probably the first, making 1264 one of only four RNAS machines with the forward oil tank. In fact, the first of the RFC's March order was delivered about the same time, and you can see a similar transition in those: 4671 had the rear tank, 4673 had the forward one. By the time they got to 4681, a little cupboard had taken the place of the old tank behind the pilot.

Another change introduced in a flurry of drawing work in May was a slightly different cowling; originally, it had been designed for the Gnome engine, but increasingly, the le Rhône engine was being used, and it needed a little more space for the valve gear.

On 6 June 1915, they received another large order for fifty from the Admiralty; this spurred Frank on to make more changes to the design, although service experience must have been fairly limited, even at this stage.

However, it is interesting that Frank's initials do not appear on any 1915 drawings (with one exception) until August, although a significant alteration to the empennage was drawn up at the end of July, and it is hard to believe Frank had not been involved in the specification, particularly since he was by then back at B&CAC full time.

August 1915 saw a major change in Frank's circumstances. Almost exactly on the first anniversary of the outbreak of the war, he was released from his RFC service and returned to official employment at B&CAC, where he was given the title of chief designer which he had been fulfilling, unofficially, for the past ten months. He immediately sought a technical assistant and recruited Leslie G. Frise, a graduate of Bristol University, having persuaded him to resign his RNAS commission. Together they started work on other design projects for the War Office now that they were open to privately designed machines. Yet first there was still a great deal of work to do on the Scout, which was their only production machine.

The span of the tail was increased by adding an extra rib on each side and it reverted to a symmetrical section. Also in August, a gap was introduced between the lower wing and fuselage in order to make it easier to judge landings, and a design drawn up for armour plate to protect the petrol tank (though there is no evidence it was actually fitted).

The second Admiralty order seems to have had a modification to the forward fuselage cover, the rear of which was raised to provide additional protection for the pilot. There is no drawing of this change, and it is not clear whether the oil tank filler cap had to be extended, but it is clearly evident on the factory photo of serial no. 526 (RNAS no. 3015) and other Admiralty machines from that batch. From 10 September 1915, the dihedral of the wings was increased from 3 to 5 per cent by amendment of the original drawing.

Finally, the space behind the pilot where the oil tank had been was filled with a tiny cupboard. How much you could fit into it seems debatable, and of course it was not accessible in flight. This was on drawing XD837, and is the last drawing to use the old XD numbering system.

But trying to keep track of which actual aeroplane incorporated which modifications is rather more difficult. Thankfully, the RFC (or Frank) became confused and, on 28 January 1916, he made a listing of what had been done to which machine (on War Office orders) for the twenty-four ordered in November 1914 and the sixty-four in March 1915. There are ten different modification states in these eighty-eight aeroplanes; weirdly, however, he seems to have missed off the position of the oil tank. One can hazard a guess about the two first Admiralty orders in December 1914 and June 1915, based on airframe serial numbers and delivery dates, but photographic evidence is better if you can get it.

Delivery of the Type 'C' trickled on for a long time; in fact, deliveries of the Types 'C' and 'D' overlapped during the last two weeks of March 1916. There were always problems with deliveries of engines, but they were having problems getting sufficient manpower in the factory and this may have contributed to the delay. Twenty-seven Type 'C' Scouts were delivered to the RFC by the end of 1915; a further forty-five were delivered in 1916, and yet at the opening of the Battle of the Somme on 1 July 1916, only six were operational. It was the Type 'C' that generally got itself into the news and into the record books, mostly with modifications that were designed locally, rather than at the factory.

RFC 1611 (factory serial 460), one of the first batch, achieved immortality when Lanoe Hawker won the first VC for aerial combat in July when he forced down three German aeroplanes in a single flight using a mount for his Lewis machine gun that he had designed himself (Fig. 36).

On 3 November 1915, Type 'C', RNAS serial 1255 (factory no. 474) became the first British landplane to successfully take off from a moving ship when Flt Lt Towler took off from the modified deck of HMS *Vindex* (Fig. 37). The Scout had lifting eyes fitted to the cabane struts, but this was unlikely to have been a factory modification.

The following spring, a Type 'C' was involved in a truly original experiment. Many of the RNAS machines were allocated to home defence duties, much of which consisted of defence against Zeppelin attack. They were not an easy target, and in an attempt to increase the range of the Scout, one was fitted to the top wing of a three-engined Porte Baby seaplane (Fig. 38). Flt Lt M. J. Day was aboard RNAS 3028, factory no. 539 when it was successfully released from the seaplane (flown by Sqn Cdr Porte) over Harwich harbour, landing later at Martlesham Heath, enabling it to considerably extend its range. This was the first time such a composite aircraft system had been successfully tried. It was not pursued because Day was killed shortly afterwards in France and because other more capable landplanes became available.

The RFC tended to issue Bristol Scouts in ones and twos to each squadron, with the result that it was reserved for the use of senior officers or exceptionally talented pilots. One such was Charles Gordon Bell, who became the only ace with five victories, all flown in Type 'C' Scouts Nos 4688 and 4675 between September and November 1915.

Bell was a colourful pre-war flier, known for his stutter and occasional use of a monocle. During the retreat from Mons in 1914, he landed up upside down in a tree. A senior staff officer with a plummy accent inspected him hanging from the seat belt and said 'Have you had an accident?' to which Bell said 'N-n-no, I always l-land like this, you damned fool'. To this, the officer responded 'What do you mean talking to me like that? Don't you know who I am?' Bell replied, 'N-no, I don't, and what's m-m-more, I don't care, and if you th-think you can come round here playing the c-comic policeman there's my number on my t-t-tail, and you can damn well b-b-bugger off.' He was killed test flying a Vickers FB16E in July 1918.[1]

It was the Type 'C' Scout (RFC serial 5312) on which the iconic ace Albert Ball scored his first victory in May 1916; he flew several others in his illustrious career.

Cecil Lewis remembers the Bristol Scout in his famous book *Sagittarius Rising*. It was the ambition of every hotshot pilot to be allowed to fly the Scout as it was the fastest, most manoeuvrable machine available. As we saw in Chapter 16, Lewis was 6 feet 4 inches (1.93 m) tall, so getting in at all was a problem, and he found (as we have all these years later) that the immediate effect is to restrict the movement of the rudder. Lewis failed to correct the drift on landing, and the Scout tripped up, turned over and was written off.

From 14 September 1915 onwards, drawings were numbered from 2001 on, and referred to the Type 'D' Scout. It seems likely that this was associated with the imminent placement for the largest order yet: eighty machines for the RFC, and Frank used this as an opportunity to update the design yet again.

Yet it was not the last time the Type 'C' was documented at Filton. In November 1915, an astonishing publication appeared. It is the full parts list for the Type 'C' discovered by Sir George White in the bottom drawer of this great grandfather's desk as described in Chapter 5. It is a wonderful summary of the type and without it, I am not sure we could have completed the rebuild of 1264.

20

Testing Times (2015–2016)

Before we could fly 1264, she would need a Permit to Fly. This is a document issued by the Civil Aviation Authority (CAA) based on the recommendation of the Light Aircraft Association (LAA). In order to get one of those, we had her inspected at various stages by Mike Smart, the LAA's local inspector. Once he had signed off all the necessary stage inspections, there would be a final inspection, and once that was passed, we would get a Permit to Test that would allow flying to take place under strictly controlled conditions authorised by the LAA. It would specify the pilots and airfields we could use, and the state of the aeroplane. Only once the test flying was complete would a Permit to Fly be issued, and we would be able to fly 1264 as we chose.

The spring of 2015 was a tense time, being sandwiched between the craftsmen who were delivering the bits we could not make such as the petrol tank and cowling, and the date when Gene DeMarco would be available in the UK for the first flight. Gene had asked, as part of the engine deal, that he be allowed to carry out the first flight, and in view of his unrivalled experience, we were happy to acquiesce.

There was another stress-raiser at this time. The trailer was completed and worked fine statically but proved to be a nightmare on the road. Indeed, the first time we took it out, towed by my trusty Škoda Octavia, it had jackknifed, and the poor old Octavia, just running in nicely with 250,000 miles on the clock, ended up in the hedge. The trailer had punched a hole in the rear wheel arch of the Octavia, but was itself undamaged, as was 1264 inside, so we managed to straighten everything up and get ourselves back to Milson without further problems.

The trailer is long and high and tends to be top-heavy thanks to the aeroplane's engine, so it was always going to be prone to snaking. On that first trip, the tow hitch was set too high and so the whole thing was grossly unstable. We altered the tow hitch height to bring the chassis level and added some nose weight in the hope that this would improve the situation.

I had also taken the decision, with enormous regret, to scrap the Octavia, since it seemed likely we would need a heavier tow vehicle. Everyone said the best vehicle of the lot was the Land Rover Discovery, so I bought a ten-year-old example from a dealer. As I drove it away, it clearly was not working correctly, and I took it straight back. They arranged to have some pretty major work done, and I got it back a couple of weeks later, by which time I had to beg a friend of a friend to tow the modified trailer for me. Suffice it to say, I never felt happy towing with the Disco, and when, six months later, it stopped 1.5 miles from home at half past midnight, I totted up all the faults and decided it had to go. It had cost £7,000 in repairs and I lost another £3,000 in the sale price, and I do not think I had ever had a complete month without a breakdown. It was replaced by a Toyota Hilux, which has been brilliant, as you will read in subsequent chapters, though the depreciation on that probably comes to another £10,000, which makes the transport arrangements a very significant proportion of the total cost of the project.

The first flight would be absolutely critical; with the sole exception of Leo Opdyke, no one in living memory had flown a Bristol Scout, and so we needed the best airfield conditions possible. This meant finding a flat grass field with as much distance as possible in every direction so that we would not be constrained by wind direction. This requirement was met by Bicester Airfield. Originally built for the RAF between the First and Second World Wars, it had, unlike almost all other RAF bases, retained its original grass field. Today, it is owned by a syndicate who are doing a fine job of restoring the hangars to their pre-war condition and turning the buildings into a centre of excellence for vintage and veteran cars; some of the old hangars are used for storage, and many of the other buildings house craftsmen who restore and maintain them. The airfield is used by a gliding club and power pilots, and has 1,000 m of grass available in every direction. It is also about halfway between us in Ludlow and Theo in Dorset, which was perfect for us.

So it was at Bicester that the final inspection took place. Normally, this would be undertaken by the inspector who had done the previous inspections, but because of the unique nature of 1264, LAA Chief Inspector Francis Donaldson wanted to be there, and asked that Jean-Michel Munn, the Shuttleworth Collection's chief engineer, be there as well.

We all met up at Bicester Airfield in June 2015, and the three of them (Mike Smart, Francis, and Jean-Michel) went over 1264 with fine-toothed combs. We were pleased and relieved that the list of things that needed fixing was relatively short and easy to achieve. A couple of weeks later, we were booked at the Bicester Flywheel event for the public unveiling.

The Flywheel event is a petrolhead's weekend when Bicester hosts hundreds of classic cars with a track where several of the most special are let loose, plus dozens of vintage aeroplanes on the airfield, and a flying display.

In 2015, the star of the show was the Second World War Bristol Blenheim bomber. Bicester had been home to Blenheims for much of the Second World War, and the sole flying example would be flying in for the first time for sixty years. It was an emotional moment when the wheels kissed the ground and it taxied in and came to a halt in front of the crowd.

Yet we had our moment in the spotlight too, as Sir George White gave a wonderful speech and signed 1264's propeller to officially endorse her as a Bristol product and we started the engine for the crowd (Fig. 39). Then for a while she sat alongside the Blenheim; these were the first and last of Frank Barnwell's designs, and they had never been seen together before, the Blenheim having been designed after the last Scout was scrapped. Only twenty years separated the two designs, and yet they were worlds apart in performance and sophistication. The rest of the weekend was spent in a happy haze as we chatted about 1264 with the crowds of people who wanted to find out about her.

On the Sunday afternoon, she was rolled into the hangar, and we knew the next time she was rolled out would be for the all-important first flight.

Gene arrived from New Zealand a couple of weeks later, together with his associate Bevan Dewes. They too wanted to conduct a very careful inspection before going flying, and it was a nervous time as the two of them crawled all over her to see if they could find any reason not to.

They did not, so we pulled 1264 out on to the grass to see if the engine would run. It did, and while they went off to get a meal, we pulled her out to the downwind end of the field in the early evening light. The conditions were absolutely perfect: clear blue skies and the tiniest of breezes with no variations or turbulence.

As Gene and Bevan came back and walked across to us, I became aware of a small sense of regret in the back of my mind. I was quietly confident that the flight itself would be successful, but I knew that this was a tipping point in the project. We had spent thirteen years working towards this moment and we had finally achieved it. Anything that came after this would be another type of experience altogether; no doubt it would be as challenging and rewarding, but it would not be the same and I knew I would miss it.

Bevan primed the engine while Gene climbed aboard. In no time at all, they were ready to go. Bevan swung the propeller and she fired first time. A few moments later, Gene waved away the chocks and opened the throttle.

I forgot to breathe as 1264's tail rose, and within a few yards the wheels were clear of the ground. As she climbed away steadily into the evening, I remembered to breathe again, and found myself completely overwhelmed with emotion. She looked entrancing, and as Gene flew overhead, her clear-doped wings in the evening light looked translucent and ephemeral—quite unlike any other Great War aeroplane I had ever seen, petite and quite beautiful.

Gene brought her in after a couple of circuits and for the first time we heard the typical sound as he used the blip switch (Fig. 40). The landing is always the most demanding part of any flight, but Gene landed 1264 as if he had been flying her all his life, she kissed the turf so gently, and Gene taxied back to us. We crowded round him, asking questions that he answered the best he could. Yet he was very happy with the setup and he did another couple of flights before the light faded. The date, 7 July 2015, is one I will never forget.

We had hoped to do some more test flying the following morning, but the wind was too strong, and Gene had other commitments thereafter. So the next time she flew was in the hands of Roger 'Dodge' Bailey (Fig. 41).

Dodge is chief test pilot of the Shuttleworth Collection and there is no one in the world better qualified for this demanding requirement. He flies every one of the Shuttleworth Collection's amazing machines, including the world's oldest airworthy aeroplane, the 1909 Blériot, and the 1910 Déperdussin. He has conquered the awesome 1934 DH88 Comet, which has a fearsome reputation among pilots as being difficult to land. He is a fully qualified test pilot, and his knowledge of the theory has earned him the nickname 'Prof'. The Shuttleworth Collection's aeroplanes are flown by the best pilots in the world, and all of them without exception regard Dodge with awe, respect, and love.

Had 1264 been a modern aeroplane, she would have required twenty-five hours of testing, but because of the limited type of flying we were expecting to do and the limited life of the engine, Francis had specified a minimum of two hours.

We had needed the minimum of changes in 1264's setup after Gene's initial flight, and Dodge was happy to leave things as they were. In fact, apart from a slight misfire on the engine at one point, the test schedule was completed with astonishing rapidity; stalling, high speed runs, a full power climb for five minutes, steep turns and a wide range of centres of gravity were all flown and found to be satisfactory.

Perhaps the biggest issue was not Dodge's but ours. The oil staining down the port side of the fuselage was much worse than we had expected and was making a complete mess of the fabric. Everything was in accordance with the drawings, and it was some small comfort to find a photograph taken in 1915 at the factory showing exactly the same pattern. Yet if we were going to keep 1264 looking even slightly decent, we would have to make changes.

The cause was not difficult to diagnose. The cowling formed a complete cylinder round the engine, with a small slot in the bottom. The exhaust valve opens well before the slot, at which point most of the oil is expelled from the cylinder. The oil therefore collects in the cowling and the rotating engine swirls it round to the port side, where it leaks back through the gap between the cowling and the firewall.

A first attempt to fit a lip seal over the gap made absolutely no difference at all, and so we decided that we would need to start modifications to the cowling. Yet here of course we ran into problems of historical accuracy. We had no pictures of 1264 showing the bottom of the cowling at that period, but we could see that one of the other Imbros machines (likely 1263) had had the lower cowling cut away so that the exhaust valve would open into clear air, and hopefully clear of the cowling. This seemed like a solution that was historically plausible, technically feasible, and more hygienic.

It was not until the winter months we had the time to get this done, but once again, Steve Moon, the aluminium magician, did a flawless job of the modification, and it certainly improved the situation a great deal.

On the final day, Dodge asked whether we would be happy for him to fly 1264 at the final Shuttleworth Air Display on 4 October 2015. This required some slick paperwork by the LAA and CAA, but the full Permit to Fly was issued the day before, and miraculously, the weather on the day of the show was perfect as we rolled 1264 out to the end of the runway accompanied by other historic Great War machines: the Bristol M.1C Monoplane and the Sopwith Pup. We had never had any problem with the engine, but we were nervous that it might play up on the big occasion.

We need not have worried. Right on cue, we pulled her over and away she went. Dodge signalled for chocks away, and opened up. She lifted into the air in front of a capacity crowd of 7,500 and Dodge treated them to a fine solo display before being joined by the Bristol F2B Fighter. They managed several formation passes, and were then joined by the Bristol M.1C Monoplane, in an attempt to get all three Great War Bristol machines in formation. In the end, the clock defeated them as they had to be down in time for the final public appearance of the Avro Vulcan. The 'tin triangle' may have been the main attraction for the crowd, but for us it was something of a support act, and we spent the rest of the day in what was becoming a rather familiar state of euphoria.

Yet this amazing week was not finished yet. We packed 1264 up and took her back to Bicester, and on Thursday, the weather was perfect for us to fly her ourselves. I was elected to go first, and once again, I was aware of a sense of regret mingled with the very considerable trepidation and excitement at what was about to happen.

There is an expectation that once-in-a-lifetime moments like these are emotionally overwhelming. Perhaps they are for others, but I can only say that I was totally absorbed in the moment: carefully completing the pre-flight inspection and thinking about my actions and possible eventualities in the minutes to come. I had gone through (indeed I had helped to edit) the pilot's notes written by Dodge Bailey and I hoped I had remembered all the advice he had given me. I had more than 500 hours flying a modern tailwheel microlight whose performance and handling were likely to be very similar, so most of my attention was focussed on the differences.

The engine seemed to be pretty well-behaved, at least by rotary standards, but was clearly very different to a modern one. I had to remember to use the blip switch for landing. The controls on a modern machine will tend to self-centre if you let go but on 1264, they definitely will not. The clinometer works in the opposite sense to a modern slip ball. I walked around her, looking for excuses not to go, but the sun shone obstinately out of a clear blue sky. There was virtually no wind and 1264 was in perfect flying condition.

I climbed into the cockpit and strapped in while Theo and Rick went through the rituals of preparation and priming. Rick swung her over, and she fired instantly. There were no more excuses.

I waved away the chocks and opened the throttle. As she rolled forward, I pushed the stick and the tail immediately came up into the flying attitude, and in no time at all, there was air under the wheels and she had begun a steady climb to circuit height. As on the ground, the sheer visceral excitement of the wind rush was perhaps the most immediate impression, but I collected my thoughts and concentrated on what she was like to fly. The first thing I noticed was how difficult it was to keep the clinometer bubble in the middle.

The practical effect of this, viewed from the ground, is that she was fishtailing around the sky—not immediately dangerous but something one needed to keep in check. The next was how quickly the stick forces built up if you were flying out of balance. In a modern aeroplane, the stick will try to self-centre under most conditions and if you let go of the controls, it will tend to resume controlled flight. With 1264, it is exactly the opposite.

If you are flying in balance the stick and rudder forces are very light, but the further you depart from a balanced condition, the greater the forces trying to make her depart from the balance point. I was trying to fly cautiously at around 45–50 kt; at that speed, the stick is pushing back, trying to make you go even slower.

This sounds worse than it was, and I felt in control, though not fully comfortable, as I cruised around for twenty minutes gradually getting the hang of things before making a perfect landing in front of the small audience that had collected. It was only then that a flood of elation overcame me. Rick and I both made three flights that momentous day, and 1264 behaved impeccably throughout. By the end, we had worked out that her comfortable flying speed was more like 60–70 kt, at which the stick was pretty much in balance and she was less inclined to fishtail. Theo was a less experienced pilot than either of us, and decided that he was not ready to take to the air just yet, but hoped to do so in the not too distant future.

A month later, we were asked to do some low-level flying for a film trailer. Still at Bicester, we rolled her out on a less than perfect day in November, and I was able to strafe the film crew standing in the middle of the airfield—something one is not normally allowed to do. It was very exciting and I even managed to get my hand out of the cockpit and on to the trigger of the replica Lewis gun, shouting 'Dakadakadaka' to myself. By the end of the day, I had gained a great deal of confidence in 1264's handling; it was easy to see why the Bristol Scout became such a popular machine with everyone who flew them.

The short days of winter are not ideal for flying, but by March, things were starting to look up, and on the 10th, we rigged 1264 at Bicester for Theo to fly. The conditions were dull and not particularly warm, but there was no wind and the drab weather meant there was no one else flying. It felt slightly strange being at the other end of the process, but all went smoothly and 1264 started first pull as usual.

Theo checked full power and waved away the chocks. If he was feeling nervous, it did not show in his take-off, which was smooth, assured, and absolutely by the book. He climbed out to about 1,000 feet and did a couple of circuits, always keeping in gliding range. Landing is always the ultimate test of a pilot's skill, and a first landing in a strange machine is doubly nerve-wracking. Yet once again, Theo's landing was by the book, and I wished I could manage them as smoothly as he did.

Theo is calm and pragmatic under almost all circumstances, but the camera mounted on the wing strut showed him leaning his head on the cockpit coaming for a long moment to come to terms with the magnitude of his achievement, followed by a most atypical expletive.

Fourteen years ago, the whole project had sprung from Theo's desire to build and fly a Great War aeroplane, and now, finally, he had achieved it. It clearly meant a great deal to him, but for me too it was one of the crowning moments of the adventure.

The following day was still calm, but with a clear sky, and when we went back to Bicester, there were more people aviating. Yet we found a quiet moment and launched Theo off again, and once more he proved himself master of the machine, with a take-off and landing that were silky smooth. As the heat was starting to create some turbulence from thermals, he wisely decided to call it a day. He had nothing more to prove.

About that time came an even more surprising phone call. Dodge Bailey rang to suggest that I might like to qualify as a display pilot in order to fly 1264 in the 2016 airshow season. Display pilots are among the best in the world, and I knew that I would be a pygmy walking among giants if I succeeded in this, but it was an opportunity I could not refuse. The requirements are quite daunting, but Dodge promised to be my mentor, and throughout that spring, I practised in my modern two-seater aeroplane doing the 'dumbbell' pattern that is the basic starting point for all non-aerobatic displays.

Dodge flew with me and was apparently confident enough to suggest I tried the same thing in the Scout. Even the simplest of routines requires lots of concentration. You have to be able to take off exactly on time, to keep the right distance and height from the crowd at all times, not to get carried away and fly manoeuvres you have not practiced, to be confident of your ability to safely manage an engine failure halfway through the routine, and to be able to land on time before the next display.

Perhaps the most challenging thing was learning to turn to the right. It was interesting to note that Granddad, exactly 100 years before, had found the same problem and noted in this logbook 'Did not like right handed turns at first, but got better towards end'. The reason for this is well known; the large rotating mass of engine and propeller create precession effects that are rather surprising. You may know the party trick when you take a toy gyroscope and spin it up with the axle horizontal. Then if you rest one end on a point support, the gyroscope stays up and rotates slowly about the point. In our case, the most noticeable effect on a rotary-engined aeroplane is that if you turn steeply to the left the nose will rise, whereas if you turn steeply to the right, it will drop. To initiate a left turn, you will use left rudder and left stick. Then when you are steeply banked the nose rises, needing more left rudder to keep flying in balance. All of this is pretty straightforward. Yet in a right turn, you use right rudder and right stick to initiate the turn, but when the nose starts to drop, you need left rudder to keep things in balance. In practice, I found that right turns would sometimes end up in a horrible sideslip and no turn, which was not much use in the middle of a low-level display.

It was a lot to take on board, but by the end of the practice week I felt pretty confident of doing a safe display, and Dodge clearly felt so too, since he recommended me for the issue of my coveted display authorisation (DA). All we needed now was for the CAA to confirm the recommendation.

21

Scout 'D' (1915–1916)

From the middle of September 1915, the order for another eighty Scouts from the War Office prompted another root and branch redesign of the Scout at B&CAC.

The drawings finally ceased to use the XD prefix and started at number 2001. Many of them are simply the old drawings traced through on to the new template, but Frank Barnwell went right through the airframe, looking at every detail.

The major changes introduced were as follows:

1. Cable and piano wire were replaced throughout. By now, it was standard practice to use what had become known as RAFwire. Developed by the Royal Aircraft Factory, RAFwires were aerofoil section steel rods with the ends forged into screw threads. The aerodynamic drag was about a tenth of the circular section cables they replaced. Internally, the cables and piano wire were replaced by threaded rods—much the same idea, but of circular cross section throughout. This necessitated the redesign of every metal fitting on the airframe.
2. Frank took the opportunity to upgrade some of the other metal fittings too; the sternpost was altered and the tailplane raised by an inch (25 mm) to give more clearance between the elevator and rudder horns. The rear chassis strut socket was beefed up and the unconventional method of keeping the axle central was replaced with more conventional guides added to the chassis foot fitting.
3. The fuel capacity was increased by making use of every available space in the forward fuselage. Previously, the petrol tank had occupied the space between the front cabane struts and the engine, and the oil tank had been between the cabane struts, with plenty of space in front and

behind it. Now there was another tank filling the entire space between the cabane struts. It was a combined tank with oil in the front and petrol in the back, with a valve operated from the cockpit to switch between tanks. The old ply cover disappeared, leaving all the tanks exposed. This eliminated the problem they had before with the leaking oil tank caused by vibration which was almost entirely inaccessible under the ply cover.

4. There was even a drawing showing a rear petrol tank in place of the cupboard, though it is not clear whether this was ever manufactured.

5. More powerful engines were becoming available and drawings were made to incorporate the 100-hp Gnome Mono and 100-hp and 110-hp Clerget engines, requiring revised engine mounts and cowlings, increased stagger of the wings to accommodate the increased engine weight, and a larger rudder.

6. A revised cowling with a more open bottom and a better securing arrangement was introduced for the standard 80-hp engines too.

7. Shorter ailerons were introduced. This was the second reduction in aileron size. On the face of it, this would have reduced the effective roll rate which might have been a disadvantage in combat, but it may have been intended to reduce adverse yaw—one of the unfortunate side effects of roll control—and not actually had much effect on roll rate. One would need to build and fly examples of both arrangements to find out.

8. Also in this spate of drawings in the last quarter of 1915 are a good many drawings for a very large spinner on the propeller boss. It was fitted on a couple of experimental machines at the request of the RFC but was not adopted for production Scouts. It did however provide the necessary data for its introduction on the Bristol M.1 monoplane in 1916.

9. Finally, in the summer of 1916, pressurised fuel and oil tanks were designed to provide a more consistent fuel supply to the engine.

By now, Frank was heavily involved in new designs for B&CAC, but many of the Scout drawings are approved by him, showing that he was still very much involved in his Baby.

Orders continued to come in, the last one being placed by the RNAS on 1 November 1916, almost exactly two years after the first order had been placed. By then, newer designs (in particular the Sopwith Pup) had been introduced along with a synchronised machine gun designed in from the start, and B&CAC were starting to manufacture the F2B Fighter—the aeroplane for which ultimately Frank became remembered. The Admiralty asked B&CAC to tender for a further forty as late as March 1917, but the offer was declined.

In total, 161 Type 'C' and 210 Type 'D' Scouts had been built between February 1915 and December 1916; these numbers are surprisingly similar to the iconic Fokker Eindecker and Dr.1 Dreidecker, and yet the Scout remains relatively unknown.

A few were sent to other countries. S/no. 1247 went to the French for evaluation. S/no. 3013 went to Greece, possibly to fly from Thassos in the hands of a Greek ace pilot, Aristedes Moraetenes. Both of these were Type Cs, but a Type 'D' (s/no. 8976) went to Australia where it was flown at Point Cook, the home of the Australian Central Flying School.

When America entered the war in 1917, their aviation industry had been brought to a complete stop by the legal action between the Wright brothers and Curtiss in regard to the patent rights, based on a claimed dispute about who had flown first. The process was ended by an out-of-court settlement in the national interest after the US entered the war.

In the immediate term, they had no suitable warplane designs available and a Major Bolling was sent across the Atlantic to research British designs that could be licence built. Among these was the Scout, which he recommended as an intermediate training machine to ease the step up from the Curtiss JN-4 Jenny to the latest fighters such as the Sopwith Camel and SE5A.

This recommendation was accepted, and by 9 August 1917, Program III included a target of 750 Scouts to be built in the USA. A month later, this figure had swollen to 900 to be manufactured by the Fisher Body Corporation of Detroit, Michigan, and the Thomas Morse company was asked to prepare drawings suitable for American production. The primary purpose of these was to convert the dimensions to imperial, the USA (along with Liberia and Myanmar) being the only countries in the world not to have adopted the metric system.

One aeroplane, B763, which was a rather tired 'bitser' (assembled from parts of a number of other machines), was sent to the US at about this time, but sat at the Thomas Morse works in pieces.

In fact, the Thomas Morse company had their own competitive design (the S4), which had flown for the first time in June; one might think it odd to ask them to manufacture under licence a machine that was directly competitive with their own, but in October that year, an order was being drawn up for them to make 500 Bristol Scouts.

By this time, they were already contracted to make fifty S4s, and another order for 500 was placed in December. By April 1918, structural weaknesses in the S4 tail structure had come to light, and although the orders for production of the Bristol Scout had by now been cancelled, the parts of B763 were transferred to McCook Field from the Thomas Morse works and reassembled. Various essential parts (including the wing struts and rigging cables) were missing and had to be manufactured, but it was assembled and ready to fly by 12 June.

It flew trials in the latter half of August from Wilbur Wright Field and on 28 August, test pilot K. L. Moore reported favourably, apart from a slight lag in rudder response in the climb, though he acknowledged that this might have been due to the age of the example flown. The following day, a directive was issued that required production of no less than 1,000 Bristol Scouts, of which 400 were to be fitted with radios, and 400 with synchronised machine guns. At this point, the shortcomings of the Thomas Morse drawings came to light, and the whole idea was abandoned. B763 belatedly got its McCook Field number, P-32, and an American serial number AS94025. It was last heard of going into storage at Wilbur Wright Field in 1921.

The drawings were preserved at the Smithsonian Institute, and these—together with the parts list held by Sir George White—provided the only source of detailed manufacturing information until 2014, when copies of many of the drawings were found in archives at British Aerospace, Filton, by the Bristol Aero Collection.

Few, if any, Bristol Scouts remained in service throughout the war, but half dozen went to Orford Ness Armament Experimental Station. One, s/no. 7053, was fitted with a synchronised Vickers gun.

However, many Scouts remained as personal runabouts until the end of the war. In his book *The Clouds Remember* (Arms & Armour Press, 1972), Oliver Stewart said:

A pilot who was able to secure one of these aeroplanes was looked upon with envy by all other pilots, and he would take very good care that his 'training' machine was never used for training and that no pilot but himself ever went near it.

I have often wondered how a modern flying club would appreciate a Bristol Scout with 80-hp le Rhône or a Sopwith Pup with 80-hp le Rhône. I believe that these machines would exercise today over the members of a flying club just as strong a fascination as they exercised over the Royal Flying Corps and Royal Naval Air Service pilots during the war. They were both great flying machines, and although of the two the Sopwith Pup was probably superior, they both gave their pilots the authentic sensations of man-controlled flight in a way that few, if any, other machines have ever done.

The Sopwith Pup managed the transition to peacetime use, being converted into the two-seat Dove, of which ten were built.

Although the B&CAC were asked to build a single example of the Bristol Scout for Spanish pilot Juan Pombo, they declined to do so. By then, it is possible much of the tooling for making the metal fittings and so on had been disposed of.

One Bristol Scout did make it to civil registration, however. Originally Type 'D', s/no. 5570, it was registered as G-EAGR and was initially kept at Hendon by Major J. A. McKelvie, who sold it in 1926 to Sqn Ldr Champion de Crespigny; a year later, it was sold to Flt Lt A. M. Wray, MC, AFC, and thence to a Mr Smith, who transferred it to the Hull Aero Club at Hedon, where it was scrapped in 1930 when its Certificate of Airworthiness was withdrawn (Fig. 42).

Therefore, the last of the Bristol Scouts died. For an aeroplane of such importance in the development of military aviation, and of such personal importance to Frank Barnwell and the Bristol Aeroplane Company, this does seem surprising, but there it is. By the end of 1930, the Bristol Scout had vanished from sight.

Granddad's War: No. 2 Wing, RNAS (1915–1918)

Granddad crossed the Channel by ferry, and then took the train to Marseilles. He saw nothing of the war in France and slept on the train. At Marseilles, they took a boat to Malta, where the CO had not heard of them and advised them to book into a hotel for the night.

The following morning, he went to the hospital to see a doctor friend to see if he could get his course of typhoid injections completed as he had left England in such a rush there had only been time for the first. He strolled leisurely back to the hotel to be told that the other pilots had already embarked on a ship that had left for Imbros, so he dashed down to the pierhead and managed to scramble on board with minutes to spare.

He arrived at the No. 2 Wing aerodrome on Imbros on 19 December 1915 (Fig. 43).

Imbros was a small Greek island about 15 miles from the Dardanelles peninsula with good harbour facilities; it was an important headquarters for the Dardanelles campaign, together with airfields used by Nos 2 and 3 Wings RNAS (together with others on Tenedos and at Mudros on Lemnos island). Today, it is part of Turkey and renamed Gökçeada.

The airfield was in the same bay as the harbour, and was a rough dirt field with canvas-covered Bessonneau hangars capable of housing four aeroplanes in each. Landings on the dust-covered area were harder than on grass because it was more difficult to judge your height.

Accommodation was basic; the officer's mess was a stone building but everyone slept in the packing cases in which the aeroplanes had been shipped from Great Britain. The cases were paper-lined with a gap between the wood and paper, and one form of entertainment was to listen carefully for scratching noises behind the paper. If you were keen of hearing, and stabbed with your penknife correctly, you could end up with a large centipede on the end.

In those days, a pilot was expected to be able to cope with many different types of aeroplane, and no significant training was given to acquaint you with the various different features or handling characteristics.

No. 2 Wing RNAS had been established at Imbros since 31 August, but was very small; on average, they only had twenty-three aeroplanes, seventeen pilots, and ten observers available. The original complement of aeroplanes—six Morane Parasols, six Caudrons, six BE2cs, and four Bristol Scouts—had been diluted by an astonishing variety of types by this time. Bunnie's logbook records an Avro 504B, Voisin III, Bristol Scout Types 'C' and 'D', Caudron G III and G IV, Nieuport 12 (Gunbus) and 11 (Scout), BE2c, and occasionally a Henri Farman HF.27—totalling ten different types.

They carried out a wide variety of tasks. The RNAS had been successful in maintaining air superiority over the Gallipoli peninsula during the invasion, and also during the evacuation that was ongoing at this time. Their observation work had reaped rich rewards when preparations for a Turkish attack on the ANZAC cove had been spotted, enabling it to be repulsed. They had pioneered the use of air-launched torpedoes against Turkish shipping with grossly underpowered Short seaplanes operated from HMS *Ark Royal* and later HMS *Ben-my-Chree*. They were also to pioneer aerial bombing of shipping.

When Bunnie arrived, much of No. 2 Wing's time was spent on artillery spotting for the large Naval ship's guns, but they also did observation work including photography, escorting of the reconnaissance two-seaters, submarine spotting (they are very easy to see underwater from an aircraft), and bombing.

Cdr Charles Samson, commander of No. 3 Wing (which was also stationed on Imbros), had successfully dropped the world's largest bomb the day before; flying a Henri Farman HF.27, he had managed to drop a bomb of no less than 500 lb on a Turkish installation.

Compared to the Western Front, the amount of air activity was relatively small, so the number of times they came across enemy aeroplanes was limited. Nevertheless, there were casualties. The first victim of air-to-air combat in the area had occurred in November, and there would be others during Bunnie's time there.

Maintenance and the provision of spares—particularly as far away as the Eastern Mediterranean—must have been difficult, and the mechanics were expected to make do and mend to a much greater extent than on the Western Front.

The decision had already been taken to abandon the Gallipoli campaign, and after three flights in an Avro 504B (an earlier variant of the definitive Avro 504K with an 80-hp engine and a fixed fin) to familiarise himself with the area, he was allocated to the Voisin III.

This was a lumbering two-seat pusher with a nacelle containing the observer (armed with a machine gun) in the front and the pilot in the back, and a clumsy four-wheel undercarriage. The position of the wheels meant that unless you made an absolutely perfect landing, it would announce your error to all and sundry by proceeding up the airfield in a series of kangaroo hops; the only way out of it was to take off again, though even then the pitching would continue for some time into the air.

Its great merit was its strength, as the frame was made of welded steel tube, so it could handle a lot of rough treatment. He made his first solo flight in the Voisin on 27 December, in which he landed on the front wheels, and learned from experience about the kangaroo hops.

He was out on his first operational mission the next day with observer Sasoon, spotting for the 8th Corps artillery over Cape Helles. The anti-aircraft fire did not trouble him much, and he 'sighted Hun and chased him a short way, but he was a long way off and far too fast'. This was the first time he had ever taken a passenger.

He flew spotting flights for the next few days, mostly for the Naval monitor ships. The machine carried a primitive wireless set with a long wire aerial that had to be unwound from a drum after take-off, allowing the observer to make Morse transmissions back to the ship. The fall of shot was observed and reported back using a grid system. Before leaving the vicinity of the airfield, a system of coloured fabric strips was rolled out on the ground in response to the radio transmissions in order to check the radio was working and to recall the aeroplane when the range had been found (typically this took three to four ranging shots). This business of communicating was so primitive, and the aeroplane so unreliable, that the spotting they did was of relatively little value compared to the tethered balloons which were operated from ships.

Yet it formed a good part of the Wing's duties, and the majority of the work during the flight was undertaken by the observer, leaving the pilot to worry about navigation and the chances of making it home in one piece.

Apart from the ever-present risk of mechanical failure, adverse weather conditions and anti-aircraft fire ('Archie'), there was an additional unexpected hazard: the ship's shells themselves. Bunnie noted one occasion when a shell came sufficiently close to cause severe turbulence as he was spotting, and Cecil Lewis said that his observer and good friend Pip lost his life in this way on the Western Front while observing with another pilot while Lewis was on leave.

On Bunnie's seventh operational flight, on 8 January 1916, he and his observer (Midshipman Burnaby) were spotting for the guns of HMS *Peterborough* in the Voisin. The engine was not performing well, and he could not get above 8,300 feet. On his way back from an excursion to 'square 29' to investigate something Burnaby had spotted and could not identify, while still over the peninsula, he was 'attacked by the Hun who came up unobserved behind and slightly above me'. Bunnie tried to manoeuvre to get his observer's Lewis gun to bear (this was not easy as it faced forward and downwards, so Burnaby lifted it off its mountings and hand held it firing over Bunnie's shoulder), but the Hun peeled off and though Bunnie tried to follow he was 'far too fast and nippy for me to bring my gun to bear on him'. The German was flying the infamous Fokker Eindecker and Bunnie reckoned afterwards that his foe might have been *Hauptmann* Hans-Joachim Buddecke, a well-known German fighter ace. Later on, we discovered he was wrong.

Bunnie found his engine misfiring, and it eventually gave out altogether, which meant that he had to make an emergency landing at the airstrip on the peninsula at Cape Helles. The Turkish guns opened up as he came in and they had to dodge the 6-inch shells as they were trying to push the Voisin into a dugout. On investigation, he found that the damage to the engine had been caused by enemy gunfire, which had wrecked one cylinder and peppered the water-cooling system, though he and Burnaby had been unaware of it at the time.

This was a not inconsiderable achievement as the approach to the strip at Helles was so cramped that it was no longer in regular use, and to manage it under fire, with a misfiring engine, on an aeroplane he had only flown half a dozen times and with a grand total of forty-six hours in his logbook showed considerable talent and coolness.

Someone took a picture from 4,000 feet that evening. You can just about make out the white wing of the Voisin in the dugout, with the shell holes in the middle of the picture (Fig. 44).

Unfortunately, Bunnie had landed on the very evening of the final evacuation of Allied troops from the peninsula, so he was told to destroy the aeroplane without setting fire to it (which might have given the game away to the Turks).

He did the best he could with 'a pick, a shovel and a sledge hammer', but he reckoned it was surprisingly difficult to inflict permanent damage in a short time with these. He was attacked sometime after 4.30 p.m. and was on board a lighter by 6.30 p.m., which departed at 1.30 a.m. and took him to SS *Partridge*, one of the last ships to leave.

You might think that with the ground forces gone, there would be nothing for the air forces to do, but he stayed on until the end of May, continuing a wide range of tasks – and the RNAS maintained a presence there throughout the war.

Ten days after the evacuation, he had his 'first flip in a fast machine': the Bristol Scout. He 'did not like right handed turns at first, but got better towards the end.... On the whole much easier to fly than I expected, though not so comfortable as pusher'. I can say from personal experience that this is something of an understatement; the trailing edge of the wing is a huge hindrance getting in or out, the cockpit is narrow enough to restrict movement of your elbows, and (for both myself and Bunnie), one's knees are jammed up under the instrument panel.

On 20 January 1915, he was 'Escorting M.F.1383 over Kithia and Fusilier Bluff':

> Flew in too slowly and pancaked on landing. It was an off day for me and although I flew with confidence and was quite comfortable the whole time I was flying damn badly. A most unsatisfactory performance. Came down 9,000 feet in 7 or 8 min. Too damn fast.

January was all escorting two-seaters doing observation work, but on 4 February, he carried four 16-lb bombs in the Scout to drop on Galata aerodrome with two Nieuports.

> Had great difficulty aiming machine as I had to fly with left hand, looking down through hole in bottom of fuselage. Dropped bombs too soon and too far to left. My first go at bomb dropping—I have never even practiced it before.

A small point to note here is that he appears routinely to have flown with his right hand on the stick, since he notes the fact that he had to use his left during the bombing run. For right-handed people, this was of course the natural way of things, and most aeroplanes were arranged with the throttle and mixture controls on the left side of the cockpit, but the Bristol had them on the right. Whether this was because they expected all pilots to be left-handed, or because the limited cockpit space meant that it was easier to reach across to the controls with one's left hand when there was not sufficient elbow room for your right hand to reach them comfortably is not clear.

The next day, he had his first go in a twin-engined Caudron G IV:

> Very heavy on rudder. Had great difficulty keeping her straight just before landing. This difficulty would probably have disappeared if I had wangled the engines. Rather unwieldy in the air, but with proper use of engines she might become fairly controllable.

By 'wangling', he means using more throttle on one engine than the other. Presumably, they found little use for it as he says it was only the second time it had been in the air. One can imagine the conversation with the CO:

Bunnie: 'Excuse me Sir, what's that machine at the back of the hangar?'

CO: 'It's the Caudron twin. Two 80-hp le Rhônes.'

'I haven't seen it out of the hangar since I've been here.'

'No, we can't find any use for it. Hopelessly slow, and difficult to fly with two engines.'

'Could I take her up, Sir? I'd like to see if I can manage her.'

'I don't understand. It's completely useless, and you might hurt yourself.'

'I should like to learn how to fly as many different types as possible, Sir."

'Well, I suppose so, Bremner. Just don't do anything silly, old chap.'

On 12 February, he was back in one of the Bristol Scouts (there were three—1259, 1262, and 1264—1263 having been lost at sea before he arrived) submarine hunting between Kephalos and Tenedos. Having taken off in calm conditions, a 40-kt wind blew up over Tenedos, but it was back to calm again when he landed. Today, GPS makes estimating the wind strength a doddle, but I am not sure how he did it then.

On 4 February, he was escorting the Maurice Farman on a reconnaissance mission but it was too cloudy to take photos. By now, he was well used to the idiosyncrasies of each machine. 'I always slip out in right handed turns with 1259 but I don't with 1264. Very queer!'

On 16 February, he carried out a reconnaissance of the Straits and landed with four bombs still under the aeroplane. Clearly, they loaded the bombs even for a reconnaissance mission just in case a target of opportunity came up. They were 16-lb bombs, so the additional load must have made a good deal of difference to the handling of the aeroplane, and indeed he himself comes to this conclusion the following day when he makes a poor landing again and blames it on the bombs. They obviously had not adopted the modern practice of dumping them before landing.

On 23 February, he was bombing a destroyer in Kilia Leman. 'Line good but dropped them too soon. About 100 yds away'.

He noted on 6 March:

Escort two H. F. and bomb shipping in straits. In dropping first bomb I pulled the machine back to 35 knots by mistake and bomb touched my axle. Machine quite reasonably steady at 35 knots, and answered at once when I put her nose down. Fairly good shooting with bomb, but I let them all off too soon. No wind, slow landing, but bounced a little. Saw quite a lot of Archie, but he never came close to me.

He commented on 11 March:

Hun reported coming from Dede Agach so (indecipherable) and I went out. Never saw any sign of him. Heard afterwards that he turned back just after we left. Glorious day up. Saw Mudros, Mytelene, Greece, Dede Agach, Gallipoli all from same spot near Samothrace (at 8300 feet). Came down in S turns and need not have used engine at all but gave her one or two touches. Nearly made a good landing but touched lightly by accident. Did not use engine and landed well and slowly after that; fair N. Breeze. Engine better.

Other work in March included chasing submarines, attempting (and failing) to intercept enemy aeroplanes and escort flights. On 17 March, he managed to get his hands on a Nieuport 11 in his pursuit of new machines to fly. His view was that it was 'A very nice machine in the air, but heavier and easier to fly than a Bristol'. Later that day, back in 1264, he flew in close formation with the Maurice Farman from Suvla to Helles. Clearly, he was becoming a confident and competent pilot.

The next day, he was practicing vertically banked turns in the morning and made a perfect landing rolling less than a foot in the strong—it must have been very strong—wind. He went up again practicing his aerobatic steep turns but his landing was a little out of wind and it tipped up on one wingtip, doing no damage. If you detect a little over-confidence creeping in, you would be right.

On his third flight of the day, the engine of 1259 cut out at 1,000 feet. He made a good circuit dead stick, but left the final turn a bit late and stalled the last few feet. The undercarriage collapsed and the aeroplane turned over on its back. Bunnie was fine, but his pride and confidence were shaken, and the machine was written off. 'My first smash. I did not mind it in the least'.

Yet his troubles were not over. The RNAS had insisted that their Bristol Scouts be fitted with the 80-hp Gnome engine because of its reputation for reliability. The newly arrived Nieuport 11 was fitted with the 80-hp le Rhône engine that, although it was nominally the same power, actually delivered a good deal more (ninety-two instead of the Gnome's sixty-five). The two engines were interchangeable, and when a new batch of Scouts was delivered with le Rhônes fitted, he had persuaded the mechanics to switch engines and propellers in 1264 so that he could keep up with the Nieuport.

Two days after his accident, he tried 1264 with the new engine, and once again tipped up on landing. This time, his confidence took a severe knock (Fig. 45).

I must have had a good deal of drift on. Why the devil didn't I see that? Two crashes in two days and I was flying very well in the air. Poor old '64. She was such a ripper and I did love her. Only two machines have I damaged in any way, and they were the two machines I loved best.

Things looked up after that. Only three days later, the mechanics had repaired 1264 and he took her up again, using the more powerful le Rhône engine once more; this time, all went well and he was able to keep up with his colleague in the Nieuport 11. Notice the detail in his observation of the changes in 1264:

> Speed the same, my engine showing 1150 and his 1175. Airspeed 80 knots. Landing again fair. She is a little nose heavy when the engine is on, but not bad in gliding. She does not drop her tail automatically the speed gets low, so she is rather harder to land.

Two days after that, he had an encounter with a Fokker Eindecker. In a letter home, he wrote:

> I waited a bit to entice him a bit further from his home, and then swung round and went straight for him. He also came straight at me and went above me. I let him do this as I guessed his game. (The usual Fokker trick is to come over a machine and then turn very sharply indeed and so swing round just behind the other machine).
>
> Sure enough just before he got to me he started to turn left. I said to myself, 'Here's a fool showing his hand in that manner.' So I judged a pause, so to speak, and then did a vertical bank left turn. In consequence, instead of his coming out on my tail, I came out jolly near his and I gave him a little dose of machine gun medicine.
>
> He started to dodge and weave all over the place like a frightened pigeon, but I was all over him and he could not get behind me, also unfortunately I could not quite get behind him, so I had to fire with a good deal of deflection and I don't think I hit him in a vital place. He then suddenly went into a devil of a nose dive and got away from me. He was flattening out a good way below and I was just starting after him when there was a flash past me and the other escort, who had been flying a bit above us, came by in a nose dive, got behind him, and gave him beans good and proper.
>
> 'I was then about 9,000 feet so I up with my tail and let her go. I had a glance at my speed indicator, but that only goes up to 95 knots, so it was not much use, and in what seemed to me to be an interval of a few seconds only, I found myself at 4,000 feet, and once more about 30 yards behind old Fokker. He had by this time dived away from my pal and I don't think he quite expected me, for it seemed to startle him somewhat when he got another dose of medicine. Again I could not quite get behind him, and he dived away and I lost sight of him.
>
> 'That dive of mine, 5,000 feet in one swoop, was one of the most exhilarating things I have done. My little bus fairly hummed down.

You cannot help but be impressed with the clear-headedness he showed. This was his first air combat, and he remained ahead of the German at all times, out-thinking and out-manoeuvring him despite the threat of death. Bear in mind that 12 per cent of the bullets he fired at the Fokker passed through his own propeller (Fig. 46). Also involved in the attack was Flt Lt Savory, who appears regularly in Bunnie's logbook.

In fact, Kenneth Savory was one of a number of distinguished officers serving with Bunnie. In April, he would be awarded a Distinguished Service Order for making a long-distance bombing attack on Constantinople, and a bar to it in 1917 when he made the most successful bombing attack on a warship up to that time.

Flying an enormous Handley Page O/100 twin-engined bomber which had been flown out from Great Britain (itself a remarkable achievement) he attacked the German battleship *Goeben* and other warships at Constantinople. They achieved hits on the *Goeben*, but managed to sink the Turkish destroyer *Yardigar-i-Milet*—the first time a warship had been sunk by aerial bombardment and a harbinger of the doom that was to await so many capital warships in the next war. He went on to become a wing commander in the RAF.

From March 1916 on, Bunnie was flying 1264 very regularly, mostly on escort duties. There are occasional days off—even ten days at one point— but very often he was flying two or three times a day (Fig. 47).

By now, we can see Bunnie's fascination with things mechanical starting to overtake his interest in prosecuting the war. On 12 April, he writes of 1264:

> Escorting gun bus on spotting trip. Started off, engine missing badly, could not make any improvement with petrol adjustment and then discovered the petrol tap leaking very badly so I came down (six minutes).
>
> I went off again and rev counter broke, but I went on brand new engine, running beautifully. I used 3 gals in 34 min. Four stays have been fitted to back bearer plate and they were a great success. The bottom two were pulled tighter than the top two and that seems to have corrected the nose heaviness a good deal. She flies hands off for quite a time now. First landing excellent, second quite fair.

As a fellow tinkerer, I am fascinated to know what these braces were since we were trying to replicate 1264 as closely as possible. However, I have racked my brains and failed to come up with a satisfactory suggestion, so our 1264 will have to remain in factory condition for now.

All of his flights in April were in 1264, but on the 29th, he got his hands on one of the batch of new Scouts. These had been significantly modified but were still defined as Type 'C'. He accurately reports the changes and finds it not as quick on the controls as 1264.

A couple of days later, on 1 May in the new Scout, he noted:

> Hun appeared early morning and I went off in pyjamas and leather gear to chase him. I lost him in the sun before starting out. He was going for Chanak. I made straight there. Nothing doing, at seaplane shed and no signs at Chanak aerodrome. I then went to Galata and got there just in time to see him land. Fitz, who started off a little before me saw him most of the way, and he took much the same route as I did.

Later the same day, he tried out the Nieuport 12 Gunbus for the first time. This was a two-seater with the pilot in front and the observer behind, the cockpits being close together to facilitate communication. 'Not a bad machine, but not a patch on a Bristol. Rather tricky on steep turns'.

He also reports on the effect of using different coloured glasses to aid landing (presumably to assist in judging one's height). He tried green and white glasses but did not have a strong view on which was better. The next day, he went as a passenger with Simpson in a BE2c to No. 3 Wing—he did not like being a passenger one bit.

On 6 May, he took 1264 with four 16-lb bombs to attack E15, which in fact was a British submarine that had run aground near Kephez Point a year before, and was torpedoed by the Royal Navy in a daring expedition a couple of days later. It is not clear why they were bombing it again at this time.

Later that day, he was in the Nieuport 12 Gunbus with his old pal Burnaby spotting for the big Naval guns; three days later, in the same machine, he told how one burst of Archie exploded within 10 or 20 yards, and they could hear the shrapnel whizzing past. The next day, back in his favourite 1264, he spotted another Hun and chased after him, but his engine was misfiring so he could not catch up with him.

On 16 May, he had his first go in the Henri Farman HF.27. They were pushers like the Voisin, but Bunnie found them a distinct improvement. The following day, he piloted it on a bombing mission, though he does not say where; the very next day, he carried out his very first night flight on this relatively strange machine on another bombing mission on enemy shipping in Chanak Bay.

His payload of three 112-lb bombs was pretty big, and he was able to see where they fell, though they seem to have dropped on the shore. Flying at night is pretty scary stuff—seeing your instrument requires special lighting, navigation was more difficult, and it was much more difficult to judge your landing—but Bunnie clearly enjoyed it very much, even though the moon had gone in by the time he landed. Acetylene lamps were used to light the landing ground.

There were changes in the organisational structure at this time. Wg Cdr E. L. Gerrard left No. 2 Wing in March to be replaced by Wg Cdr F. R. Scarlett, but at the end of May, it was split into three flights. 'A' Flight (Capt. Kilner) was detached to Thassos off the Greek coast, 'B' Flight went to Mytilene, and 'C' Flight remained at Imbros. Bunnie was attached to 'A' Flight.

On 30 May, he made the 90-mile flight to Thassos in 1264, almost all over water for about ninety minutes with an engine that he describes as vibrating very badly. Navigation was made easier by the line of warships stationed along the route, but even so, it is a flight that would give most modern sport aviators the collywobbles (Fig. 48).

We have the map he used for the flight, with the name of the other pilots faintly visible on the back. A Farman HF.27 arrived first and tipped up on landing. Bunnie's 1264 was regarded as a particularly valuable machine and he had been told to wait until someone had made a successful landing before following them in. Yet he decided to look for himself and concluded that a ground feature that looked like a ditch across the field (which the HF.27 had tried to avoid) was in fact just an optical illusion, so he landed across it without any problems. They joined a small detachment of French pilots who had flown in from the Greek mainland a few days previously. The French commanding officer of the Thassos detachment was a talented watercolourist called Lt René Prejelan, who turned his talents to recording the goings-on there. There's one particular picture which we like to think shows Granddad wearing his solar topee (Figs 49 and 50).

They had flown to Thassos to bring the war to Bulgaria, and they did this mostly by bombing—sometimes towns (on 8 June, they attacked Xanthi)—and sometimes crops, using incendiary bombs. His logbook becomes more and more involved with the technical details: getting the engines to run nicely, adjusting the airframe to get them properly trimmed, and so on.

I assume this is because he had met Bartolomeo (Meo) Costantini, the Italian racing driver who was serving with the French detachment. Costantini was a very gifted mechanic and advised Bunnie on the way to get the best out of his engine. He also gave Bunnie a German Bosch magneto which he had acquired through his racing contacts. It was regarded as being much more reliable than the Avia ones fitted as standard, and Bunnie switched it to every machine he flew after that. There is an interesting codicil to this story, which will be covered in the next chapter.

Among the other interesting characters, he worked with was Sam Kinkead. Although he was not mentioned in the logbooks, they are mentioned together in the diary of Flt Sub Lt R. S. W. Dickinson who served in No. 2 Wing at Imbros at the same time. Sam went on to fly on the

Western Front, and commanded a squadron of Sopwith Camels providing support for the White Russians in southern Russia in 1919. The squadron was moved from airfield to airfield using a train of special wagons. Then in the 1920s, he joined the high-speed flight, a special RAF unit dedicated to competing for the Schneider Trophy in very high-powered seaplanes. Sam was killed on 28 March 1928 on a test flight in a Supermarine S5 over the Solent.

At the end of July 1916, Bunnie was invalided back with a persistent and ill-defined sickness (possibly related to the malaria and dysentery that were endemic in the area) that resulted in heart irregularities. Scout 1264 was being returned to HMS *Ark Royal* for refurbishment about the same time, and Bunnie took three souvenirs home with him: the stick, rudder bar, and that Bosch magneto.

He was only declared fit for ground duties in March 1917 and was posted as first lieutenant of RNAS Redcar. He instituted a potato patch which provided spuds for the men and was serviced by the defaulters.

By March 1918, he was posted as experimental officer to the Experimental Station at Orford Ness, which was adjacent to Martlesham Heath. Martlesham was where they tested all the new aircraft; Orford Ness carried out experiments on other equipment. Bunnie carried out testing of parachutes to see how much damage they could sustain before they became unusable, and the optimum type of underwater explosive to use on air-dropped torpedoes.

He was in distinguished company. Professor Lindemann (who later became the Prime Minister's scientific adviser in the Second World War) and Dr R. V. Jones (who became head of the Air Ministry's Scientific Branch) both worked there. The pilots who tested the experiments were a particular breed too; one pilot named Hill came up with a scheme for reinforcing the leading edges of the wings of an aeroplane so that they could cut through the cables of balloons.

He was persuaded to test the theory out first using separate steel extensions to the wings. Unfortunately, they had forgotten about the effect of static electricity, and when he tried it out there was a blinding flash and the aeroplane was thrown into a spin. It was a miracle that there was no fire.

Bunnie finally got a clean bill of health to go flying on 4 April 1918, by which time he had been a captain in the RAF for three days (which was formed on the 1st). He made a few flights in April and May of that year but never resumed combat flying. He had a total of about 140 hours in his logbook.

23

Island of Dreams
(2012–2016)

While the three of us spent so many hours together working together on the build, we talked a good deal about the things we would like to do when it was finished.

One of the dreams we talked about was to revisit the locations Granddad had flown from: Imbros and Thassos, and so I was particularly interested to read an article in *Cross and Cockade* magazine by Paschalis Palavouzis about a memorial to the airmen who flew from Thassos as well as an upcoming article about another pilot who flew from Thassos just after Granddad and who in fact flew some of the same aeroplanes as him. I was given Paschalis's contact details by the magazine's editor, Mick Davis, and just after Christmas 2012, we got in touch. It was like lighting the blue touch paper on a firework.

Paschalis obtained a degree in computer science in London and is now head of the Technical College in the port of Kavala, which was occupied by the Bulgarians in August 1916 and is directly opposite the island of Thassos where Granddad was stationed. He is also an acknowledged expert on the air war in this little-known theatre of operations in the Great War, and the result was a flurry of emails that advanced our understanding of Granddad's war by several orders of magnitude.

Looking at Paschalis's original email of 30 December 2012, I see that he says 'I am really dreaming of ... watching the Scout up in the air, here at Thasos, where your grandfather once flew and fought'. This was an idea we had never seriously considered; going there ourselves was one thing, taking 1264 was something altogether different and quite beyond the scope of our imaginations. The suggestion was filed away in the 'daydreams' category.

Paschalis and I exchanged views and information and with Paschalis's knowledge of the area and the war and my knowledge of aviation, I felt I could actually fly with Granddad on many of the missions he flew. Over the following couple of years, we kept up a regular correspondence and became good friends in a virtual sort of way.

By Christmas 2014, the idea of taking 1264 to the Greek islands was starting to coalesce from a daydream into a vague idea and I asked Paschalis for suggestions about where this might be possible. He first broached the idea of taking her to the very spot on Thassos where Granddad flew in 1916.

Six months later, in July 2015, shortly after 1264's first flight, Paschalis came up with the astounding news that he had taken it upon himself to float the idea of the Thassos flight with a retired Hellenic Air Force Col. Panagiotis (Panos) Georgiadis, who like Paschalis belonged to a group researching local aviation history, and the Mayor of Thassos; they were all willing to help to get this off the ground. The projected date was June 2016, timed to coincide with the local airshow at Kavala (of which Panos happened to be the organiser). From there on, the project rapidly focused and moved from a dream into an idea.

We started looking at how to get 1264 out there, and any issues relating to the various permissions required. The aeroplane's Permit to Fly is a British approval, which might or might not be acceptable in Greece. My pilot's licence was internationally recognised and so should be acceptable. We started investigating shipping agents to get 1264 to Thassos.

By November, Paschalis and Panos were working on the head of the Macedonia and Thrace Prefecture and even the Greek President's office to gain official approval for the project, and we had arranged to visit Thassos in January 2016 to assess the local conditions.

A couple of years previously, we had met up with Stephen Saunders, a BAFTA-nominated film producer who was making a documentary about 1264. By now, he was a regular visitor to the project, but for him the trip to Thassos was going to form the culmination of the film and the most expensive bit of filming. It was critically important that he come to Thassos to weigh up the situation and make sure that everything was in place when we arrived in June.

So on 13 January, Stephen and I met Paschalis and Panos for the first time as they drove us from Thessaloniki airport to Kavala. It was a great experience to meet both of them; I felt I knew Paschalis so well via our email correspondence, and in person he was everything I had come to expect; warm, generous, and a bottomless pit of knowledge on our shared enthusiasm.

Panos also lived fully up to expectations; compact and energetic, it was impossible to imagine him as anything other than a fighter pilot. I later learned that he is regarded with considerable respect among his peers, having flown many interceptions in his F5 against hostile aircraft across the Aegean Sea and survived an ejection following an engine failure.

They explained that the project had now received official government backing and would form part of the Kavala airshow. While it is tempting to think that it was laid on for our personal benefit, this was not in fact the case. When the RNAS had flown in on 31 May 1916, they were accompanied by a detachment of French pilots and aeroplanes. Later, they were supported by Greek pilots who were trained up and flew the British and French machines; these Greek pilots formed the kernel of the independent Greek Air Force.

Yet Granddad, the first British pilot to land successfully on Thassos, was a valid focal point for the festivities, particularly if he would be represented by his grandson flying his original machine. They explained that there would be a formal ceremony involving flypasts, one of which would be by 1264. One of the benefits of this arrangement was that it removed all possible pitfalls in obtaining permission to fly; we would be fully covered by the military authority granted to Panos as director of the Kavala airshow.

The following day, we took the ferry across to Thassos and met the mayor, who was very hospitable and clearly enthusiastic about the project. The island of Thassos is small, mountainous, and very beautiful. It is most famous for its marble quarries that have provided the best quality marble since the time of the ancient Greeks; in fact, the Acropolis is built of marble from Thassos.

There is a memorial to the Great War aviators killed in operations from Thassos located on the ferry terminal at Prinos, only a stone's throw from the airfield. We paid our respects and Paschalis told us the stories of some of those commemorated there.

The airfield is immediately behind the village of Prinos on the north western corner of Thassos and is more or less the only piece of land on the entire island that is flat enough for any sort of airfield. Today, the island's main industry is tourism, and it seems astonishing that it has not been built over many years ago. Yet after the Great War, the airfield was decommissioned and in the uncertain period thereafter, locals started fencing off and cultivating parts of it so that ownership became somewhat muddled. Also, the land is marshy and poorly drained.

When we arrived in January, the fields were mostly empty, but much of the area was covered in grass and reeds more than 2 m high. In the middle of this was a 250 m by 10 m strip constructed by a local microlight pilot. It was made of compacted marble dust, and while it was just about long enough, it was definitely too narrow. We made a survey and identified an area that was clear of cultivated fields and drainage ditches and large enough for our purposes, and Panos promised to get the Greek military involved in clearing the area.

With that done, I had a little time to myself to think about Granddad and the other aviators who had been there nearly 100 years before. The landscape is barely altered; the hills that restricted the landing approach are still there, and it is easy to visualise the exact spot where the canvas Bessonneau hangars once stood in the shade of the olive trees that are still harvested by the locals. It was a magical moment.

After that, we met John, a private pilot whose grandmother had helped clear the airfield for use before the RNAS arrived. We all went to look at an amazing collection of Sopwith Camel parts the aviation history society had found on a hillside above Prinos.

On our return to the mainland, we met the head of the prefecture who was also enthusiastic about the project. It seemed that the Greeks had met their half of the bargain; all we had to do was get ourselves and 1264 there.

Up to this point, we had planned that our trailer would be loaded on to an articulated trailer and hauled out in the week before the show, but this was starting to look something of a problem. It would take a week there and a week back. The Kavala show was fixed for the week 26–27 June, and we needed to be there for a week beforehand to be sure of getting preparations complete and some suitable weather. The Navy Days display at Shuttleworth at which 1264 would be a participant was on 5 June, and we were also due to receive the 'Preservationist of the Year' award from the Transport Trust, presented by Prince Michael of Kent.

It had also been Theo's long-term ambition to fly over the Somme on 1 July 2016 to commemorate the opening day of that most fatal of days in the history of the British Army. It was clear that the week's journey in the articulated truck, coupled with the need to meet up with it and load and unload, was going to mean that something would have to give.

By now, I had switched from the Land Rover Discovery to the Toyota Hilux and we were altogether more comfortable with it as a tow vehicle that might make it all the way to Greece and back, and might even get to the Somme as well. We started to do the sums, and it became apparent that it might be possible to fit in the whole shooting match if we were lucky. In only a few months, daydreams had morphed into ideas and were fast crystallizing into a plan. Meanwhile, historian Paschalis had been continuing his researches into Granddad and 1264.

Shortly after we returned from Thassos, he emailed us about the time Granddad was shot down over the Helles peninsula on Gallipoli. Granddad thought he might have been shot down by *Hauptmann* Hans-Joachim Buddecke, a German fighter pilot who had become an ace, and was reasonably well known. Looking at Buddecke's records on line, I had reckoned that was quite conceivable: Buddecke had shot down a two-seater the day before, and it was possible the dates and type of plane had been entered in error. Yet if you want to know the truth, ask Paschalis. He said that although Buddecke was indeed flying a Fokker Eindecker from the right airfield (Chanak, on the Asian side of the Dardanelles), his records show that Granddad was actually shot down by *Oberleutnant* Theo Croneiss.

Later that month, he said that he had come to the rather startling conclusion that Granddad's story about the magneto having been given to him by racing driver Meo Costantini was wrong. Yet Granddad was not a liar; the story is much more entertaining than that.

Paschalis said that although Meo Costantini was a pilot in the Great War, he could find no record of his having served on the Macedonian Front or Thassos. The only possible alternative was a Dominique Felix Pierre Costantini, who was not a racing driver. How could this be squared with Granddad's story? We were both confused.

Paschalis is not one to let a mystery like this stand, however, and contacted David Mechin, a French historian colleague. Between them, they unearthed the true story. Pierre Costantini was born in Sartène (Corsica), on 16 February 1889. He became a military pilot in late 1913, fighting in Escadrilles D4, DM36, and MS26 in 1914–1915, gaining two Mentions in Despatches.

He was transferred to Salonika with Escadrille N91 on 28 September 1915. It is hard to know why for certain, but many pilots were sent to Salonika at that time because their commanding officers wanted to get rid of potential trouble-makers.

In Salonika, he went to Escadrille N87 on 8 December 1915, then Escadrille V83, then Escadrille V90, was shot down by flak on 23 March 1916, and escaped capture by the Bulgarians. He was sent to the Thassos detachment in May 1916, where he presumably pretended to be Meo Costantini, the famous racing driver for Bugatti before the war. Like so many others on the Macedonian Front (including Granddad), he contracted malaria.

Back in France in early 1917, he served in several units—perhaps a clue that he was a difficult man to handle: Avord Flying School 20 January 1917, Escadrilles N83 on 1 March 1917, N79 on 6 September 1917, SOP134 on 10 September 1917, and N102 on 30 September 1917. Then on 9 November 1917, he was shot down and captured in Diksmuide, and escaped on 30 May 1918.

Between the wars, he became a journalist, but in the Second World War, he served as a major with the French *Armée de l'Air* reserve. He also wrote two books about his fellow Corsican, Napoléon Bonaparte, and founded the collaborationist French League following the controversial sinking of the French fleet at Mers-el-Kébir by the Royal Navy. He also founded the Union of anti-Masonic Journalists and the collaborationist militia the *Légion des volontaires français contre le bolchévisme* (LVF). In 1944, after the D-Day landings, he fled to Germany.

Condemned to fifteen years in prison for collaboration in 1952, he was adjudged to be of unsound mind and spent several years in a psychiatric asylum after which he returned to journalism and published more works on his hero Napoléon. He died in 1986, three years after Granddad.

It was hard to know what to make of this new slant on one of our favourite stories. Surely if anyone (French or English) on Thassos or in Salonika had known his true identity, he would have been exposed immediately? Also, if he was not a racing driver, where had the magneto come from?

The first question remains something of a mystery. His true identity is recorded in all the official documents for the time, so it is not clear how he could have continued to perpetrate such a deception to the extent that it clearly took in my Granddad. The only plausible solution I can come up with is that the official records were all kept at Salonika, and it might have been possible to maintain the pretence on the little outpost at Thassos. Nevertheless, it is still pretty intriguing.

As for the second question, Paschalis suggests that at least four Albatros C.I aeroplanes were shot down on the Salonika front in the first quarter of 1916, and were displayed at the 'White Tower' in Salonika, and that the magneto likely came from one of these. If so, it adds a further patina to the parts used on 1264.

So Paschalis had uncovered the truth about the magneto. His next mission was to discover more details about 1264's last movements, and in July 2016, he came up with the goods. The best source book for this type of information is the snappily titled *Royal Navy Aircraft Serials and Units 1911–1919* by Ray Sturtivant and Gordon Page. It says 'To Malta 6.16 for recovering; but lost on return to Thasos when ship sunk. Deleted 8.16'. Other accounts mention Egypt and Athens as possible destinations.

The first stage of clarification came from Granddad's logbook. His last flight in 1264 was on 9 June 1916, and ten days later, he was flying 3036 fitted with his old engine, so it seems pretty definite she was taken out of service between those dates. It must also be the point at which Granddad liberated his souvenirs: the magneto (which was his personal property), the stick (which he had extended for his personal use), and the rudder bar. She was going for complete refurbishment, so no one would have objected.

From here on in, Paschalis provided much additional information, and even another possible photograph. It is most likely that 1264 was put on to lighter K19, based at Stavros on the mainland and shipped to HMS *Ark Royal*, the world's first aircraft carrier that had been based in the Aegean since the start of the Gallipoli campaign. She had a reasonably extensive hangar and good repair facilities, and her logbook for 27 June shows her receiving an aeroplane. The following week, the Weekly Operations report states that Thassos had one Bristol Scout beyond local repair and the *Ark Royal* was repairing Nieuport machines. A week after that, Thassos had no Bristol machine beyond repair, and the *Ark Royal* was undertaking the repair of Nieuport and Bristol machines.

By week ending 28 July, the Weekly Operations Report stated that 'it is hoped to have another Scout which has been rebuilt in HMS *Ark Royal* ready for duty in two days'. On 2 August, a Bristol Scout was transferred to HMS *Clacton*, a merchant ship that had been impressed into the Royal Navy; she left for the mainland port of Stavros to transfer stores. Yet as she was coming alongside HMS *Grafton* at 8.33 a.m. on 3 August, she was torpedoed and sank, having on board 'a Bristol Scout which had been completely rebuilt in *Ark Royal*'. The same report states 'The Bristol Scout was raised and sent to Thassos on Sunday, 6 August'. Paschalis has combed through the records and although it was never positively identified as 1264, no other Bristol Scout was lost in that period. It must be assumed that a survey was carried out on Thassos of the bedraggled wreck, no doubt further damaged during the recovery; she was written off.

There are no records of her final disposal, but Paschalis says that they were typically ferried back to HMS *Ark Royal* where anything useful was removed, and then taken to the island of Ispatho (known as Koukonesi today) for burning. That might have been the end of the story, if it were not for Granddad's souvenirs.

24

Scout Armament (1914–1916)

It had been clear from the start that the Bristol Scout needed armament; there were three high-performance Scouts in service, all privately designed: the Sopwith Tabloid, the Martinsyde S1, and the Bristol. There was no doubt that it was the Bristol they all lusted after. It had immediately been nicknamed Bullet (and that was how my Granddad always referred to it) because it was the fastest and most manoeuvrable.

This speed and manoeuvrability immediately rendered the War Office's idea of an unarmed single-seat scout obsolete. If you were flying something as fast and precisely manoeuvrable as this, it was axiomatic that you would want to take armament with you and have a pot shot at the enemy.

Guns

The first solution to the problem was to take handheld guns, either pistols or (if there was enough space to stow it) a rifle. Experiments by the RNAS at Eastchurch involved three Webley-Fosbery pistols attached to the fuselage with a lanyard, which were semi-automatic. These were chosen as although they fired multiple shots with a single pull of the trigger, they did not eject the cartridge cases, which might have done more damage to your own aeroplane than to the enemy. Thereafter, they moved on to the Holland and Holland Aero 12-bore shotguns loaded with buckshot and chain shot in an attempt to rip holes in the target's wing fabric.[1]

Manoeuvring the aeroplane as well as aiming a handheld gun was asking a bit much; very soon, the pilots worked out ways of mounting a gun on the aeroplane itself, realising that the aeroplane was so manoeuvrable that it would be perfectly possible to get a good shot at the enemy.

The two Type Bs had had extempore mounts made for rifles on the fuselage side firing outwards and downwards (although the only victory was achieved using a pistol), but in May 1915, Frank Barnwell at the B&CAC office was producing drawing XD821 showing a mounting for an infantry Lewis gun, and there is photographic evidence of it being fitted.

It has a hinged mounting bolted to the rear starboard cabane strut and forward supports fixed to the longeron and the front cabane strut. The gun is mounted at eye level and in the firing position, it fires obliquely forward outside the propeller arc. The butt protrudes into the cockpit space, and the barrel can be swung inwards against the cabane struts to at least give the pilot a fighting chance of getting in or out of the cockpit.

Frank drew this one himself, and also approved XD830 dated 11 August showing the aircraft-pattern Lewis without the cooling tube. The most entertaining is XD824 dated 11 June, showing mountings for no less than a duck gun—was this a spot of whimsy by the draughtsman on a quiet afternoon, or had he heard of the 12-bore shotgun trials? AG, whoever he was, approved his own drawing, but it is referred to on XD830, so perhaps it was serious and Frank was aware of it (Fig. 51).

A duck (or punt) gun was a very large bore shotgun which delivered a fearsome load of chainshot over a wide area. It was traditionally mounted on a shallow draught punt, partly for concealment in the rushes at the edge of a pond, and partly because its fearsome recoil would have been far more dangerous to the shooter than the duck if it had been handheld. Presumably this particular gun was breech-loaded, otherwise one would presumably have only had a single shot at the enemy.

Even so, there is no magazine, so it would have needed reloading for each shot, but perhaps the most imaginative detail is the use of loops of undercarriage bungee to allow for the awesome recoil. It might have reduced the loads on the cabane strut (already dangerously weakened by the bolts passing through it) but the butt of the gun would almost certainly have delivered a knockout punch to the pilot's jaw.

Meanwhile, the pilots at the front all had their own ideas. The Martinsyde and Tabloid seemed to standardise on a mount on the centre section of the top wing. It was easy to install, clear of the propeller and fired in the line of flight or a bit above it. But it required a remote trigger mechanism and reloading it was difficult or impossible. The most famous example of this is Louis Strange, who stood up in his Martinsyde to change his ammunition drum and ended up hanging from the ammunition drum when the aeroplane turned upside down. He managed to manoeuvre himself into a position where he could kick the stick forward so that the machine righted itself, and then get back into the cockpit to return to the airfield none the worse for his experience.

Yet the Bristol seemed to inspire all sorts of alternative ideas. Some did indeed have the gun mounted on the top centre section, and there are pictures of two or three different mountings, some fixed, and some capable of being rotated backwards to allow reloading.

The two Type Bs had rifles mounted pointing out and down. Lanoe Hawker, who was a brilliant pilot and a capable engineer, mounted a Lewis gun on his aeroplane, Type 'C', s/no. 1611, also pointing out and down. In July, while other ideas were being drawn up in Bristol, he used it to force down three Germans in one flight—an action that earned him the VC, the first to be awarded for aerial combat (Fig. 36).

The RNAS at Eastchurch also experimented with an unsynchronised Lewis gun mounted on the fuselage firing directly forward.

> Two or three holes could be made with impunity and the propeller bound up with sticky tape after landing. If there were more than three holes the propeller was scrapped. Firing through the propeller became too extravagant with propellers, so a metal deflector was clipped on to the blade. That idea was soon dropped because too many useful bullets were wasted.[1]

There was another unusual installation found in Egypt: two Lewis guns on hinged brackets mounted midway between the wings and well away from the fuselage. The line of fire would have been straight ahead, and access to the butt of the gun was by hinging them inwards. Of course, this solution (wing-mounted guns) anticipates the Spitfire and Hurricane by some twenty years.

Yet the period from August 1915 to April 1916 became known as the Fokker Scourge, owing to the Fokker Eindecker, a monoplane based on a French pre-war racing design of rather indifferent performance, but single-seat and manoeuvrable enough that, when fitted with a mechanism to synchronise the firing of a Spandau machine gun with the rotation of the propeller enabling the pilot to aim the whole aeroplane at the enemy, it caused devastation among the Allied air forces.

Fokker introduced the idea following the shooting down of Frenchman Roland Garros, who had also tried the metal deflector blade idea and had some initial success, but it was not really satisfactory and Fokker was lucky to come up with a more viable solution than the Allies. It is interesting to speculate what would have happened if Anthony Fokker, the wayward genius designer from Holland, had had his offer to work for the British at the outbreak of the war accepted. Yet the synchronising gear was not reliable, and the first German ace to use the Fokker Eindecker, Max Immelmann, probably died shooting his own propeller off.

The Fokker Scourge was so bad that Noel Pemberton Billing, who had earlier been taught to fly by Harold Barnwell and was now an MP, actually accused the War Office of murder on account of their official policy of only ordering aircraft designed by the Royal Aircraft Factory—namely, the BE2c.

During this period, the RNAS in the Aegean had an eclectic collection of aeroplanes, but it included probably the largest number of Bristol Scouts in any one place. Although there was little opposition, it included a number of Fokker Eindeckers.

They adopted the Eastchurch solution of unsynchronised Lewis guns firing through the propeller but doped fabric on to the propeller to limit the amount of splintering since they were short of spare propellers (Fig. 52). They mounted guns on one or sometimes both sides of the fuselage, firing directly forward through the propeller, and sometimes with a third above the centre section. By my calculations, the chances of a bullet hitting were about 1 in 10 so loosing off a forty-seven-round drum of ammunition would have taken about six seconds, by which time on average you would have three rounds in each blade. Perhaps that was why they told pilots the propeller was still safe with two or three rounds per blade in it.

It was not until December 1915—seven months after the Germans— that the British developed their own synchronising gear, and it was the Bristol Scout that was the first to go to France fitted with the Vickers-Challenger gear.

It arrived on 25 March 1916 at 13 Squadron, base of the young Albert Ball, soon to become a legend. Mechanical synchronising gear was generally unreliable; Ball had to return from a patrol with a damaged propeller after the gear failed. One missive from a squadron complained that the gear had been set up incorrectly, and ground trials had shown that *every* bullet went into the propeller.

Also, it's not often noted that in addition to its unreliability, it halved the rate of fire and therefore halved the chances of a hit. Even in 1917, pilots in 45 Squadron RFC flying the Sopwith 1 1/2 strutter equipped with the Ross synchronising gear would deliberately turn off the synchronising in combat, coming home with up to twenty holes in the propeller.

We have carried out our own experiments on a dummy propeller blade, and firing a standard 0.303 round at point blank range causes minimal damage because the bullet is travelling so fast. Three holes per blade seems eminently survivable, and the ten holes reported by 45 Sqn pilots seems possible, though pretty risky.

Perhaps this unreliability explains why the RNAS felt that the risks of an unsynchronised gun were acceptable.

Trials were also carried out on the Bristol Scout with the Scarff-Dibovski and the ARSIAD systems. None seems to have been successful, possibly because the Scout's structure—and its tiny cockpit in particular—made installation problematic.

The CC (Constantinescu-Colley) system, which used a hydraulic rather than a mechanical link between engine and gun, would have been compatible but was not introduced until August 1916 by which time the Scout had been superseded by other aeroplanes such as the Sopwith Pup.

Other Armaments

One idea that seems to have been quite widely adopted was the use of Ranken darts for attacking Zeppelins, though I have yet to come across any Bristol drawings. The idea arose from the RNAS, who were tasked with home defence. After the Zeppelin raids in June 1915, the Scout was one of the few machines with any hope of attacking them, though even the Scout could not match the Zeppelin's rate of climb or endurance.

Ranken darts were simple dart-shaped projectiles with a 1-lb explosive charge designed to be dropped on an airship and penetrate the gasbags. They came in packs of twenty-four and could be dropped individually or all together.

The darts were loaded into launch tubes fitted on the outside of the fuselage or internally alongside the seat. There are no records of successes with this weapon, though Zeppelin LG17 was attacked by Flt Lt C. T. Freeman in Scout Type 'D', s/no. 8953 on 2 August 1916 flying from HMS *Vindex* without success; it was difficult enough to get in position above the Zeppelin, despite the airship obligingly waiting around for the forty-seven minutes it took to gain the necessary altitude. Despite three attacking runs, during which he thought one hit the LG17, it failed to detonate and no harm was done. Freeman had to ditch in the North Sea in the absence of a landing deck on HMS *Vindex* and was rescued by a Belgian steamer.

The Ranken Dart was superseded by 0.303-inch incendiary ammunition suitable for the Lewis and Vickers machine guns, and one wonders if that was the intended use for another installation, in which the gun is mounted on the fuselage side pointing downwards between the fuselage and wing and presumably missing the undercarriage (Fig. 53). The photograph indicates that this was taken on HMS *Vindex*. The target was clearly therefore Zeppelins, and while it would seem at first glance to be odd to have to climb above the target with all the difficulties that brings, at least you would be shielded from attack by the Zeppelin's crew in the gondola below.

Bombs were fitted to some RNAS machines. In 1915 two Bristol Scouts dropped six 20-lb bombs and a dozen hand grenades on a damaged Zeppelin that was being towed back to Ostend harbour by a German ship.

No. 2 Wing RNAS fitted a small bomb rack underneath the fuselage just behind the engine. On this they could mount four 16-lb Hales or 20-lb Mills bombs. The only known photograph is not very clear, but as we have seen in Chapter 22 on one of Granddad's bombing missions, he dropped them at too slow a speed and the bombs bounced off his undercarriage axle.

One other possible fitment was a 3.45-inch launch tube for incendiary bombs, known to have been fitted to Scout Type 'C', s/no. 5292. The bombs had hooks designed to catch in an enemy aircraft's fabric and apparently, an attack by Lt D. A. Glen on an observation balloon on 30 October 1915 using such armament was unsuccessful.

Conclusion

The sheer variety of ammunition fitted was simply astonishing; I have found evidence of no fewer than seven different methods of mounting an unsynchronised Lewis gun, a couple for a rifle, and one for a punt gun. There was one trial with a synchronised Lewis gun and a couple with the Vickers gun. Then there were two types of installation for the Ranken darts and possibly an incendiary bomb launch tube.

I doubt any other Great War design had so many different types of armament fitted, and it indicates the passion with which pilots wished to do so. The fact that none of them went into production is not a criticism of the basic design; it was just that its original specification was outdated.

25

Dreams Come True (2016)

By May 2016, our schedule for the following month was pretty much set; my Display Authorisation had been approved by the CAA and the Transport Trust's award ceremony was set for the day after the Shuttleworth Navy Days display.

The month of June looked as follows:

Saturday 4 June: Interview and photo session at Old Warden. Prepare 1264 and self for air display.

Sunday 5 June: Fly Navy air display at Old Warden. Immediately dismantle 1264 and drive to the Brooklands circuit at Weybridge, Surrey.

Monday 6 June: Erect 1264 in front of the old clubhouse at Brooklands. 11 a.m.: Transport Trust Preservationist of the Year presentation by HRH Prince Michael of Kent. Dismantle 1264 again and drive to Bicester.

Tuesday 14 June: Drive to Bicester, collect trailer, and drive to Portsmouth to sail on Le Havre overnight ferry.

Wednesday 15 June: Overnight stop near Mâcon, France.

Thursday 16 June: Drive through Mont Blanc tunnel. Overnight stop near Milan, Italy.

Friday 17 June: Overnight ferry Ancona–Igoumenitsa, Greece, while the rest of the team—Theo, my wife Sue, film producer Stephen Saunders, his wife Clare, and three film crew—fly to Thessaloniki and thence by car to Thassos.

Saturday 18 June: Drive to Kavala.

Sunday 19 June: Ferry to Prinos on Thassos island. Check airfield and hangarage. Rig 1264.

Monday 20–Thursday 23 June: Flying and filming at Thassos.

Friday 24 June: Air Display at Prinos.

Monday 27 June: Depart for France.

All of this depended on the weather and the serviceability of 1264, the trailer, the Hilux, and the various ferries, as well as the Greek authorities.

Things started well; the weather at Old Warden, home of the Shuttleworth Trust, over the weekend of 4–5 June seemed fair, and we had a good day on the Saturday, talking about 1264 and watching the preparations for the Sunday. A huge marquee was being erected to house the Fly Navy Heritage Trust, and a large Naval helicopter landed alongside as a static display for the day.

The Sunday dawned bright and calm, and the morning was spent talking with the public about Granddad's war, 1264, and building and flying her. Halfway through, we were joined by Ian Tibbitt and Jock Alexander, both retired admirals and vice-chairman and chairman respectively of the Fly Navy Heritage Trust.

They had generously provided assistance for our historic trip to Greece and came to pay their respects and the money, which I gave to Sue for safe keeping. They took us across to the marquee, where we were introduced to a bewildering variety of the great and good, among whom who was the Assistant Chief of Naval Staff (aviation and carriers), who is also the Rear Admiral of the Fleet Air Arm, Keith Blount, OBE, RN. He shook me warmly by the hand and introduced himself firmly as Keith. A long time ago, I was a very junior Naval officer, and this did not come naturally to me.

All too soon, it was time to get 1264 down to the southern end of the runway to be sure to be ready for our slot. Theo and I went down with Theo's schoolfriend Richard Chillingford (Chill), who had replaced Rick as ground crew, Rick having got married to Marian a couple of weeks before and decided to step back from the project now the build was completed.

As always, it was a matter of hurry up and wait, and once we had fussed around 1264 and gone through as much of the pre-start ritual as possible, we lounged about in the sun and kept a wary eye on the wind, which was blowing gently straight down the runway.

The plan was that I would do around five minutes solo, and then be joined by the Bristol F2B Fighter, flown by Paul Shakespeare, who is a test pilot at the Empire Test Pilot School. All too soon, our time came; I clambered into the cockpit while Theo and Chill got ready to start her up at the same time as Paul clambered up into the F2B to get her started and warmed through.

The take-off was absolutely fine and I started my display. For a slow non-aerobatic machine like this, it is important to keep as low and as close to the crowd as you are allowed, so the majority of your attention is being given to that imaginary line on the ground you must keep close to without ever crossing, and keeping just above the level of the trees. You maintain full power throughout the display, and at each end do a 'dumbbell' turn: turn away from the wind about 45 degrees, then a 270-degree turn into wind, and a final 45-degree turn back on to the display line, while adjusting your height to get back down to the minimum allowed. There are a number of variations you can make—a 360-degree turn away from the crowd or a 'topside' pass, where you keep the aeroplane tilted towards the crowd by doing a gentle turn down the display line so that people can see the top of the machine.

All this went fine, and I watched as Paul took off in the F2B. He was going to try and formate on me but never seemed to catch up, and when my time was up, I made a wider circuit and landed in front of the crowd. After I had landed, the engine would not respond to control inputs so I shut it down and found the linkage had come undone.

It was a sublime moment; never in my entire flying career had I expected to be flying in a proper display, and when I was applauded as we neared the crowd, I felt I would not need an aeroplane to go flying. Paul Shakespeare joined me after he had landed and said I had been turning too tightly for him to follow in the much larger and less manoeuvrable F2B.

Here I was, discussing on more or less equal terms display flying with a test pilot who was absolutely at the top of his profession when I was flying a rotary engine aeroplane that he never had. My head swelled to more or less twice its normal size.

Yet there was not time for too much self-congratulation. As soon as Theo and Chill had returned from the far end of the field, we set to dismantling 1264 and putting her in the trailer before heading away from Old Warden—Theo to go home to Dorset, while Sue and I headed for Brooklands near Weybridge for the Transport Trust's presentation ceremony, which was due to start at 11 a.m. We arrived late at night and parked the trailer up by the clubhouse before heading to the bed and breakfast accommodation a mile or so away.

In the morning, it was quite a rush to get 1264 rigged and parked outside the clubhouse in time, but she looked great with a Bristol car alongside, and a magnificent racing version of a Model 'T' Ford and a vintage bus there as well.

Nevertheless, Sue and I, along with Theo and his partner Fran, were all 'poshed up' by the time HRH Prince Michael of Kent arrived. With him were long-time supporters of the Transport Trust, Lord and Lady McAlpine, and they all spent a good deal of time looking 1264 over. The presentation ceremony itself was very enjoyable; we were surrounded by some very meritorious efforts indeed. Yet ours was the premier award; it is a stunning silver model of the SS *Great Britain* mounted on an original piece of the deck. It was created in honour of the original recipient, Sir Jack Haward, who arranged for her recovery from the Falkland Islands in 1970 (Fig. 54).

I made a short acceptance speech in which I suggested that my great-great-great-great-great-uncle, James Bremner of Wick, might be considered for a posthumous award since he refloated the *Great Britain* after she had been stranded on the sands of Dundrum Bay in Northern Ireland in 1856.

Over a buffet lunch, we spent some time chatting to the McAlpines, Prince Michael, and the others. Theo spent time with Prince Michael discussing the information on our display boards. Then it was time to pack up, and poor 1264 was yet again dismantled with the assistance of the staff from the Brooklands Museum. We knew that the next time she was rigged would be on Thassos.

Having left the trailer at Bicester, I had just a week to do some work and get the last-minute arrangements completed. A week later, film producer Stephen Saunders and cameraman Elliott Bell came to our home with a car boot full of very expensive camera equipment. We loaded the equipment into the back of the Hilux and set off for Bicester to pick up the trailer, then Portsmouth where we met up with Theo's brother Noel who was acting as co-driver (since Theo had to be away this week and would join us in Thassos).

The ferry arrived the following morning in Le Havre and we headed south-east at a steady 55 mph. The GPS routed us around the outskirts of Paris and down a route that had a height limit of 2 m, so we spent some time fiddling through little suburban roads trying not to hit anything with the trailer. There was a good view of the Eiffel Tower, but given the choice, we would have managed without that.

The following day, we had to get through the Mont Blanc tunnel. The climb up to it was long and in places very steep, and we were glad of all the Hilux's muscle, but we arrived at the top safely and the views were spectacular. The tunnel itself is pretty straightforward, but descending on the Italian side is even more eye-popping than the French side.

The following afternoon we arrived at Ancona for the ferry to Igoumenitsa in north-west Greece. We had been warned that the loading process was chaotic, and boy was it. There seemed to be no pattern at all, and all the vehicles were being shouted at in stereo. We were no exception, and when we finally drove up the ramp, the man on the middle deck shouted at me at the top of his voice in a mixture of Italian, English and one or two very rude words in French.

I was not sure what he was trying to achieve, so it was difficult to obey fast enough. Yet after a while, it became clear that he wanted us to make a U-turn and then reverse into a narrow slot next to an articulated lorry.

When the shouting and swearing ceased, we were simply astonished to discover that we were parked absolutely parallel to, and less than 100 mm from, the articulated lorry.

We arrived at Igoumenitsa the next morning and the contrast could not have been greater—a deserted wharf and a civilised and calm disembarkation. We had been forewarned that fuel stations were at something of a premium, so we topped up before we headed west. The road from Igoumenitsa to Turkey is something of an engineering miracle, and the first half seemingly cuts straight through the huge mountain range, so we spent more than half the time in tunnels.

It took pretty much all day, but as we got closer to Kavala we were contacted by Paschalis who gave us directions for meeting up. As we turned off the main road, an escort was waiting to meet us, and our little convoy headed into the military barracks, courtesy of retired Air Force Colonel Panos.

We left the trailer there and headed back to the hotel where we relaxed for the first time after a journey of around 1,300 miles with Panos and Paschalis, together with English couple Tony and Carol Henwood, who had come all the way to see us there. Tony's great uncle was Norman Starbuck, another pilot flying from Thassos in 1916.

The next day was Sunday and we collected the trailer and headed for the little ferry going to Prinos on Thassos Island. Loading this time was civilised, even though it required reversing. We saw Theo, Stephen Saunders and the film crew on the ferry as it docked, and it was a huge pleasure to see them again.

The journey across was smooth enough, but when I started to drive off under the instruction of the ferry crew, a corner of the trailer hit the rear light of a black Mercedes in the next row. This resulted in a protracted conversation at maximum volume between the ferry skipper, retired Col. Panos, and the owner of the Mercedes, who turned out to be a current Air Force colonel who apparently pulled rank on all the others.

We watched on the sidelines until it all went quiet, and then drove the mile or so to our hotel, which was only a short walk from the airfield. We went to have a look. The original 250 m × 10 m hard strip had been enlarged to about 650 m × 100 m, using a grader to clear the weeds. This was a good start, but a couple of drainage ditches had not been filled, reducing the usable length to around 400 m, and the surface was still very rough and consisted of dry loose dust (Fig. 55).

The hangar that we had been promised was only just big enough in length and width, and far too low to get the aeroplane in. Yet the immediate problem was that the access road was inaccessible so that no vehicle could get in or out. The problem was further exacerbated by the fact that Monday was a Bank Holiday, making it unlikely that anything would happen much before then.

We returned to the bar in the hotel and I was finally able to say hello to Sue, who had flown out with Theo and Stephen and the remainder of the film crew. Paschalis invited us all to a wonderful restaurant in the hills, and we had a leisurely Greek lunch that lasted most of the afternoon and served to cement friendships. As we came back, we were delighted to see work going on to make the access road to the airfield passable. This was most impressive.

Due to the Bank Holiday, the Monday was an enforced day off, which we spent around the hotel. The Tuesday morning was taken up by a press conference in Greek in the hotel, which was well-attended by representatives of the Greek press. All appeared to go well, and by the evening, sufficient work had taken place on the strip that we could move the trailer round and get 1264 rigged and into her rather ramshackle shelter.

The shelter had no sides, and we parked the trailer as close as we could to it on the upwind side to provide a bit more protection. Yet it was still a risky business getting her in and out of the shelter; once the canvas at the front had been rolled up, two poles had to be removed, and then manipulated manually to keep the roof from sagging on to the top wing as she was rolled out. It took four or five people to move the aeroplane, and two weightlifters to hold the roof up.

The weather was beautifully calm, and we wondered about getting an evening flight in. But for once the engine seemed unwilling to start, and by the time it did and we rolled her to the take-off position, it was all getting too late, so we decided to leave it until the morning. We had lots to do; we needed to get as much flying footage as possible for the film and I wanted to make sure that I could do the display on Friday, but we still had two days and we thought it was not impossible.

Wednesday morning broke the spell and left us all with a feeling of deep gloom. It might have been okay 100 years ago to fly in all sorts of weather, but then they were operating under military conditions where risks were acceptable and there were plenty of spare machines if one got broken. For us, flying was always going to be limited to morning and evening, since the midday heat generated powerful thermals that would throw us about all over the place. So far, mornings and evenings had been perfect, and we had been led to believe this was normal for this time of year.

The forecast predicted the imminent and unseasonal arrival of the Meltemi, a strong hot north-easterly which would blow for several days. Our display flight on Friday was supposed to be at 11 a.m., and the chances of this happening now seemed vanishingly remote. Worse than this, it seemed entirely likely that we would be unable to get any flying in at all, which would be a huge disappointment.

We went down to the strip and managed to sort out the starting problems (the considerable heat made the priming evaporate off quickly, so we changed our routine to make sure she was started immediately after priming, and all went well), but the wind was blowing at 45 degrees to the strip and so no flying was possible. We decided our only hope of flying lay in getting up before dawn on the following morning and hoping that the wind had not increased already. With 1264 put away, Sue and Clare Saunders headed for the beach, while Theo and Noel and I took a tour round the island.

The alarm went at 5 a.m. on Thursday morning and we all headed down to the airfield with a pretty strong feeling of foreboding in the pit of our stomachs. In the half-light, the wind was still reasonably strong, but at least it was straight down the strip, and we rolled 1264 out of the shelter. There were more people there than we might have expected: Sue of course and the film crew, but somehow Paschalis and Tony and Carol Henwood had made it across from the mainland for this ungodly hour.

Theo and I took a long, careful look at the surface and tried driving up and down it to assess its smoothness. The result was not encouraging. The Scout lands at about 40 mph, and it was hard to get to that sort of speed in the Hilux without risking your head banging on the roof. Barring a miracle, there would be no other opportunity to fly. The dust and grit would cause havoc to the propeller and engine. As the morning light crept across the eastern sky, we walked and talked.

Then Theo suggested that we use the original strip to take off. It was firm and smooth; also, we would be able to control the direction sufficiently. The landing would have to be on the rough stuff, but provided I kept the speed under control so that it did not float on, it gave us the best chance of a successful outcome.

The decision was taken. We rolled 1264 out, and while I climbed aboard, strapped in, and settled my thoughts, Theo and Noel primed the engine and she started first pull. I ran her up as quickly as possible to limit the damage to the engine, and then I was off. The take-off was smooth and the engine pulling well. I knew we needed as much film material as possible, so I made several low passes, but quickly found the air, even at that time in the morning, was very bumpy—so bumpy that at one point I could feel splashes of petrol from the vent pipe on the petrol tank in front of me (Fig. 56).

After a while, aware that this would be the only chance I would get to fly, I started to climb up to try and have time to think about Granddad and the flying he did. Yet the turbulence got worse, if anything, and after ten minutes, I decided this was not worth the risk, and I reluctantly headed back to the airfield for what would be one of the most challenging landings of my flying career.

Coming in, I could see that the wind had not shifted direction, which was good, but the turbulence would always be a worry. I lined up on the rough dirt and tried to keep as low and slow on the approach as I dared, blipping the throttle as necessary. The far end of the strip seemed awfully close, but although I managed to get the wheels down reasonably early, they immediately caught a bump and we were back in the air. Thankfully, I was going reasonably slowly and we settled down again more or less straight away, and in a straight line. We stopped after a short run of only about 20 m (Fig. 57).

I had made it. Theo came bounding up and we were both pretty much speechless with relief and pride. Shortly afterwards, Sue joined us, and it was time for a huge hug and a kiss. Paschalis was there too, a huge beam across his face. The film crew interviewed all of us, and within half an hour the wind had risen well outside safe limits. We rolled 1264 back into the shelter and headed back to the hotel for a quick breakfast before going back to the airfield for a live interview on Greek TV. It was a moment to savour, and we did so over a beer or three.

The next day was to be the official ceremony at the Prinos War Memorial attended by many dignitaries headed by the Minister of Defence and the Chief of the Air Force. We were represented by Sue Bremner and Clare Saunders. We hoped for a miracle reduction in the wind, but it only got stronger and stronger, and so it was decided that we would welcome everyone on the island to come and look at 1264 in her shelter.

The weather was hot and the wind increasing as large numbers of police and army vehicles arrived on the airfield. A while later, two military helicopters arrived in a huge swirl of dust, and shortly after that a mob of brass hats approached, with the Minister of Defence, Panos Kammenos, and the Chief of the Hellenic Air Force General Staff, Lt-Gen. Christos Vaitsis at the fore. There was no opportunity to change or even wash our hands, but they were very interested in 1264 and how we had managed so far.

They were swept off in the convoy of cars to the commemoration ceremony at the Prinos pier just the other side of the airfield boundary fence, and we waited, frustrated that we would be unable to play our part. Theo and I had a brief moment to get changed and wash our hands before getting back to 1264's shelter and the ever-increasing wind.

We could not hear the majority of the ceremony, except for the Greek F16 fighters that roared overhead in a 'missing man' formation, and an aerobatic display, but shortly afterwards people started arriving at the airfield to come and have a look at us. More and more of them came until we were entirely surrounded by people, all jostling to ask about 1264 and have their photographs taken with us. For an hour or so, it was madness, Theo, Sue, and I in the middle of this surging crowd, all eager to meet us, to see 1264 and all full of praise. Is this what it is like to be a celebrity? It was a very strange sensation—not quite heady, but very pleasant.

Standing out in the crowd was the crisp white uniform of the British Naval *attaché*, Captain Richard Pocock, and his charming wife, and it was great to have a couple of minutes to chat to someone from home.

Suddenly, Panos Georgiadis was at my elbow, insisting that I get into a car to go to the hotel, where there was a reception. He quickly arranged for local police to ensure 1264's safety, and then we were off to the conference centre in the hotel. I had no idea what was coming and was sat, slightly nonplussed, in the front row with Captain Pocock beside me.

We chatted for a moment or two until the band struck up. After this, they showed a short film of the history of the airfield at Prinos, and a three-minute video of yesterday's flight hurriedly put together by Stephen Saunders' team, which won applause for the take-off and landing. The Minister of Defence then said that the Greek government had decided to award Granddad the Hellenic Commendation Star of Merit and Honour, and I was asked to accept it on his behalf. Thankfully, I was not asked to make any response other than to thank him for what was a very rare and special honour to Granddad.

Yet we were not finished. Next in line was the Mayor of Thassos, who awarded me the freedom of the island; coming a day after the UK's decision to leave the EU, we felt this had the potential to be of real practical use. This was our moment in the sun, and by the time we all left for the buffet lunch, my head had once more swelled to about double its size. It was not to last.

After lunch, Theo and I drove to the airfield to put the front back on 1264's shelter. The ever-rising wind was giving us some concern, and we wanted to make sure that she was not completely covered in dust. Yet when we got there, our breath stopped in our throats. As we pulled up, we could see that the back half of the shelter was completely missing, and a moment's search showed that it was upside down, about 20 m away in the reeds. What had happened to 1264? We ran over to have a look and could not believe what we saw. There was not a mark on her. Amazingly, the shelter seemed to have lifted clean over the top of 1264's tail before blowing away.

Yet she was still in imminent danger. Although she was protected from the full force of the wind by the trailer, the rudder was slatting from side to side and she was being covered in dust from the regular dust devils during which it was difficult to breathe. The other half of the shelter looked to be in imminent danger of collapse, and there was no way we could move her outside to de-rig her, and so we removed the rudder and called for help, which arrived shortly afterwards in the person of the deputy mayor, Babis. Together, we decided that the only way to secure the situation was to park another large vehicle in front of the shelter to provide more protection from the wind, and a strongpoint to which the shelter could be attached. Babis got on the phone and within a few minutes, a garbage truck was parked alongside the shelter. As the sun set, we scrambled on top to tie ropes from it to the shelter to try and ensure its overnight security.

We had hoped to be able to re-erect the shelter the following morning, but it quickly became clear that it was too damaged and the wind was still too strong. We reluctantly took the decision that the only safe place for 1264 was back in her trailer. Even this was not straightforward as we had to do this inside the shelter; it involved some tricky moments as the wings were removed to make sure they were not damaged by the shelter or blown away in the wind that was still whipping around us.

Did we feel disappointed? Well, we hardly had time to feel anything as we were invited to witness the main Kavala airshow from the roof of the local government offices. The show was slick and very entertaining, and the ancient port of Kavala formed a perfect backdrop. All the other VIPs there were keen to meet us and have their photographs taken with us, and I even got interviewed at length by Bulgarian television.

The following morning was the Sunday and with no aeroplane to fly, we had time to reflect on the month's momentous events. I was disappointed that we had not managed to get more filming done, and that Theo had not managed to fly. Yet slowly these feelings were replaced by a feeling of quiet pride, with gratitude to all of those who had contributed so much to the effort.

We had rebuilt a 100-year-old aeroplane—Granddad's favourite—and flown it. It was, and remains, the only airworthy Bristol Scout in the world. We were members of a very select band of pilots (probably less than a dozen in the UK) who had flown a rotary-engined Great War aeroplane and I had even flown one in a public airshow. Most of them operate for around half an hour a year.

We had flown 1264 for no less than nine hours. I had managed to fly Granddad's aeroplane, using Granddad's original stick and rudder bar, from the very spot Granddad flew from, exactly 100 years after he did. We had met some truly amazing people along the way, and been treated like Hollywood celebrities. Most miraculous of all, we still had an airworthy machine in the trailer, ready for the next adventure. If you had told us thirteen years previously that we would have achieved all these things, we would have laughed in your face.

Most of us found history lessons at school terminally dull, and while politicians and statesmen surely need to have a firm grasp of the grand sweep of history to inform current decision-making, the finer detail, such as we have explored in this project, is less likely to be relevant.

However, be in no doubt, it exerts a powerful fascination for people of all ages and has undoubtedly inspired many of those who have come to visit us at static displays. For most, it is a pleasant way of spending half an hour reading the background and asking questions. For some, it may lead them to further investigation of the engineering and aeronautical challenges it presents or broadened their knowledge of a little-known theatre of war.

For me, it has been an unprecedented opportunity to get to know my grandfather in a level of detail that few are granted. His is not an outstanding military career by any measure, and yet he made great sacrifices and showed an uncommon level of skill in what he did. I feel that in addition to knowing him through eyes of a grandson, I have been able to get to know him on more equal terms, as a colleague and pilot.

I have also learned to marvel at the sophistication of the aeroplanes that were coming off the drawing board only five or six years after the start of practical powered aeroplanes in 1908. Comparing the performance between the 1913 Bristol Scout and my 2003 Escapade, I find that weight, horsepower, minimum and maximum speeds, and rates of climb and glide are all pretty much identical. The chief difference is that the modern engine is light enough to allow the Escapade to carry a passenger.

Sat there, in a hotel on Thassos, I felt nothing but gratitude to fate and all the people who had helped along the way for where this incredible adventure had taken us.

Epilogue

The Barnwells

The Barnwell boys, Harold and Frank, contributed more to the world of aviation than most. Talented, fearless Harold proved to be a good instructor and a valuable test pilot. Quiet, introspective Frank introduced intellectual rigour to the process of aeroplane design, and led a team of designers at the Filton works to produce a list of iconic aeroplanes: the Bristol F2B Fighter that served the RFC and RAF from 1917 to the end of the 1920s; the fastest Great War fighter aeroplane in the 132-mph M.1C Monoplane; the Bulldog; and the Blenheim bomber.
Yet they did not have long, happy, and fulfilling lives.

Harold was killed in 1917 test flying the prototype FB26 Vampire, a night-flying variant of the Gunbus format. He had taken off from the Vickers airfield on 25 August at Joyce Green in Kent where so much of his work took place, and the aeroplane never recovered from a spin. Harold had suffered a bout of flu the week before and it is thought that he may have suffered a relapse and collapsed at the controls, although later service trials with the other early production machines showed it to have poor handling qualities. He was only thirty-eight. Only four Vampires were built.

There is a memorial to Harold at Joyce Green paid for by his siblings. The fact that Harold left his not inconsiderable estate to Frank shows how close they had remained despite their lives having taken separate paths. Harold was a naturally talented pilot, but all his attempts at aeroplane design were less than successful.

Frank was a mirror image; his aeroplane designs, from the 1911 monoplane that won the Laws prize, were all successful while his career as a pilot was less so. In his book *Bristol Fashion*, published in 1960, author John Pudney says of Frank: 'The line of Barnwell crashes is too long to be enumerated.' He also mentions the trip he made to the front in France in a F2B to see first-hand what the pilots thought of it. He took a passenger with him on one leg, and in the crash, Barnwell broke both ankles, thereafter walking with a limp. History does not relate what happened to the passenger.

In 1919, he took the flying surfaces from a Badger (a proposed development of the F2B fighter) and made up a cheap slab-sided fuselage for experimental work. The whole thing cost £250 to build and was known as the Badger X (and unofficially Barnwell's weekender).

It became the first aeroplane to appear on the UK civil register as G-EABU on 30 May 1919, by which time Barnwell had turned it over on the golf course adjacent to the Filton airfield. He was left unharmed but angry, hanging from the straps; he got even angrier when someone released his straps before getting hold of him, meaning he landed on his head.

Later that year, he crashed the MR1 (the first all-metal airframe produced by Bristol and a development of the F2B) into a tree at Farnborough, successfully decapitating the tree and writing the airframe off in the process.

In 1927, a lightweight two-seater called the Brownie, built for the Lympne ultralight trials and much modified as a prospective basic trainer for the Air Ministry, had been allocated to Barnwell as his personal runabout. He flew it in all weathers, on one occasion remaining in view for over an hour from Filton as he battled enormous easterly headwinds over the Cotswolds. In March 1928, he crashed it at Farnborough, only yards from his decapitated tree.

In all his crashes, he had escaped serious injury, but in 1938, having been banned from flying company's aeroplanes, he had designed his own lightweight runabout called the BSW1, which he had built by the local Aero Club. It stalled and spun on its second flight and Barnwell was killed at the scene. He was fifty-eight. He and Marjorie had three sons. All joined the RAF and all were killed in the early years of the Second World War. Pilot Officer John Barnwell, 29 Squadron, died aged twenty on 19 June 1940; Flight Lieutenant Richard Barnwell, 102 Squadron, died aged twenty-four on 29 October 1940; and Pilot Officer David Barnwell, DFC, 607 Squadron, died aged nineteen on 14 October 1941. One wonders what his widow Marjorie thought of flying, having lost her brother-in-law, husband, and all three sons to its service.

An obituary at the time of his death in 1938 was penned by his friend C. M. Poulsen, who was the editor of *Flight International*. Poulsen says:

There may be designers who are greater technicians in some particular sphere and on some particular aspect of aircraft design, but it can be said quite truthfully that there is no designer who has had the confidence and loyalty of his entire staff to a greater degree. It is literally true that there was not one member of the Bristol staff who would not do anything in the world for Capt. Barnwell. Service was given him, not through fear, for Barnwell was the most gentle of men, but because everyone felt that it was a privilege to be allowed to work for him.

In his work Capt. Barnwell was one of the neatest and most methodical men. It did not matter whether he was doing an elaborate calculation or merely a simple memorandum; they were all written in his peculiar large, neat handwriting and carefully filed away.

As an example of how Barnwell worked, perhaps I may be permitted to quote a personal experience. I had been worrying him for many months to write me an article for our monthly technical supplement, The Aircraft Engineer, but he had been far too busy to spare the time. Then one day I received a letter from him informing me that he was doing an article and that I should be receiving it after the Easter holidays. It duly arrived, and I found it to be written entirely in his own handwriting, and all the charts and graphs done by himself. He had spent the Easter holidays doing it at home. I had naturally assumed that in the archives of the Bristol company there would be much material which could be turned into an article, with very little trouble, by his assistants. But no, that was not Barnwell's way. He set to work and did the whole thing himself from 'A' to 'Z'.

It has been my good fortune to know Frank Barnwell since about 1913 or so, and before that I was privileged to count among my friends his brother, Harold Barnwell, who was chief test pilot to Vickers and lost his life in a flying accident in 1917. Although very dissimilar in appearance and in many other respects, the two brothers had in common a charm which made one treasure their friendship. Frank was rather shy and retiring and would never suffer the limelight of publicity to be pointed in his direction. If asked to write an article or deliver a lecture he usually refused because, as he said, there were lots of people much better qualified than he. And that was not a pose; he meant it quite sincerely. He was modest to a fault.

The Bristol Scout

The Bristol Scout was an important aeroplane in at least three different ways and deserves a more prominent place in the history books.

Firstly, since 1908, the French had been the supreme player in the world of aviation. They had been the first, apart from the Wright brothers, to develop a practical heavier-than-air flying machine, and for six years, they had been the undisputed leaders in airframes, engines, and pilots. Yet in April 1914, that supremacy was broken for the first time by a British machine, the Sopwith Tabloid, which turned in such a spectacular time in the Schneider Cup that all the other entrants simply retired, knowing they had no hope of coming even close.

The Bristol Scout had flown a couple of months before, more than matching the Tabloid's performance, and the two of them were seen as evidence that British manufacturers had caught up with—and overtaken—their rivals across the Channel. In that sense, the Scout can be seen as the first fruits of forty to fifty years of British pre-eminence in aeroplane design.

In the second place, that pre-eminence was the result of outstanding work by a generation of British aeroplane designers, among whom Frank Barnwell was one of the most respected. Frank's work on the Scout—the only production aeroplane he designed entirely himself—led directly to the seminal paper read to Glasgow University in the autumn of 1914 that would provide a methodological backbone to the work of all other designers after him.

There was never a definitive showdown in peacetime between the Tabloid and the Scout, but in wartime, it was the Scout that proved to be the faster, the more manoeuvrable, and the better liked of the two, therefore continuing in production the longest.

The Tabloid and Martinsyde Scout were capable machines with guns mounted above the top wing, but they did not have the performance of the Bristol and did not inspire the pilots in the same way. They also did not inspire the pilots to experiment with the myriad different forms of armament that were tried on the Scout, and neither was ever tried with synchronised guns like the Scout. For the first year of the war, it was the fastest warplane, and for the first eighteen months, it was the machine they all hankered after.

The fact that it never made the transition from single-seat scout to single-seat fighter is not a sign of a flaw in the design; as an unarmed Scout, it was designed to be as fast and light as possible, and the tiny cockpit and relatively lightweight structure were perfectly suited for that role. Having demonstrated the viability of fixed armament, it was apparent a new aeroplane design would be needed to house the mechanism for the synchronised machine gun and to give the pilot sufficient room to operate it.

These days, the Bristol Scout tends to get forgotten in the light of its later, more glamorous offspring: the Sopwith Pup, the Sopwith Camel, and the SE5A (and on the German side, the Fokker Eindecker and Dreidecker (triplane)). Yet all of them owe a debt of gratitude to the Bristol Scout, which, more than any other type, showed the way in the early months of the war and demonstrated the viability of a single-seat aeroplane with a fixed forward-firing machine gun as a way of maintaining all-important air superiority in air-to-air combat. This, more than any other thing, cements the Bristol Scout's place in the history books.

While none of the Scout airframe features was revolutionary, it was probably the first time this combination of features—taildragger tractor biplane, wood and wire structure, steel tail feathers, simple vee-strut undercarriage, rotary engine, and four double-acting ailerons—had been used in combination; the fact that most Allied aeroplane designs throughout the Great War copied this combination shows how practical it was.

The Somme

For us, the Greek adventure was only half of the story; we had always hoped to fly over the Somme in July, but it was clear that the actual centenary on the 1st would be so heavily regulated there would be absolutely no possibility of our getting into the air.

Yet as a result of a chance contact with Stephen Slater, chief executive of the LAA and co-owner of a replica BE2c, we had been contracted by the Department of Tourism and Culture, along with two other Great War aeroplanes—the Albatros D.V (representing the Germans) and BE2e (representing the British), both operated by the World War I Aviation Heritage Trust—to carry out a flypast as part of the centenary commemoration of the start of the Battle of the Somme on 1 July. We were representing the French, on account of the French cockades thoughtfully painted on the Scout by the RNAS 100 years before.

This had always been a personal ambition of mine, since Granddad's first cousin, after whom I am named, had been fatally injured in that first terrible hour. David was a second lieutenant in the 1st Battalion, Border Regiment, and was in the support trench about 100 m from the Newfoundland Regiment near Beaumont Hamel at the northern end of the line. As a result, his trench has been preserved as part of what is now Newfoundland Park, and I often think about his unsung heroism and sacrifice on that day (Fig 58).

It seems grossly unjust that Granddad, who got to play with all the latest machinery, and whose war had lots of variety and adventure, is remembered, while David, whose war had none of those things and who paid the ultimate price, is lost among the 57,000 who suffered with him on that day.

At 7.20 a.m., the Hawthorn Ridge mine blew a short distance away over his left shoulder. At 7.30 a.m., the South Wales Borderers in the front line went over the top. The Germans, having had ten minutes' warning that something was up, lined their machine guns up on the gaps in the barbed wire, and none of them got more than about 50 yards. Thirty-five minutes later, David had to order his men over the top (Fig. 59).

By now, the support trenches were completely choked with the dead and dying, and they had to make their way under fire from the support trench to the wooden bridges over the front line. These focal points formed an ideal aiming point on the skyline for the German machine guns, and those that managed to make their way through here were picked off as they made their way through their own barbed wire. A few of them did manage to form up and march forward in line, but though they maintained their ranks magnificently, they were picked off long before they made it to the German lines at the bottom of the hill.

At 7.30 a.m., there were 811 men and twenty-three officers in David's battalion. An hour later, there were 202 men and three officers; the rest were dead, injured, or missing. David, unlike so many of his colleagues, was recovered and sent to the hospital at Doullens, where he died a week later.

So we had one spare day at Thassos to relax, and then it was time to head off back up to the airport at Albert, where we were to meet up with the other aeroplanes. The journey, with four of us in the cab, was tiring but went smoothly. Getting on to the airfield presented quite a challenge since it was where most of the British attending the event would be arriving, to be ferried to the Thiepval Memorial by an army of coaches lined up on the airfield. Thankfully, I had made contact with the young enthusiastic and capable operations manager, Morgan-Jeffery Hugon, and he managed to cut through the layers of red tape so that we were able to get 1264 rigged under cover and into the hangar.

At least we arrived by trailer. Jean-Michel Munn in the BE2e and Rob Gauld-Galliers in the Albatros had flown across the Channel. They were safely tucked away in a hangar there and 1264 joined them. Even accommodation was a challenge, and we only managed to get the necessary rooms in a hotel about an hour away in Cambrai thanks to a personal contact of Stephen Saunders.

The day itself was cool and blustery and we arrived early in the morning hoping that the wind would drop out in the afternoon when we were slated to fly. We sat and watched the Royal family arrive in their Royal flight aircraft, cautiously eyeing up the snipers located on all the hangar roofs.

At 11.30 a.m., we had to make the decision whether to fly, and the three pilots looked at the windsock blowing obstinately at 45 degrees to the runway and unanimously decided that it was just too dangerous.

It was a hammer blow. We had driven all the way to Greece and France and only achieved one ten-minute flight in pretty scary conditions. Theo had not flown at all. Would this be the sum total of our achievement? Both Theo and I felt absolutely shattered and went back to the hotel to drown our sorrows and to cherish the faint hope that at least we could fly on the morrow, though the forecast for our remaining days there did not look particularly promising.

The following day, we headed back to Albert, where security had eased off very considerably. All three aeroplanes were hauled outside for engine runs. Jean-Michel Munn discovered a crack in one-cylinder head of the BE2e, which was clearly therefore grounded. Rob Gauld-Galliers discovered a faulty magneto in the Albatros, which was therefore also grounded. Scout 1264 ran flawlessly, and my cousin Claude Michenau, who had made a six-hour journey to see us, sat in the cockpit.

Yet that wind was still too brisk and variable and the controllers in the tower were unwilling to let us go flying without a radio, so we decided to see if things settled down after 6 p.m., by which time the tower would have gone home and we would have unrestricted access to the grass strip used by the gliders. As we sat outside in the sunshine, we were outwardly relaxed but there was an inward tension crackling beneath the surface.

Gradually, the thermal activity eased back, and by 5 p.m., it was clear the wind would be blowing gently and steadily straight down the strip. The tension eased, and we started to prepare the aeroplane and the camera equipment for what would be a very historic occasion.

Cousin Claude was promoted to *pompier* and put in charge of the fire extinguisher, and Theo and Noel adopted their familiar roles in charge of preparing the engine while I clambered into the cockpit and put David's picture in the map holder so that he could be with me on this trip. With the cameras all rolling, Theo swung the propeller and she fired first time.

Power checks done, I waved away the chocks and opened up. Scout 1264 lifted willingly into the calm air and for the first time in her life, I pointed her nose determinedly away from the airfield. This was the first time she had ever strayed beyond gliding range. The le Rhône was pulling eagerly, and I gained confidence as we headed off across the historic blood-soaked fields of the Somme valley towards the Thiepval monument easily visible on the skyline.

From any angle, it is an imposing sight, and I thought about the countless names carved on its many faces as I circled round as we had hoped to do the day before. After I had been around a few times to try and make sure we had good footage, I headed the few miles to the Newfoundland Park which was likewise easy to spot from the air. For the first time on this trip, I had sufficient time to think about David. His serious young face was looking at me and I hoped his spirit was looking down on me as I thought about him and all his comrades, so many of whom were still buried under that soil.

I returned to Albert feeling deeply, deeply grateful for the privilege I had been given. Scout 1264 was behaving beautifully, so I indulged in some gentle twists and turns over the airfield to gently let off steam. When I landed, there was one more thing to achieve.

Theo had set this whole project in motion with a desire to fly a Great War aeroplane over the Somme in emulation of his childhood hero Biggles. He is a cautious flyer and it took a little persuasion to get him into the cockpit; eventually, we succeeded. I swung the propeller and he took off into the clear evening air. He did not feel the need to go outside gliding range, but he flew as cautiously and carefully as he always does, and after ten minutes or so, he made an absolutely perfect landing. The circle was closed (Fig. 60).

Endnotes

Chapter 1

1. Probate Calendar, Anne Barnwell, 1894. *ancestry.co.uk* (Accessed 6 April 2014).
2. 'Richard Barnwell Obituary', *The Engineer*, p. 238 (7 March 1898).
3. Baptism records. *FHL* Film no. 994177 item 1 page 69, Lewisham, Kent: St Marks Church (1879).
4. Frank Sowter Barnwell RAF Service Record, *National Archives* (19 Jan 1919).
5. Census, 11 Darnly Road, Lewisham, Lewisham, Kent: *National Archives* (1881).
6. Census, Elchro House, Balfron, Glasgow, *National Archives* (1891).
7. Frank Barnwell Biography, *Undiscovered Scotland* (Accessed 4 April 2014).
8. Census, *op. cit.* (1891).
9. Census, 5 Wemyss Place, Edinburgh, Edinburgh: *National Archives* (1891).
10. Fettes College roll of honour, *edinburghs-war.ed.ac.uk* (Accessed 10 June 2014).
11. 'Richard Barnwell Obituary', *op. cit.*
12. Probate Calendar, Anne Barnwell, *op. cit.*
13. 'Deaths—Frederick Crofts Barnwell', *The Morning Post*, p. 1 (17 April 1897).
14. 'Richard Barnwell Obituary', *op. cit.*
15. 'Frank Barnwell Biography', *op. cit.*
16. 'Richard Barnwell Will', *The Morning Post*, p. 4 (19 May 1898).
17. Census, 4 Park Terrace, Govan, Glasgow: *National Archives* (1901).
18. Frank Barnwell Biography, *universitystory.gla.ac.uk* (Accessed 4 April 2014).
19. Goodall A. T. M., *British Aircraft before the Great War*, p. 36 (Schiffer, 2001).
20. Frank Barnwell Biography, *Undiscovered Scotland. op. cit.*
21. Frank Sowter Barnwell, RAF Service Record, *op. cit.*
22. Frank Barnwell Biography, *Undiscovered Scotland. op. cit.*

Chapter 3

1. Bulman M. G. P., Memorial Lecture, *Flight*, pp. 338–342 (19 March 1954).
2. Goodall A. T. M., *British Aircraft before the Great War*, p 36.
3. Barnwell's First Aircraft, *SCRAN*, Dec. 1908 (Accessed 4 April 2014).

4. 'A Scottish Aeroplane—Experiments at Stirling', *The Aberdeen Daily Journal*, p. 4 (2 Dec. 1908).
5. *Ibid.*
6. Goodall A. T. M., *British Aircraft before the Great War*, p 36.
7. 'Flying Machine Experiments', *The Evening Telegraph and Post*, p. 2 (29 July 1909).
8. Goodall A. T. M., *op. cit.*
9. 'City's Tribute to flight pioneers', 27 April 2005, BBC (Accessed 25 August 2018).
10. Though strangely enough, we have been unable to find any documentary evidence of it or their marriage.
11. Census, 28 Lion Hill, Clifton, Bristol: *National Archives* (1911).
12. 'City's Tribute to flight pioneers', *op. cit.*

Chapter 5

1. Barnes C. H., *Bristol Aircraft since 1910* (Putnam, 1964), p. 20.
2. Driver H., *The Birth of Military Aviation: Britain, 1903–1914*, p. 76 (The Boydell Press, 1997).

Chapter 8

1. 'Salisbury Plain, Bristol School', *Flight*, 29 June 1912, p. 587.
2. 'Vickers School', *Flight*, 23 November 1912, p. 1,082.
3. Dallas Brett, R., *The History of British Aviation 1908–1914 Vol. 1*, p. 202 (Aviation Book Club, 1934).

Chapter 10

1. Bruce J. M., *Windsock Datafile 44*: Bristol Scout (Albatros Publications, 1994).
2. *Ibid.*
3. Driver H., *The Birth of Military Aviation: Britain, 1903–1914*, p. 188.
4. Sykes M. F. H., 'Military Aviation', *Flight*, p. 277 (8 March 1913).
5. Bruce J. M., *op. cit.*

Chapter 11

1. 'The New 80hp Bristol Speed Scout', *Aero and Hydro*, p. 225 (1 August 1914).

Chapter 13

1. War Office, 'Tests for Aeroplanes of Private Design,' *Flight*, p. 184 (21 February 1914).
2. Barnwell F. S., *Aeroplane Design* (McBride, Nast, 1917).
3. 'Olympia Exhibition Report', *Flight*, pp. 261–274 (14 March 1914).
4. Barnes C. H., *Bristol Aircraft since 1910*, p. 81.

Chapter 14

1. Driver H., *The Birth of Military Aviation: Britain, 1903–1914*, p. 127.
2. Andrews C. and Morgan, E. B., *Vickers Aircraft since 1908* (Putnam 1988).

3. Green W., *The Complete Book of Fighters* (Salamander Books, 2001).
4. *Flight*, p. 889 (19 November 1915).

Chapter 17

1. Driver H., *The Birth of Military Aviation: Britain, 1903–1914*, p. 121.
2. Barnes C. H., *Bristol Aircraft since 1910*, p. 25.
3. Minutes, 30 November 1914, B&CAC Papers.
4. Frank Sowter Barnwell, RAF Service Record, *op. cit.*

Chapter 19

1. Pudney J., *Bristol Fashion*, p. 74.

Chapter 24

1. Moore W. G., *Early Bird*, p. 15 (Putnam, 1963).

Further Reading

B&CAC

White, Sir G. B., *Tramlines to the Stars—George White of Bristol* (Redcliffe Press, 1995).

Bristol Scout

Barnes C. H., *Bristol Aircraft since 1910* (Putnam, 1964)
Barnwell, F. S. and others, *Design notebooks and calculations in B&CAC Collection* National Aerospace Library, Farnborough.
Bristol Scout FaceBook page, *@BristolScout*
Bristol Scout Twitter page, *@ScoutBuilder*
Bruce, J. M., 'Bristol's Fighter Manqué', *Air Enthusiast* (December 1986 to April 1987).
Bruce, J. M., *Collection of photographs, RAF Museum*, Hendon.
Bruce, J. M., 'The Bristol Scout' (four parts), *Flight* (26 September–24 October 1958).
Bruce, J. M., *The Bristol Scouts C & D*. No. 139 (Profile Publications, 1967).
Cole, C., *Royal Flying Corps 1915–1916* (William Kimber 1969).
David Bremner's blog, *www.bristolscout.wordpress.com*
Davis, M & Henshaw, T., 'RFC Bristol Scouts', *Cross & Cockade* vols 43/1 to 44/1 (2012–2013).
Lewis *British Aircraft 1809–1914* (Putnam, 1962).
Lewis C. S., *Sagittarius Rising* (Warner Books, 1993).
Lukins A. H., *The Book of Bristol Aircraft* (Harborough, 1946)
Nahum, A., *The Rotary Aero Engine* (HMSO, 1987)
Pudney, J., *Bristol Fashion* (Putnam, 1960)
Sturtivant and Page, *Royal Navy Aircraft Serials and Units 1911–1919* (Air Britain, 1992).

F. D. H. Bremner

Bremner, D., 'Oral History', *iwm.org.uk/collections/item/object/80000004*.
Bremner, F. D. H. Capt., *Private papers and flying logbooks*, Documents ref 7219. RAF Imperial War Museum.

'Flights of Fancy', *Radio Times*, p. 69. (27 September–3 October 1975).
Lance, D., 'Naval Pilot in the Aegean—1916', *Cross & Cockade*, Vol. 5 no. 4, pp. 179–184 (1974).
Lewis, B., *A Few of the First* (Leo Cooper, 1997).
Smith, M., *Voices in Flight: The Royal Naval Air Service during the Great War* Part 5, pp. 114–170. (Pen and Sword, 2014).

The Air War in the Aegean

Ash, E., *Sir Frederick Sykes and the Air Revolution, 1912–1918* (Routledge, 1999).
Heydemarck, Haupt., *War Flying in Macedonia* (Naval and Military Press).
Palavouzis, P., 'P K Fowler: His Service in the Aegean', *Cross & Cockade*, Vol. 44/1 (2013).
Palavouzis, P., *Thassos: The Unknown Aerodrome* (Razor, 2016) (Greek language only).